OPERATION
ROLLBACK

OPERATION ROLLBACK

America's
Secret
War
Behind
the Iron Curtain

Peter Grose

Houghton Mifflin Company

Boston · New York / 2000

For information about permission to reproduce selections from this book,
write to Permissions, Houghton Mifflin Company,
215 Park Avenue South, New York, New York   10003.

Library of Congress Cataloging-in-Publication Data
Grose, Peter, date.
Operation Rollback : America's secret war behind the Iron Curtain / Peter Grose.
p.   cm.
Includes index.
ISBN 0-395-51606-4
1. United States — Foreign relations — Soviet Union. 2. Soviet Union — Foreign
relations — United States. 3. United States — Foreign relations — 1945–1989.
4. United States — Foreign relations — Communist countries. 5. Communist
countries — Foreign relations — United States. 6. Cold War. 7. Kennan, George
Frost, 1904– 8. Espionage, American — Communist countries — History.
9. Sabotage — Communist countries — History. 10. Subversive activities —
Communist countries — History.   I. Title.
E183.8.S65 G76 2000
327.1273'01717 — dc21   99-089830

Printed in the United States of America

Book design by David Ford

QUM 10 9 8 7 6 5 4 3 2 1

Again, with love for M.K.,
who manages to endure a curmudgeon

Contents

Overture: The Vexing "Mr. X"   1

The two visions of George F. Kennan

I

AN IRON CURTAIN OVER EUROPE

1   Nazis and Communists   11

"People of whom we know nothing" . . . unilateral disarmament of intelligence . . . the secret of "Wild Bill" . . . Russians: allies or enemies? . . . Germans: enemies or allies? . . . the "rat line"

2   Resistance   32

Crackly radio signals from the Baltics to the Balkans . . . the Forest Brothers . . . Romania's load of plenty . . . Hungary's Scarlet Pimpernel . . . "bandits" from Ukraine . . . bothersome Russian émigrés

II

WASHINGTON AT PEACE

3   Liberals and Conservatives   53

Ideological ferment in a sleepy town . . . an unwelcome visitor . . . unwelcome testimony . . . the FBI finds new bearings against communism . . . the public perplexed

4   "Did I Do Right?"   69

The president perplexed . . . a New Dealer visits Moscow . . .
clandestine operatives in action . . . political
operatives in action

III

POLITICAL WARFARE

5   Kennan's Design   87

The Soviet enemy discovered . . . the Long Telegram . . .
Truman reaches out . . . Kennan conceives
a plan . . . NSC 10/2

6   The Secret Game   100

A special agency hidden within the government . . . an
expansive Frank Wisner . . . money: "the heart and soul of
covert operations" . . . Congress looks the other way

IV

GUERRILLAS, SABOTAGE, AND SUBVERSION

7   Starting with Intellectuals   121

"Organization X" . . . émigrés in harness . . . fussing and
feuding in exile . . . Mike Josselson and the Congress
for Cultural Freedom

8   Into Battle   144

Is there a "CIA type"? . . . Frank Lindsay, the
businessman . . . William Sloan Coffin, the divinity
student . . . Michael Burke, the entrepreneur . . .
failing the test case in Albania

9   Combat High and Low   164

*Blowback from Romania . . . low-flying unmarked planes . . .
parachute drops . . . arrests, accusations, denials . . .
deception in Poland ... mischief in Ukraine . . . the perils
and travails of the NTS*

V

AFTERMATH

10   Anticommunism on the Hustings   193

*"Liberating the Captive Nations" . . . the FBI turns against
the White House . . . ethnic politics ... the troublesome
Congressman Kersten . . . John Foster Dulles takes power . . .
Kennan is moved out*

11   Legacy   211

*Rollback frays at the edges . . . and at the core . . . restraint
in Berlin . . . in Hungary . . . a devastating verdict on covert
action . . . Glasnost and Rollback*

Notes on Sources   225

Author's Note   241

Index   245

East Central Europe After World War II

OPERATION
ROLLBACK

Overture: The Vexing "Mr. X"

THE TIMING WAS AWKWARD but, as it turned out, auspicious. At the turn of 1946, just as the new American president, Harry Truman, was growing skeptical about continuing the uneasy wartime cooperation with Soviet Russia, the United States embassy in Moscow was in the temporary care of a moody and troublesome journeyman, a midcareer diplomat hitherto unnoticed by the powers in Washington.

His ambassador, W. Averell Harriman, millionaire disburser of Lend-Lease aid to the Soviet Union for the common cause against Hitler, had worn out his welcome in Moscow — and had exhausted his own patience in trying to sustain cordial relations with Stalin while putting up with daily life under communism. Late in January 1946, Harriman turned over the embassy to his deputy. Old money and high politics tend to patronize careerists: "You're in charge now," Harriman told the earnest caretaker. "Now you can send all the telegrams you want."

Just a few days short of his forty-second birthday, George F. Kennan had waited a long time for his main chance. He had served powerful ambassadors across Europe through the 1920s and 1930s with unsung competence, working his way uncomfortably through the social obligations that constituted the diplomacy of the era, chafing at the bureaucratic concerns of those he considered intellectual inferiors. He had a way of trying people's patience with his propensity for obtuse musing. "Almost everyone got annoyed with Kennan after they first got to know him," said Loy Henderson, a senior diplomat whom Kennan actually admired. "He was so engrossed in his own ideas that he never learned how to go along or get along."

Kennan had graduated from Princeton in 1925 and had lived abroad

1

almost continually after 1926; that was an era when the diplomatic career was a rarefied preserve cut off from American life. His postings included Geneva, Berlin, and the Baltic states of Estonia, Latvia, and Lithuania, the American diplomatic missions closest to the still-unrecognized Soviet Union. Tapped at the beginning of his professional career for special training in Soviet affairs (an uncle, for whom he was named, had been a recognized scholar of Tsarist Russia at the turn of the century), the pensive youth from Milwaukee had grown more conversant with the culture and politics of Russia than of his native land.

He had become a minor and idiosyncratic member of an exclusive cadre of Soviet specialists in the State Department, unknown to the general public or indeed to anyone outside his own circle. Almost to a man (no women had diplomatic careers at that time, of course), these tightly focused experts were contemptuous of Bolshevik manners and pretensions, contemptuous even more of American liberals of that era who looked upon Soviet Russia as a laboratory of social reform.

In the New Deal years of the 1930s, intellectuals sympathetic to the Soviet experiment had gained an upper hand in Washington, from President Franklin D. Roosevelt on down. Dispatches from the likes of this Kennan, about purges and the murderous rampages of collectivization and communization, threatened the prevailing wisdom. Kennan would have had no interest in getting along or going along with such left-wing contemporaries in the State Department as Noel Field or Alger Hiss, for instance.

Kennan began serving in Moscow under Harriman in 1944 and, along with disenchanted colleagues like the chief of the military liaison mission, General John Russell Deane, bombarded the lower levels of Washington bureaucracy with analyses of communist evil — reports that went unread by the senior officials pursuing Roosevelt's vision of alliance with the Soviet Union. As victory over Hitler became assured, however, the simmerings of anti-Soviet thought began surfacing in Washington again. Even Roosevelt, the week before he died, began to doubt that he could go on doing business with Stalin in building a secure peace.

President Truman came into office uninhibited by the reforming zeal of the old New Deal. Once the victories in Europe and the Pacific were confirmed in the course of 1945, his fledgling administration opened new eyes upon the Soviet Union: an ally for six years, was it now to be an adversary?

In February 1946, just after Ambassador Harriman had withdrawn, the State Department and the Treasury sent two modest inquiries to the Moscow embassy left in Kennan's care. Washington needed an "interpretive analysis" of recent Soviet statements about international financial institutions, for the purpose of fashioning American policy. Such inquiries were routine, the normal format for discussion between a capital and its diplomatic outposts. What was unusual was that this time the officer responsible for replying was George Kennan.

After a few days of thought, the chargé d'affaires *ad interim* decided to seize the opening that had eluded him through all his years of bureaucratic servitude. "Now, suddenly, my opinion was being asked," he wrote, looking back on the moment. "It was no good trying to brush the question off with a couple of routine sentences describing Soviet views on such things as world banks and international monetary funds. It would not do to give them just a fragment of the truth. Here was a case where nothing but the whole truth would do. They had asked for it. Now, by God, they would have it."[1]

At nine P.M. on February 22, Kennan sent a telegram to Washington — 8,000 words in length but broken into five parts, as its author described it, "like an eighteenth-century Protestant sermon." (More to the immediate point, he split up the text so as not to burden the primitive communications channels of the day and so that it "would not look so outrageously long.") Here was Kennan on his own — analysis both elegant and prolix, lucid in language but not always clear on the practical points he was trying to make. It was the sort of thoughtful essay that over the years had stirred the respect, and the irritation, of busy superiors and men of politics.

Your inquiry, Kennan began, "involves questions so intricate, so delicate, so strange to our form of thought, . . . that I cannot compress answers into single brief message without yielding to what I feel would be dangerous degree of over-simplification." Readers thus warned, the flow of words poured forth: Soviet behavior patterns scrutinized for both academic and operational import; the Kremlin's "neurotic view of world affairs"; the "traditional and instinctive Russian sense of insecurity"; the implications for American policy arising from the neuroses of the Russian soul. Kennan released all the intellectual emotions of his diplomatic colleagues steeped in Soviet affairs, pent up as they had been under the disinterest of the Roosevelt years. As it turned out, his musings that February evening in 1946 rang down the final curtain on the alliance of wartime convenience between Soviet communism and western democracy.

In the later annals of the Cold War, Kennan's dispatch no. 511 became known simply as the Long Telegram — "probably the most important, and influential, message ever sent to Washington by an American diplomat," in the words of Clark Clifford, then a modest Truman aide in the White House. In the State Department, a wary staff assistant warned the secretary of state that "this telegram from George Kennan in Moscow is not subject to condensation." The hard-driving secretary of the navy, James V. Forrestal, clipped a copy of the diplomatic dispatch to his personal journal and, ignoring its Secret classification, passed it around the government.

From his later stature as an elder statesman, Kennan remarked, "If none of my previous literary efforts had seemed to evoke even the faintest tinkle from the bell at which they were aimed, this one, to my astonishment, struck it squarely and set it vibrating." For the Long Telegram told Washington what it was finally ready to hear: the Soviet Union, an ally in war, was becoming an adversary in peace.

Kennan was due for home leave after his overseas service during World War II, and upon the arrival of a new ambassador that spring he returned to the unfamiliar terrain of Washington. There he found that quite a few important people wanted to meet the author of the Long Telegram. Assigned to a sabbatical at the National War College, Kennan made the rounds of policymakers and commentators known to him previously only from newspapers and shortwave radio broadcasts.

Forrestal asked him for a further memo clarifying what the thoughts of the Long Telegram meant for America's long-term strategy. Sitting in a northwest corner room at Washington's Fort McNair, hacking away at a typewriter (as he later pictured himself), Kennan churned out a new essay, which, with Forrestal's permission, he submitted to the prestigious New York journal *Foreign Affairs*. Unexpectedly, however, he was recalled onto active State Department duty; he tried to withdraw the article, then in press, for fear that it would be taken as an official policy statement. He reluctantly agreed to permit publication under the pseudonym "X."

The "X article" of July 1947 addressed a general public confused about the Soviet Union; it had all the impact in intellectual circles that the Long Telegram had registered within the government a year earlier. As the author's identity quickly became known, the State Department tried to dismiss the article, unconvincingly, as merely the views of a scholar on leave.

"The main element of any United States policy toward the Soviet Union must be that of a long-term, patient but firm and vigilant containment of Russian expansive tendencies," Kennan as "X" argued. "Soviet pressure against the free institutions of the Western world is something that can be contained by the adroit and vigilant application of counterforce at a series of constantly shifting geographical and political points."[2]

The elucidation was nuanced and elegant, but the argument rode roughshod over all those in Washington who still clung to the hope that the wartime alliance could be sustained in the postwar era. It proposed nothing less than a fundamental realignment of all the assumptions held by the American people about the nation's foreign policy. Understandably, and to the discomfort of its author, the "X article" provoked an enduring storm of criticism from both left and right.

From the prevailing liberal perspective, the first onslaught came from the era's most influential commentator on public affairs, Walter Lippmann, who lambasted "Mr. X" in fourteen successive columns published in newspapers across the nation that autumn. (The columnist, an intimate in Washington political circles, knew full well the identity of the author he was criticizing and, indeed, regarded him as a personal friend.) Lippmann challenged the facts, the logic, and the implications of the article. Containment, Lippmann argued, was a "strategic monstrosity" that would require unending military pressure, straining America's political and economic resources to the breaking point. The policy was doomed to fail.

Painful though this assault was to Kennan, a private person unaccustomed to public criticism, an even more strident response came from the conservative opinion centers of Washington, New York, and the midwestern heartland, where generations of emigrants from eastern Europe had made their new lives. Containment reeked of appeasement, they complained, and amounted to the abandonment of eastern Europe to communism.

As eloquent on this side as Lippmann on his was James Burnham, a then-prominent polemicist holding forth from the philosophy faculty of New York University. Containment, he declared, was merely "bureaucratic verbalization of a policy of drift — its inner law is: Let history do it." Burnham and his cohorts on the right were not content with drift when it came to confronting communism; they wanted action! "Containment is a variant of the defensive," Burnham argued, "and a defensive policy . . . can never win."[3]

The rhetoric soared as the controversy raged over the coming years. Burnham belittled containment as a "teacup edition" of what ordinary Americans wanted from their foreign policy; the doctrine, as he understood it, drew a magic line behind which "every communist, like a Brunhilde behind a wall of fire that even Siegfried has sworn to respect, can sleep secure." Alexander Wiley, the powerful Republican senator from Wisconsin, denounced Kennan and his State Department colleagues for pursuing what he made bold to call "panty-waist diplomacy."[4]

Kennan did not reply to these critics (though years later he commented sadly that his friend Lippmann had argued upon a "misunderstanding almost tragic in its dimensions"). Kennan's was not the style of the radio discussion programs that were starting to make an impact among Americans far from the intellectual centers. Moreover, he was once again a serving United States diplomat, restricted by protocol from speaking out on his own.

Only four decades later did another reason for Kennan's reticence come to light. Commentators and even powerful senators were not privy to some most unusual policy discussions proceeding in deep secrecy within the top echelons of the Truman administration. Even as containment was being scorned as appeasement and timidity in the first months of 1948, a high-level staff within the State Department was devising a remarkable initiative to confront communism aggressively through clandestine action. The secret program would start with innocuous propaganda and persuasion, then proceed directly into sabotage, subversion, and paramilitary engagement.

While critics were lambasting what they considered the defensive doctrine of containment, its author was at work designing a massive offensive. When the diplomatic archives were finally unsealed, they revealed the architect and champion of American covert action against east European communism to be "Mr. X" himself, George F. Kennan.

*

Among Kennan's many idiosyncrasies was a fascination, rare for a conventional diplomat, with the practice and product of intelligence as it was then understood — the clandestine collection of secret information. As early as September 1945, while serving as the ambassador's deputy in the Moscow embassy, Kennan had been impressed with the work of the American intelligence officer serving in the Soviet Union under diplomatic cover. Since "the normal channels and facilities now available to us" were not turning up the most important and sensitive information, he informed the State Department, using the euphemisms of polite diplomats, "large scale special efforts on various lines . . . are therefore justified."[5]

His sabbatical abruptly terminated at the end of 1947, Kennan became head of the State Department's new Policy Planning Staff. Kennan turned to one theme of Mr. X's exposition that his militant critics tended to overlook: containment, to be effective, required "adroit and vigilant application of counterforce." Lippmann was one who did spot this point, and warned that it would require "recruiting, subsidizing and supporting a heterogeneous array of satellites, clients, dependents and puppets." Lippmann may have been appalled by that prospect, but it seemed just fine to Kennan. Seeking useful tasks to perform, he set his planning staff to the design of the counterforce. In the process, he expanded the practice of traditional intelligence into a new realm of political cold warfare.

An early Policy Planning product, a memo of February 5, 1948, called policymakers' attention to hundreds of thousands of refugees from eastern Europe and the Soviet Union languishing as war-displaced persons in western Europe. Kennan's staff urged that they be mobilized "to fill the gaps in our current official intelligence, in public information, and in our politico-psychological operations."[6] That was a modest beginning.

By April, Kennan was ready with a more ambitious comprehensive program for "organized political warfare." He shared the draft of his bold initiative with a few trusted colleagues among the department's Soviet specialists, including his old mentor Loy Henderson and a promising contemporary, Charles E. Bohlen. Kennan's proposal was submitted to the National Security Council (NSC), the top policymaking body of the Truman administration, even as the "teacup" image of Mr. X's containment was gaining public currency.

On June 18, 1948, Truman and his NSC formally committed the United States government to an unprecedented program of counter-force against communism, moving beyond propaganda and economic warfare to authorize "preventive direct action, including sabotage, anti-sabotage, demolition and evacuation measures" and then even "subversion against hostile states, including assistance to underground resistance movements, guerrillas and refugee liberation groups." And all of these activities were to be carried out under such ruses and deceptions, the Truman administration directed, that the U.S. government could "plausibly disclaim any responsibility."[7]

Thus was drawn the first battle line of the Cold War, without the knowledge of the public and, indeed, contrary to what the public believed its government's foreign policy to be. Kennan's secret operational plan for the counterforce quickly took on a life of its own across the government, caroming wildly out of its author's control. By the 1950s right-wing ideologists, little knowing what the defeated Democratic administration had already attempted, pounded the hustings with the battle cry of rolling back the Iron Curtain.

Years later, looking back in dismay on the whole sorry episode, Kennan portrayed himself as "one who has inadvertently loosened a large boulder from the top of a cliff and now helplessly witnesses its path of destruction in the valley below, shuddering and wincing at each successive glimpse of disaster."[8]

PART I

An Iron Curtain over Europe

1

Nazis and Communists

As THE NAZI REICH was crumbling all around him early in 1945, Joseph Goebbels, creative propagandist for Hitler, shared his forebodings with the German people in an editorial. The Russians were poised to occupy all of eastern Europe, Goebbels declared in late February, and "an iron curtain would at once descend."

Goebbels's warning, carried on shortwave radio, caught the attention of a literary stylist on the other side of the war: Winston Churchill, prime minister of Britain. Perhaps without remembering its source, Churchill used the ominous image in his first message to President Truman not three months later: "An iron curtain is drawn down upon [the Soviet] front; we do not know what is going on behind." Striving to impress the new president, with whom he yet had no personal rapport, he then cabled on June 4: "I view with profound misgivings . . . the descent of an iron curtain between us and everything to the eastward." And nine months later, when Churchill, by then out of office, spoke at a small college in Fulton, Missouri, Truman's home state, the image finally caught on, to become the singular metaphor for the gathering Cold War. Churchill declared:

> From Stettin in the Baltic to Trieste in the Adriatic, an Iron Curtain has descended across the continent. Behind that line lie all the capitals of the ancient states of central and eastern Europe — Warsaw, Berlin, Prague, Vienna, Budapest, Bucharest, and Sofia; all these famous cities and their populations around them lie in what I might call the Soviet sphere, and all are subject, in one form or another, not only to Soviet influence but to a very high and in some cases increasing measure of control from Moscow.[1]

Few Americans who heard Churchill that day could have confidently placed Stettin, Trieste, or any of the other named cities on the map. If one drew a 600-mile-long line from Stettin in the north to Trieste in the south, dividing the European continent at its narrowest, all of the cities except Berlin would be east of the line. Stettin, by then known as Polish Szczecin, was the capital of Pomerania, on the western bank of the Oder, less than a hundred miles northeast of Berlin. German settlers had built the town in the twelfth century. In 1945 nearly four million Pomeranian Germans had fled toward the West to escape the Red Army in its advance against the disintegrating Third Reich. Cosmopolitan Trieste was the Adriatic port that had given the old Austro-Hungarian Empire access to the seas. By the end of World War II, it was effectively integrated into Yugoslavia under the control of the communist partisans led by Josip Broz Tito.

For the purposes of Churchill's rhetoric, the line was a natural demarcation, but the realities on the ground in 1946 required modest adjustments. Vienna, capital of Austria, was east of the direct line, as Churchill said, yet American, British, and French troops, as well as Russians, controlled the venerable (and vulnerable) city under a four-power occupation authority. Prague and the lands of the Czechs — Bohemia and Moravia — were actually a little to the west of Churchill's line, but they were occupied by the Red Army alone. Also to the west were the German *länder* around Berlin; under Soviet occupation, they soon would become the German Democratic Republic (East Germany).

With those adjustments, the line that Churchill drew that day in Missouri endured intact for forty years, for all the overt and covert efforts of the most anticommunist Americans to roll it back. What had over time been called central Europe disappeared for half a century, absorbed into a rigid delineation between East and West.

Just eight years before, Churchill's predecessor, Neville Chamberlain, had dismissed a crisis in this central ground as "a quarrel in a faraway country between people of whom we know nothing."[2] (Chamberlain's dismissive statement was uttered only 650 miles from Czechoslovakia; Americans were another 3,600 miles farther away.) The disparate nations behind this curtain were not prominent in United States foreign policy, save among ethnic and academic specialists whose interests rarely intruded upon general public perceptions. The diverse nations of eastern Europe faded into an undifferentiated and hostile land mass under communism, monolithic and, it was said, dangerous to America's global interests.

To be sure, Poland enjoyed an enduring hold on the American imagination — tenacious, throbbing, and Roman Catholic, fabled for Chopin and Paderewski and its nineteenth-century struggle for nationhood against the vise grip of Russia and Germany. From the waves of migration early in the twentieth century, Polish immigrants had built a strong political presence in the United States, backed by the Roman Catholic hierarchy, as Roosevelt and Democratic Party strategists were ever mindful. The acts of the traditional predators upon Poland drew Britain and France into the war against Hitler; once the war was won some five years later, Stalin's designs moved the Polish state bodily westward. Poland absorbed Pomerania and the Baltic coast; in return, Polish lands in the east passed into the Soviet Union. Polish nationalism was a culture resting on a shifting territorial base.

Czechoslovakia, by contrast, was a relatively new cause. From his years as a practicing historian, Woodrow Wilson had been intrigued by the Slavs, predominant in central Europe before the invasions of the German knights and merchants. At the Paris Peace Conference of 1919, the uneasy merger of Czech and Slovak nationalisms found voice in the remarkable political skills of Tomaš Masaryk and Edvard Beneš, diplomatic charmers who knew how to flatter the sensitivities of the western democracies to gain privileged status for their artificial homeland. Yet by the time Hitler sought to unite into his Reich the long-established and industrious German population of the Sudetenland, ringing the Czech heartland, Britain and the western democracies could not summon up sufficient sympathy to bestir themselves for this "far-away" land.

Hungarians were Magyars, not Slavs, remembered by Americans of idealistic inclination for the uprising of Lajos Kossuth in the heady revolutions of 1848. The Magyars had allied themselves uneasily with the triumphant Germanic culture of the Hapsburg Empire in the mid-nineteenth century, and they joined the Nazis at the start in fighting the western allies and Russia. Hungary was occupied by Nazi Germany in 1944. Though Hungary was well to the east of Churchill's line, the western allies did not initially regard it as lost to a Soviet sphere of influence.

Hugging the eastern shore of the Baltic, Lutheran Estonia and Latvia, geographically and politically beholden to Soviet power, clung to the vision of independent nationhood that they had enjoyed between the two world wars. Like neighboring but Catholic Lithuania, with its cultural and political ties to Poland, they hoped for western support against Soviet Russia.

The South Slavs, joined together in the Yugoslav Federation, were nonetheless fractured between Orthodox Serbs, who had resisted Hitler, and Catholic Croatians, who had readily embraced Nazism in its local manifestations. The Slavs farther east, Ukrainians and Belorussians, lived on lands truly uncharted to most Americans — save the active Ukrainian population in the United States (and Canada), which struggled to make their national identity a cause of interest.

Given this perplexing diversity, American policymakers seemed inclined, like Chamberlain, to dismiss the whole area. In 1943, Czech president Beneš urged Americans to accept the eventual predominance of the Soviet Union in eastern Europe. Later that year Roosevelt breezily informed the troubled archbishop of New York, Cardinal Spellman, that even if regions of particular Catholic interest — he cited Austria, Hungary, and Croatia — fell under Soviet "protection" after the war, twenty or thirty years of European influence would make the Russians "less barbarous."[3]

Early in 1945 some voices in the wilderness, such as those of navy secretary Forrestal and Republican senator Arthur Vandenberg, tried to turn official attention to the plight of eastern Europe. Their motivations for concern were not altruistic: Forrestal, formerly of Wall Street, was growing obsessed with the communist threat to capitalism; Vandenberg had a large Michigan constituency of immigrants from eastern Europe. A measure of their loneliness in political life was Walter Lippmann's dismissive remark as late as the start of 1946 that acceptance of a Soviet sphere of influence in eastern Europe was only realistic. After all, he told his millions of readers, this was only "one small specific area of the globe."[4]

In this small specific area, these faraway countries of which Americans knew so little, American political and strategic thought found its focus in the first decade after World War II. Here was the first battlefield of the Cold War, the campaign to roll back the Iron Curtain. The weaponry to be deployed would come from the new (to Americans) arsenals of intelligence, subversion, and espionage.

Once the United States became established in the 1950s as a superpower of the Cold War, the government could summon up sources and methods for acquiring accurate, real-time, on-the-ground information about lands and peoples hitherto unfamiliar. But in May 1945, America was on its way to unilateral disarmament in the realm of strategic intelligence.

"Intelligence," so called, was a fractured pursuit, combining visions of high purpose with low-life transactions in dark alleys, with military officers and civilian professionals competing for the attentions of policymakers and the services of agents in the field. The military intelligence teams that had supported the Allied invasion across France and into Germany found themselves after the Nazi surrender with a fundamentally altered mission. Instead of assembling the order of battle and tactical intelligence necessary for an advancing fighting army, they were tasked with supporting an army of occupation. Clinging for the first postwar months to the image of Germans as enemies, the Army G-2 staff pursued suspected remnants of the fallen Nazi regime across the ruined German countryside.

Another military branch, the Counter-Intelligence Corps (CIC), should have been better equipped for the local security missions of an occupation administration. CIC detachments, after all, were accustomed to the freewheeling ways and nonaccountable practices endemic to the running of spies. But the CIC was, like the rest of the armed forces, a corps of ordinary Americans, drafted into service for the duration, with neither dedication nor ambition in the tradecraft of intelligence. Weary from fighting a war, too many officers and men of the CIC succumbed to the venal motives of an occupying army. Discipline was lax, and anyone with casual access to CIC insignia could pursue nefarious, self-enriching missions without the nuisance of official orders. Stories of black-marketing and looting of art works and other civilian treasures came to mar the reputation of the CIC in occupied Europe.

Most complicating of all in 1945 was the upstart civilian intelligence agency, the Office of Strategic Services (OSS). Later generations of American intelligence professionals liked to trace their lineage not from the military branches but from the broad-ranging OSS. Created by Roosevelt to remedy the haphazard and uncoordinated gathering of information that had allowed the surprise attack on Pearl Harbor, the OSS became in just four years an expansive, inclusive, and erratic intelligence apparatus, distinct from the traditional and confined intelligence staffs of the uniformed services, responsible to no one but a preoccupied president. Businessmen, partisan fighters, professors, technicians clever at devices for sabotage, all worked side by side in the OSS. Exploits of both derring-do and sophisticated analysis were subsequently and appropriately heralded in the popular and professional literature. But with the end of the war, the OSS seemed a strange hybrid in a morass of conflicting purposes.

Its founding director, the dynamic William J. Donovan, was ever difficult to place in a bureaucracy. A restive corporate lawyer from Buffalo, New York, he was already fifty-eight when Roosevelt called him to active duty in 1941. Twice he had run as a Republican for public office, including the governorship of New York in 1932, and twice he had lost. But he was a veteran of foreign wars, a cavalry officer on the Mexican border in 1916 (where he picked up the sobriquet "Wild Bill"), a Medal of Honor winner in World War I. Innovative and hyperactive, he had shown a penchant for secret missions during the Russian civil war in 1919, the Italian campaign against Ethiopia, the Spanish civil war, and diverse military missions to Czechoslovakia and the Balkans in the late 1930s, even as he gained stature as a Wall Street lawyer and pulled in clients for his firm, Donovan and Leisure. He had an undeniable gift for cutting through petty obstructions, for energizing talents and getting things done — not necessarily in an orderly way, but getting them done.

Energy, smoke, mirrors, and imagination had built an unprecedented civilian intelligence service for the United States in World War II. To his credit, Donovan recognized the demands that would be made upon the broad profession of intelligence in the postwar era. But his proposal in November 1944 to turn his agency into a peacetime instrument of government backfired in a blaze of tendentious publicity from the anti-Roosevelt press.* Donovan always pursued several purposes at the same time — a virtue for a master of spies, self-defeating for a man of politics.

---

* The story of this public self-destruction remains a point of contention within the intelligence community. The Donovan plan was destroyed by a leak to the right-wing

From early in the war, the OSS faced the dilemma of whether or not to collect intelligence about the Soviet Union as well as about the Nazi enemy. Roosevelt, determined to maintain Stalin's alliance and trust, ordered Donovan to restrain his people — and himself. For instance, even though a chance encounter gave the OSS secret access to the private secretary of the Soviet ambassador in Washington, Donovan broke off the contact. Early in 1943, he was tempted by a proposition to develop sources on Soviet activities in cooperation with the less inhibited British intelligence agencies. But the State Department honored the presidential edict and declined to get involved in undercover activity, refusing to provide diplomatic cover for an OSS officer in the Moscow embassy. (Later that year, however, a single OSS analyst, Thomas Whitney, quietly joined the embassy staff, with the concurrence of Ambassador Harriman. He became a trusted colleague of George Kennan's.)

Donovan was never a man to settle for a tightly circumscribed mission. If he could not target the Soviet Union, he would take the opposite tack in seeking to enhance his agency's effectiveness: cooperation with the Soviet ally against the common enemy. On Christmas Eve, 1943, Donovan flew to Moscow for professional discussions with the Soviet external intelligence services. The astonished Russians quizzed Donovan in detail "about the particular methods of spying, American style." How did Americans introduce agents into enemy territory? How were these secret agents trained? What equipment did they carry? Donovan responded in his expansive way. The Russians volunteered no information about spying, Soviet style.

The Soviet government delayed a formal reply to the American offer of cooperation, and during that six-week interim early in 1944 more sober minds prevailed in Washington. Even Roosevelt concurred in the judgment of J. Edgar Hoover, who as director of the Federal Bureau of Investigation was responsible for internal security, that cooperation with

---

Chicago Tribune; OSS men jumped to the conclusion, which they perpetuated through decades of storytelling, that the source of the damaging news stories was J. Edgar Hoover, Donovan's jealous rival in intelligence. Years later the *Tribune* reporter admitted to a historian of the Central Intelligence Agency that his source had been not Hoover or similar suspects but Roosevelt himself, through his press secretary, Stephen Early, who said "FDR wanted the story out." Thomas Troy conveys this disclosure, without comment, in *Donovan and the CIA* (Frederick, Md.: University Publications of America, 1981), p. vi.

Moscow on matters of espionage and intelligence risked becoming, at the least, counterproductive.

In 1944, swept up in the end-game enthusiasm of the invasion of continental Europe and eager to serve the triumphant military, Donovan turned his intelligence service in a less visible but ultimately more fateful direction, to the urgent tasks of tactical military intelligence rather than the strategic political intelligence for which it had been assembled. His OSS parachuted men behind the lines and built networks in France and the Low Countries as the Allies pushed toward the Rhine. Inside Germany itself the OSS tried to develop fifth columns and resistance to the disintegrating power of the Nazis. This change of mission risked provoking the existing rivalry between the civilian OSS and the military intelligence staffs, of course. But Donovan knew what he was doing, even if his rivals did not.

One of the most tightly guarded secrets of the war was a special asset available to the OSS and not to the other intelligence services. This was SIGINT, or signals intelligence: intercepts of German army and police communications that the British had been collecting and exploiting since early in the war. Churchill had agreed in 1942 to share this invaluable real-time intelligence with the United States but, to guard the secret to the fullest, with only one select, specially classified agency. Created for the purpose was a counterespionage branch of the OSS called X-2. Donovan's agency was thus uniquely equipped to provide Eisenhower's advancing forces with accurate and detailed intelligence of the names and locations of resistance networks. The military intelligence staffs were not apprised of the source of this sensitive data; the OSS relished the power of its special, mysterious asset, which came at the bureaucratic expense of its rivals.

The crucial military decision in the last weeks of the war can be traced to information provided by Donovan. In diverting the Anglo-American drive away from conquest of the accessible capitals — Berlin and Prague — and turning his land armada toward southern Germany, Eisenhower was acting on OSS intelligence. Donovan's agents had assembled clues that the Nazis were building an underground army of 35,000 to 40,000 guerrilla fighters, with a last-ditch military redoubt in the Alps, to fight on even after the fall of the Nazi capital. The Americans succeeded in cutting Bavaria off from the rest of Germany, but found there no organized guerrilla units, no Alpine redoubt.

The OSS "played a key role in the redoubt myth," wrote one irreverent Donovan aide, William J. Casey, years later. "We were unable to explode it and we should have, easily. We had a dozen teams in the redoubt area and none of them reported anything justifying belief that enough military strength could be generated in that pastoral, undeveloped country to resist five million Allied troops for more than a few weeks."[5]

Casey, who became director of intelligence under President Ronald Reagan in 1980, was one conservative who harbored enduring suspicion about this seeming intelligence failure. Eisenhower's 1945 decision to chase the mythical Nazi guerrillas and their redoubt gave the advancing Russians opportunity to capture cities and territory in central Europe that otherwise could have fallen to the armies of the West. Cold War anticommunists who saw conspiracies all around them suspected that left-leaning officers of the OSS might have contaminated the evaluation of tactical intelligence over the winter and spring of 1945, for the postwar benefit of the Soviet Union.

American intelligence lost its most powerful advantage with the Nazi surrender in May 1945, when its access to secret German communications became irrelevant. No information source remotely comparable was available about the Red Army occupation forces in eastern Europe or the Soviet Union itself. Having lost his special asset, Donovan then lost his patron as well: Roosevelt may have relished the skullduggery that Donovan promoted, but Truman had no use for it nor for the overreaching Donovan himself. Acting on impulse, in the style that characterized his early presidency, Truman abruptly fired Donovan and abolished the OSS in September 1945.

The European continent was a pit of human and physical misery after the six years of World War II. It was "the most violent and frightening decade in European history," in the words of the British historian Alan Bullock.[6] Beyond the millions who had perished in war, no less than 60 million persons had been uprooted from their homes, nearly half removed to some other country to serve as slave labor for the Nazi war machine or to escape marauding armies of victors and vanquished alike. The occupiers of the fallen Reich found some 10 million homeless Germans, mostly uprooted city dwellers foraging the countryside for food and shelter. A further 12 million who had fled or been expelled from Germany's eastern territories poured into the western occupation zones, mainly the American zone of Bavaria, arriving, at one point in 1945, at the rate of 40,000 per week. Another 7 million lingered in German prisoner-of-war camps, for which the occupation regimes had to assume sudden responsibility.

Among these displaced persons were men, women, and children from the Soviet Union, including ethnic Russians, Ukrainians, Cossacks, citizens of the Baltic states, and Poles whose home villages had been incorporated into Soviet territory. Some 5 million Soviet nationals were found across western and central Europe, including 2.8 million forced laborers and 1.15 million captured Soviet troops who had survived in POW camps. Intermingled were a million other Soviet citizens who had volunteered to fight under Nazi command against their own communist government; these people surrendered to the western armies rather than face a vindictive welcome home from Stalin.

Even before V-E Day, the western allies had wondered about these renegade Russians. Britain's Special Operations Executive (SOE) mounted a clandestine deception operation in 1944, dropping fake documents and subversive equipment to pinpointed locations in France, Belgium, Denmark, and Norway where the Russian units were known to be deployed — hoping to make their German officers suspect an anti-Nazi resistance movement among the Russian soldiers. In at least one case, the SOE believed that their mischief mission had caused the German command in northern France to replace the Russians with SS fighting units.[7]

As victory approached, the western allies became concerned about the fate of these Russian volunteer units. At first Soviet spokesmen affected disinterest, claiming that too few men were involved to be a matter for government concern. As British historian Nikolai Tolstoy concluded, "the Soviet Union was reluctant to admit publicly that any of its subjects were opposed to their Marxist government." Yet when he met Roosevelt and Churchill at Yalta, Stalin obtained their agreement to a seemingly routine "housekeeping" measure committing the western allies to the repatriation of Soviet citizens found in the various territories liberated from Nazi rule. This commitment, signed at the working level by the American military attaché in Moscow, Major General Deane, and a Red Army counterpart, was not made public until a year or so later.

With the war's end, the enormous scope of the problem came into view. The western allies demanded a routine order-of-battle report from the captured Nazi high command, and two weeks after the surrender General Alfred Jodl issued a pathetic accounting, documenting the anarchy that had befallen the armies of the Third Reich in its closing days. When he last heard from them, the Nazi commander in captivity reported, Russian volunteer units (presumably anticommunists all) were as follows: "a) 599th Russian Brigade, appr. 13,000 men, on march from Denmark southwards . . .; b) 600th Russian Infantry Division, appr. 12,000 men, last reported in Bohemia-Moravia; c) 650th Russian Infantry Division, appr. 18,000 men, last reported on march from Muesingen to the Linz [Austria] area."[8] On and on went the meticulous but feckless accounting.

Western observers saw the problem in human terms. When the novelist George Orwell visited a POW camp outside Munich as a British war correspondent, he reported:

> Prisoners were passing through it from day to day, but at a given moment the number there was about 100,000. According to the American officer in charge, the prisoners were on average 10 percent non-German, mostly Russians and Hungarians. The Russians were being sorted by asking the simple question, "Do you want to go back to Russia or not?" A respectable proportion — of course, I have no exact figures — answered "not," and these were regarded as Germans and kept in the camp, while the others were released.[9]

By the end of June 1945, 1.5 million Soviet nationals had been returned to Red Army detachments in eastern Germany. Up to this point, contemporary reports indicate, the repatriation proceeded without incident or resistance. But as the months passed, news spread through the camps of displaced persons about the fate befalling those who had been returned to the Soviet Union: arrest as traitors, sentences of hard labor, even execution on the spot immediately after the western escorts had withdrawn from the sites of transfer. Scarcely noted by the British and American public at the time, this repatriation later became one of the most searing controversies of the early Cold War. Honoring a commitment at Yalta undertaken before they understood the nature of the problem, the western allies eventually employed military force to dispatch hundreds of thousands of Soviet nationals back to the mercy of the Red Army, to certain punishment or death.

*

Churchill had slightly overstated the case when he complained to Truman that "we do not know what is going on" in the lands conquered by the Red Army. Ill coordinated and sporadic, British and American intelligence teams had in fact made numerous feints into eastern Europe before the war's end.

As early as March 1943, Donovan had sent a three-man mission to Budapest to try breaking Hungary from its alliance with Hitler; the men were promptly incarcerated. Late in 1944 a young OSS lawyer, Frank G. Wisner, reported from Romania that the advancing Red Army had deliberately let two Nazi divisions out of a trap, freeing them to fight the British and Americans in the Ardennes campaign on the western front.

The OSS and the British SOE fielded a joint mission behind German lines in northwest Moravia (Czechoslovakia) in February 1945, aimed at opening radio contact with London and preparing landing fields for larger teams. The team ultimately made its way to Prague, but not in time to set up a deterrence to the Soviet occupation of the capital. The American Third Army under General George S. Patton crossed into western Czechoslovakia in the first days of May, but Eisenhower, acting in good faith about the understandings of Yalta, ordered his general to halt the advance along a line drawn through Karlsbad, Pilsen, and Budweis. The restraining order angered Patton, but at least the names had a pleasant resonance among American troops who knew good German beers.

British teams were ahead of Donovan's men in clandestine missions to penetrate Nazi Germany and organize networks of agents and informers for the occupation. One SOE agent named Fordwick actually made his way into Germany in October 1944 from a clandestine base in Denmark, contacting Danish workers in German industrial centers to start spreading defeatist propaganda. Learning of the mission, the British Foreign Office ordered it scuttled, fearful of undermining the allied policy of unconditional surrender, and reprimanded an SOE case officer serving under diplomatic cover in Stockholm.[10]

Once the Nazi Reich surrendered, and intelligence about the Red Army finally became a priority for the western occupiers, front-line officers confronted a stark reality that posed moral and practical dilemmas for which they were not prepared. It became evident in the first months after the war that Germans, Nazi or not, possessed a great deal more intelligence and expertise about Soviet Russia and the Red Army than any other source.

American conservatives, who, after the World War I armistice, had collected reports by the defeated German General Staff about Bolshevik atrocities, had long been impressed by the expertise of Germans about Russia and eastern Europe. In the 1920s, financiers such as Hjalmar Schacht, seeking American loans to rebuild German industry, fed their interest. As early as 1920, the National City Bank of New York circulated a report originating (anonymously) from Schacht and his business associates arguing that America could benefit from "the exact knowledge of Russian conditions possessed by Germany, which the United States will be able to successfully avail themselves of."[11]

Developing their instincts for self-preservation as the Nazi enterprise collapsed in 1945, German officers recognized that their expertise about the East could be a vehicle for ingratiating themselves with the conquering allies. Intelligence on the Soviet Union soon became the coin of the realm, with any former Nazi of gumption claiming special knowledge, even control of secret networks of agents in eastern Europe who could be mobilized to serve the western allies just as they had served the Nazis. The summer of 1945 opened the era of fabricators and paper mills in American intelligence, with real and, more often, fictitious sources of information dangled before the Americans in return for favorable treatment from the war crimes courts.

Lacking other access to developments within the Soviet zones of occupation, the Americans in Europe were tempted by these information sources, for all the absence of quality control. Within a month after the Nazi surrender, the X-2 branch of OSS, charged with hunting down war criminals, received three separate offers from former members of the Nazi intelligence services to turn over their agent networks in Soviet-occupied territory. The officers involved fell into the "automatic arrest" category, and X-2 flatly rejected the offers.

Other American intelligence organizations were not so scrupulous. At the POW camp of Wörgl, near Kitzbühel, a forty-three-year-old German general struck American military interrogators as more interesting than the rest of the unruly crowd of war prisoners. Reinhard Gehlen had turned himself in to the American army on May 22. Humility was not a common trait within the German General Staff, and Gehlen did not hesitate to express his irritation at the lack of respect shown to his person by the Americans. Gradually, successive interrogators begin to appreciate that this prisoner, while probably not as important as he said he was, deserved special attention for the services he could provide. For Gehlen, who had been head of Hitler's military intelligence on the eastern front, possessed a card-file memory of agents and locations and a scholarly familiarity with the Red Army and the Soviet system of warfare and government.

Transferred to more comfortable captivity than the routine POW camps, Gehlen began to open up the project that he had been devising for the past six months.[12] Secretly, for any sign of defeatism in the ranks would have brought immediate execution by the SS, Gehlen had been spiriting away from his military headquarters files and documents about Soviet affairs in eastern Europe, which he buried in a mountain hideout in Bavaria near the Czech border. Through June this wily Wehrmacht general dribbled out more and more data and insights to American intelligence on what was becoming their topic of greatest concern — on condition that he and his closest associates in conspiracy not be treated with the contempt meted out to all the rest who had worn the Nazi uniform.

By mid-July American interrogators were sufficiently impressed with the prize that had fallen into their grasp: Gehlen's name was discreetly removed from the circulated lists of German officers subject to automatic arrest, and a special alert about his potential value was passed up the line to General Edwin Sibert, chief of army intelligence (G-2) in the U.S. occupation zone. Sibert was a man sophisticated enough in the business of intelligence to have understood the disadvantage his G-2 staff had been operating under during the last year of the war, lacking the valuable asset of SIGINT. He was determined not to let such a liability recur and to grab for his own service any asset that seemed a promising source of intelligence. Holding to none of the X-2 inhibitions about traffic with the Nazi enemy, Sibert had already shown interest in German intelligence professionals whom the rest of the army considered war criminals. He did not bother to inform the OSS or any other intelligence service of his catch.

Unlike lower-ranking intelligence officers, however, Sibert understood the necessity of working within the chain of command, and he arranged for Gehlen and a few of his closest associates to be spirited out of Germany and flown in disguise to the army's interrogation center at Fort Hunt, Virginia, for further interrogation, cross-checking, and testing of credentials. For ten months Gehlen was held under wraps in the United States. When he was allowed back into Germany in June 1946, he returned with secret status and authority within the intelligence apparatus of the American military government.

By the summer of 1946, Washington's top military intelligence officers had abandoned the fervor of de-Nazification and were arranging for ex-Nazis with "special" qualifications, such as expertise in rocket science and other high technology, to be excused from the indignities of prisoner-of-war status and join the service of the United States for the demands of the postwar era. Included among these special qualifications was demonstrable expertise on the USSR. As Major General Stephen J. Chamberlin, director of army intelligence in Washington, informed Eisenhower, "valuable intelligence on Russia and Russian dominated countries can be developed more rapidly by this method than any other." In the less formal language of an American staff officer in Frankfurt, speaking to journalist John Gunther, "Are we dealing with our former enemies, or our future allies? We have not yet decided whether we want to win the last war or the next one."[13]

Between World War III and a Fourth Reich, Americans in Germany saw the former as the greater threat. If the United States was to learn what was happening behind the Iron Curtain, they believed, they must start with the expertise of the Nazis.

*

Weapons systems are difficult to dismantle even when they no longer serve the purpose for which they were devised. The superpower combatants found this out about their stockpiles of nuclear weapons when the Cold War was over in the 1990s, and the United States found it out concerning its weapons of intelligence at the end of World War II. President Truman could abolish the OSS with a stroke of his pen; more difficult was deciding what to do with the field agents and communications channels established in a war that was over.

At its demise at the end of September 1945, the OSS had on its duty rolls 10,390 persons, including nearly 6,000 abroad, distributed among nine overseas missions. Those involved with research and analysis (including the important wartime Foreign Nationalities Branch) were transferred to the supervision of the State Department. The actual "spies," agents in the field and the case officers who ran them, were reassigned to the War Department in a section specially set up to receive them, the Strategic Services Unit. The SSU represented the remnant of an intelligence apparatus in decay; by December 1 it numbered no more than 1,900 officers.*

The SSU's mandate was to demobilize and disperse these wartime assets. Yet from the start, the unit's intelligence professionals were determined to keep a structure in readiness, secretly, for a future "efficient peacetime clandestine intelligence agency." They first signaled their intent on October 25, 1945, in a memorandum to their chief, marked "for American eyes only," in which they proposed to preserve capabilities for "support of underground forces" and "clandestine subversion of enemy morale."[14] None of them yet envisaged a campaign to overthrow communist governments but they believed there was no harm in stockpiling the weapons.

Encountering no resistance from "American eyes," the surviving intelligence officers spelled out the details of their undercover design in January 1946 for a tightly restricted audience in Washington: The SSU would maintain up-to-date rosters of "recoverable personnel" who had returned to private life but could be called back on duty when needed; "local agents who have served American secret intelligence purposes well have been 'sealed off,' with arrangements made to resume contact in the future"; and a central file was assembled on more than four hundred thousand individuals, known agents of foreign intelligence services and other secret organizations "whose activities are or may be inimical to American interests."[15]

* This surely represented a low-water mark for modern American intelligence, in both resources and stature. Interviewed late in the 1990s, in retirement at his Arlington apartment, the SSU commander, General William Quinn, told me, "It's been forty years since anyone has asked me about the SSU days."

All these preparations were for an undefined future. In the field those first months after the war, the dwindling arsenal of intelligence was a jumble of overlapping missions, competing jurisdictions, and inter-agency rivalries. The SSU, Army G-2, and CIC maintained separate re-porting channels to Washington; seldom did they communicate with each other, and never with the intelligence services of the British and French in their own zones of occupation.

In Munich no less than ten American army and military government units were pursuing distinct and uncoordinated activities; in one case, three of them conducted separate reliability investigations of the same potential informer. In Berlin the SSU retained a former Gestapo officer named Karl Krull, who strolled the streets to pick out former Nazi com-rades who were either looking for a job (most of them) or, more omi-nously, had already signed on with the Soviets to spy on the western occupation — for the Russians also were engaged in building new intel-ligence networks. When fingered by Krull, former Nazi officers would be "turned" by the Americans to serve as double agents in the new war of espionage.

Sometimes the demands of intelligence clashed with official policy imperatives. When the American military government ordered a former Nazi evicted from his comfortable apartment to provide housing for a family of displaced persons, the American occupation officers had no way of knowing that the officer, one Heinz Schmalsläger, was already employed by SSU and was providing reams of documents on Soviet in-telligence methods and networks in eastern Europe. Schmalsläger was allowed to keep his flat; the DPs had to wait for other quarters.

Scattered down the chains of command of American military intelli-gence were officers who were unwilling to depend solely on the rem-nants of Nazi networks. Though they had to start from zero, various CIC units in occupied Germany and Austria set out to build their own access to information.

The destitute refugees and POWs were a humanitarian problem for the occupation authorities, but these displaced persons also represented potential sources of information about the Red Army and the Soviet in-frastructure. The CIC established elaborate interrogation procedures to systematically assemble data about industrial and military facilities from POWs, forced laborers, and Red Army defectors who could provide firsthand descriptions of what they had seen and experienced. Countless stories of humanity in upheaval show through the interrogation files: the thirty-five-year-old teacher of science and mathematics in Odessa who defected from his artillery regiment at the Hungarian border; his parents had perished in the Ukrainian famine of the 1930s, and he had no other family; the twenty-four-year-old lieutenant in the Red Army signal corps, veteran of the battles for Budapest and Vienna, who, after being ordered back to Moscow, decided that surrender to the Americans might bring him the chance of a better life; the Pole from Belorussia liberated from a German POW camp in Czechoslovakia who had witnessed the Red Army massacres of Polish officers at Katyn Forest in 1940 and had resolved never to return to the Soviet Union.

Immediately upon the German surrender, the American army commandeered a former Luftwaffe camp at Oberursel, outside Frankfurt, where Nazi intelligence officers had grilled captured British and American fliers. Some forty American interrogators, fluent in German, Russian, French, Italian, Polish, Czech, Hungarian, Spanish, and Dutch (even one who could handle Japanese, mainly when cursing), settled in at Oberursel.[16] A similar center was established across the Austrian border in Salzburg.

At first the interrogators sought evidence of lingering Nazi guerrilla activity. As this line of questioning dried up, the Americans turned their attention to what could be learned about the Soviet Union. The first problem they faced was determining the bona fides of each individual. "The interrogators . . . were always on the lookout for [Soviet intelligence] agents in disguise," explained one veteran of the operations, "men who would present themselves in the West as refugees from communism and would learn every detail they could of American intelligence proceedings, the identities of American officers, the places they used for their business."[17] The Kremlin never tired in its curiosity about spying "American-style."

After many months of interrogating the destitute homeless, the American officers confronted the problem of what was not so politely called their "disposal." The Americans had learned enough by early 1947 about the fate of displaced Soviet nationals repatriated to the Red Army.

Though most of their interrogation subjects were willing to take their chances in returning to their former homes, others did not want to go back.

At a level far below the vision of the statesmen, the human treasure of postwar Europe had been taken in hand by particular interests. All sides — British, American, Russian — were seeking technicians of Nazi enterprises to contribute scientific expertise for new national ventures in high technology. The builders of a future Jewish homeland, Zionists, combed the DP camps starting as early as the summer of 1945 for fighters and intellectuals ready to be smuggled out of Europe to populate and develop Palestine.

The 430th CIC detachment in Austria devised a novel method of disposing of defectors and informants from Soviet-occupied lands. These officers were accustomed to operating on their own, without documentation or reference to the higher occupation authorities. The commander, Colonel James Milano, son of Italian immigrants in West Virginia, resolved in the summer of 1947 to set up a route for smuggling truly displaced persons to South America, where they would establish new identities, secure from the hit men of Soviet intelligence.[18]

Latter-day United States government investigators described the mechanism, apparently unknown to higher authorities, as "a sort of underground railroad, dubbed a 'rat line,' and it ran from Austria to Italy, where it relied on a Croatian priest, Father Krunoslav Dragonovic, who was attached to a seminary in Rome where Croatian youths studied for the priesthood."[19] After an official investigation in the 1980s, Milano came forward to tell his long-secret story without the euphemisms of government officials.

Father Dragonovic was "completely corrupt," Milano's chief of operations told him, "runs a visa racket on the side . . . will sell them for fifteen hundred cash no questions asked." But what caught the alert officers' eyes was an American citizen associated with the Catholic father in his lucrative pursuits. This American's daytime job was in the eligibility office of the politically respected International Refugee Organization in Rome; he clearly knew all the devices for getting visas for foreign countries for persons of shady provenance.

If the CIC men in Austria could have compared notes with the remnants of the old OSS and consulted those card files assembled by the

SSU, they might have learned a good deal about this particular American. His name was Robert Bishop, and he was a veteran of undercover exploits in wartime Romania. Presumably to protect the secrets of American Cold War intelligence, his name was deleted from the official investigation of the "rat line." Bishop would later figure prominently in the effort to roll back the Iron Curtain, but for Milano and the men of the CIC in 1947 he was a disappointment. He "suddenly lost his mental stability," as the evaluations put it, became an alcoholic, and had to be confined to the psychiatric unit of an American military hospital.

The 430th CIC detachment in Salzburg nonetheless decided to pay Dragonovic the then-extravagant fee of $1,500 from their unvouchered funds to "dispose" of each defector from Soviet justice, once their use as intelligence sources was exhausted; the Americans called each one a "visitor" or a "VIP." All records of previous identities were erased as the men disappeared into new lives, families, and livelihoods in Bolivia, Argentina, and other South American countries. Nothing was put in writing about a minor American army intelligence operation — or almost nothing. One contemporary report survives, a rambling assessment by CIC operations officer Captain Paul Lyon:

> [Dragonovic] is known and recorded as a fascist, war criminal, etc., and his contacts with South American diplomats of a similar class are not generally approved by US State Department officials, plus the fact that in the light of security, it is better that we may be able to state, if forced, that the turning over of a DP to a welfare organization falls in line with our democratic way of thinking and that we are not engaged in illegal disposition of war criminals, defectees and the like.[20]

The refugees of the rat line surely numbered only in the dozens — many more, at $1,500 a head, would have raised questions even in the unvouchered funds of the CIC. But the demonstrated efficacy of this novel escape route proved tempting beyond measure for a different sort of "disposal."

Sent along to Dragonovic and then to safety in South America was one particular intelligence asset for the United States in the gathering Cold War, a Nazi war criminal named Klaus Barbie. He was indeed a defector, but not from communism. Both the French and American systems of justice were on his trail, but he had also provided much useful data to American intelligence. Rather than face the consequences of legal and public disclosure of the connection, the CIC decided to "dispose" of him. Barbie, called the "butcher of Lyons" for his role in Nazi atrocities in France, lived for the next thirty-three years as a free man in Bolivia. Only in 1983 was he discovered under his new identity and deported; tried for crimes against humanity in 1987 and sentenced to life imprisonment, he died in a French prison in 1991.

2

Resistance

THE MILLIONS OF MEN, women, and children foraging across central Europe overwhelmed the young American soldiers who had taken on the unfamiliar task of caring for peoples they knew little about. But within the tide of refugees and defectors, the intelligence units of the occupying armies began encountering persons who sought contact with the western democracies for more than shelter and daily sustenance.

From the forests and plain of the Baltic north down across the Carpathian Mountains and into the Balkans came signs that not everything was going smoothly for the Red Army and the political commissars. Resistance to communism was trying to make itself heard by the world outside. A few British and American intelligence field units were listening, whether or not their governments were ready to pay attention. What they heard became the foundations for American policy at the dawn of the Cold War.

Even before the final Nazi surrender, a British monitoring station picked up crackly radio signals from partisan bands deep within the Courland forest of Latvia. Agents of the Czechoslovak Second (Intelligence) Bureau slipped across the Bavarian border into the American zone of occupation during the summer of 1945. During the war they had worked in secret against the Nazis; now they offered to serve against the Red Army "liberators." Refugees from Hungary sought the support of the West against local communists under Moscow's discipline. In Romania, agents recruited by the OSS persistently promoted noncommunist politicians in efforts to prevent the Red Army occupation from turning into a despotic civil government. Polish partisans worked openly against

Soviet Russia, and western intelligence learned that the communist security forces were collecting dossiers on American citizens resident in
Poland — and even on Poles who had at any time visited the United
States. Refugees from Russia itself congregated inside the barracks and
barbed wire of DP camps in the American and British zones of Germany, organizing cells of shadowy political parties eager to overthrow
communist rule.

❋

It took a couple of years for the ingenues of America's halting intelligence agencies to appreciate the diversity of the nations and cultures
"behind the Iron Curtain."

Midway between Stettin and Trieste was Czechoslovakia, an early
victim of Hitler's expansion to the east. Of all the eastern European republics between the world wars, only here had the culture of parliamentary democracy taken hold. The Czech capital of Prague had been allowed to fall under Red Army occupation, to be sure, as Eisenhower
held advancing American troops back at the Sudeten mountain region
on the country's western edge. Yet heirs to the democratic tradition of
Tomaš Masaryk held uneasy sway over the postwar government; three-
quarters of Czechoslovakia's trade in 1946 and 1947 went to the West,
flowing away from the Soviet market. Soviet efforts to reverse this trade
pattern, incidentally, also provided cover for intelligence missions, both
to install a communist government in Czechoslovakia and to mount
sabotage operations in western Europe and the Middle East. Moscow's
station chief or *rezident* operated his network of agents as an export-im-
port enterprise producing world-famous Czech costume jewelry.

For the first three years after the war, internal security was not under
communist control, and the 165-mile Czech border with Bavaria became a porous route of transit for refugees and agents from Poland and
points east who were escaping communist domination or returning under cover on missions of espionage.

Though they failed to appreciate it in time, the western intelligence
services had a rare and fully functioning resource on this stretch of the
Soviet front: the security apparatus of one of the most active intelligence
professionals of the era, General Frantisek Moravec, head of the Czech
Second Bureau before the war, who transplanted his operational head-

quarters to London when Hitler arrived in 1939. With the Nazi defeat, Moravec and his team returned intact to their homeland to defend the noncommunist regime of Edvard Beneš in its futile effort to get along with Stalin while maintaining parliamentary democracy. But because of his ties and affinities to British intelligence, Moravec fled his country a second time after the Czech communists seized power in February 1948. Turning up amid about fifty refugees in the American zone of occupation, Moravec was ignored. American field officers knew nothing of his background in political intelligence; they interrogated him only for technical details of the Soviet order of battle, leaving his wealth of information about the land and politics of Czechoslovakia unexploited.[1]

The coastline of Estonia, Latvia, and Lithuania served British intelligence much the way the Czech-Bavarian border served the Americans. Inlets and harbors along the Baltic coast were easily accessible to motor launches from Sweden, Finland, and even Britain itself. Traffic, overt and covert, was established and commonplace, both under the Nazis and in the early years of the Soviet era.

As the Red Army pushed the Nazi occupiers back from eastern Europe through 1944, Soviet security forces in military formations advanced alongside. Intelligence units reached the Estonian capital of Tallinn, for instance, even before the regular troops, and stumbled upon files conveniently left behind by the retreating Nazis, containing names, addresses, and notes on the personal foibles of the partisan fighters. In Lithuania, the advancing Russians confronted bands of resistance fighters living clandestinely in the forests, numbering in the first years after the war as many as 30,000.[2]

Called locally the "Forest Brothers," these dropouts held fast to their romantic memories of the national independence they had known before the six years of Nazi occupation. They defied the Nazis, then, newly armed with weapons and ammunition left by the retreating Germans, they pursued resistance, but this time against the Russians. News of ambushes of Soviet military patrols reached the West in the summer of 1945; in Estonia the communist Central Committee held an emergency meeting in August to devise battle tactics against "bandits" from the forests. Over the coming months, units of British intelligence started training refugees from the Baltic states for penetration missions behind the Iron Curtain, hoping to make contact with the Forest Brothers. From ports in Sweden and Finland, small craft crossing the Baltic offloaded men and materiel into the thick forests of Courland.

Long afterward, an Estonian named Ants Saulep recalled an incident typical of the furtive encounters managed by undercover agents from the West:

> My old friend Hansen came up one day and asked me if I wanted to go for a drive. I realized that something was afoot, but I agreed anyway. First we drove onto a forest road and Hansen said, "Stop here." Two men with a huge knapsack emerged from the forest and got into the car. We kept driving. Hansen said, "Just drive right through Rapla." There were lots of stories making the rounds . . . so I had a pretty good idea who these men were. I said, "You're crazy. That town's crawling with Reds." Hansen replied, "That's why we're going through Rapla, because no one would think of looking for us there." So we drove to the forest behind Rapla. [The two strangers] stepped out with their bundle, stayed away for a while and then returned.[3]

The savvy Saulep was in no doubt that he had just aided two "bandits" make radio contact with western intelligence from a remote site, and he did it again several times afterward.

Only gradually did the western case officers realize that their clandestine missions were falling into the grip of double agents, the chronic trap of undercover work that would plague the Rollback operations to the end. From 1945 to 1949, British-sponsored penetration missions into the Baltic forests were in fact compromised in an elaborate Soviet design to turn agents from the West into deep-cover agents of the East.[4]

One early double agent was a Latvian named Augusts Bergmanis, a radio operator for the occupying German army during the war who had also established secret communications with the nationalist resistance movement in Sweden. In October of 1945, British intelligence sent a speedboat with four well-equipped Latvian partisans from Sweden to the Courland coast. Communist border patrols spotted the landing and captured the men as they dispersed through the forest — along with the invaluable prize of their communications gear and special ciphers. Meanwhile, Soviet intelligence had identified Bergmanis in a POW camp, recognizing that his wartime Swedish radio contacts could be turned to good advantage. They induced him to cooperate while still posing as the faithful contact of the nationalist underground. Equipped with the newly captured transmitter and codes, Bergmanis made contact with the British intelligence outpost in Stockholm, tentatively at first, then more confidently as his messages seemed to be gaining credibility with the British case officers; his Soviet handlers watched with satisfaction as their deception took hold.

Over the coming months, into 1946, more British agents were dispatched to the Latvian coast to try making contact with the Forest Brothers. When one two-man team encountered transmitter difficulty that September, the British handlers suggested they make contact with this man Bergmanis in Riga, whose communications gear seemed to be in good working order. Within weeks, Bergmanis had gained the confidence of the new arrivals, and Soviet intelligence had gained lists and details of British penetration operations.

A second Soviet double agent, a former student at Riga University named Vidvuds Sveics, penetrated the British infiltration operations even more dramatically. Sveics had been a popular and convivial scholar before the war, and he carried his social contacts with him into army duty. As a nationalist and anticommunist he readily accepted the Nazi occupation in 1939. But Nazi atrocities and the Latvian collaboration in German war crimes apparently soured him on the independence movement. In October 1948, Soviet intelligence arranged for their new recruit Sveics to "escape" to Sweden, where he contacted anticommunist nationalists, ingratiated himself at the undercover training camps, and was chosen by British case officers to lead an ambitious mission to infiltrate agents into Estonia and Lithuania as well as his native Latvia.

Late in April 1949, Sveics led a six-man mission in a fast speedboat to the Lithuanian shore near Palanga. Landing on May 1, the Soviet communist holiday, their white speedboat and rubber landing craft eluded the border patrols. Sveics separated from his colleagues, which was standard procedure, but instead of seeking out the Forest Brothers, he reported to the security authorities. The mission was wiped out within days, but Sveics sent back a properly coded message reporting his "miraculous" escape and readiness to act on further instructions.

The Soviet game of deception was complete. Subsequent penetration missions were compromised before they even began. Moscow's control over the restive Baltic republics repressed the partisan resistance of the

Forest Brothers before British and American intelligence services could be confident that any genuine partisan force even existed.

✳

As the western intelligence services fumbled along in this new postwar order (Soviet intelligence was far ahead, having never interrupted its surveillance of the capitalist societies), Czechoslovakia and the Baltic states fell naturally into the British sphere of operations. But when American intelligence officers looked at Romania, the budding New World operatives in Old World conspiracy thought they knew what they were doing. After all, in the last months of the war the OSS had built a network of imaginative anticommunist agents in Bucharest, run by the dynamic and aggressive naval lieutenant commander Frank Wisner.

Romania had joined the Nazi Axis in 1941, in time to regain the territories of Bessarabia and northern Bukovina as the German armies advanced into the Soviet Union. When the battle lines reversed and the Red Army was poised to reinvade in August 1944, an antifascist coup led by the young King Michael seized power. At this juncture Wisner and the OSS arrived. Their mission, code-named the HAMMERHEAD, plunged into operation with a gusto that left professionals who were more seasoned in Balkan intrigues somewhat bemused. From a 1944 mission report to Washington: "This place is wild with information and Wisner is in his glory. We have a beautiful entree to the government and a place to use it fast while it is available and hot stuff."[5]

One member of Wisner's team, Major Robert Bishop, relished the life of the eager spies as the war entered its final stages of upheaval and destruction: "Romanian tables groaned under the load of plenty. We feasted on fresh caviar from the Delta Danube, sliced salami, smoked sturgeon, chicken roasts and cakes dripping with cream."

The situation for HAMMERHEAD became a little more somber when a proper diplomat from the State Department arrived in November 1944, followed by an official American military mission headed by an elegant West Pointer named Brigadier General Courtlandt Van Rensselaer Schuyler. The OSS seemed superfluous in such company, and Wisner packed up and left Bucharest to wait for more enticing intelligence opportunities. But Romania remained in the institutional memory as a rich and lush land, a land of gypsies and merriment, women and plenty. It huddled directly under the Russian bear, to be sure, but it was blessed by a pliable and pragmatic populace. And the intelligence networks assembled in the months while Frank Wisner was there never stopped humming.

Major Bishop, for one, became a target of controversy over the early Cold War years, with analysts and then historians calling him either prescient or, alternatively, crazed. The assessments he conveyed in 1944 and 1945, some 800 reports to Washington, fed the anti-Soviet passions that had been kept under wraps during the New Deal era. Bishop knew no inhibitions about expressing unfashionable sentiments.[6]

From Chicago, where right-wing anti-Roosevelt sentiments were strong, Bishop, who had been a newspaperman in the 1930s, was one of the gadfly intelligentsia drawn to the OSS for patriotic duty. In Romania as a counterintelligence specialist, he developed contacts with secret agents operating for all sides, as was routine in his position. Most effective were his networks within the counterespionage service of King Michael's new government, which had been preoccupied even during the fascist period with the activities of the Romanian communist party.

Bishop's impressive haul of information included captured Nazi documents, Soviet military training manuals, specifications of weapons used by the Red Army, and topographical maps of terrain totally unfamiliar to the western armies. Restless with this sort of technical data, he directed his scrutiny into grand politics: specifically, the aims of the Soviet Union in postwar Europe. On February 2, 1945, he reported that the Russians planned to set up a puppet government in Germany (in Berlin if possible, otherwise Breslau) once the Nazi regime collapsed. His sources encouraged him to warn that agents of the Communist International, or Comintern, were descending on Italy to foment revolution. As for Romania, the Russians had declared this to be a "reactionary country," Bishop reported, which, for all its pro-western factions, should be incorporated into "the Soviet communist style system as soon as possible."

General Schuyler, Bishop's commanding officer after Wisner departed, was impressed by his access to communist secrets, but the Chicago scoop artist seemed to be turning a bit obsessive in his politics — and, amid the opulence of Bucharest, in his personal life as well. When he left the American military mission under a cloud in April, he branded his colleagues as "reds" and, more troubling, used official transport to smuggle out of the country his mistress, a Romanian woman widely regarded as first a Nazi and then a Soviet agent.

Threatened with court-martial, Bishop managed to secure a job with the International Refugee Organization in Rome, devising devious means to smuggle anticommunists to havens in South America. For this task, collaboration with the nefarious Father Dragonovic on the "rat line" was mutually rewarding. Between bouts of alcoholism and psychiatric therapy, Bishop sold American intelligence officers on the notion of assembling "large numbers of underground troops, military supplies, sea evacuation, air evacuation and the like" — the sorts of facilities that would be necessary if a campaign to roll back the Iron Curtain ever got under way. (Bishop was recruited for the Central Intelligence Agency in 1950, under his old partner in the carousings of Bucharest, Frank Wisner).

Bishop's reports to the OSS in the spring of 1945 are remembered as the first substantive signals to Washington that the alliance with Soviet Russia would not survive into peacetime. But at the time OSS officers reviewed the so-called Bishop Traffic with skeptical eyes. Bishop had produced "a mass of false information and half-truths, false predictions and sinister insinuations," concluded an OSS analyst in August 1945. "Since he had a few dealings with some Russians and had some reliable Russian agents, he will undoubtedly pose as an authority." This officer believed "that any reports written by him on the Russians should be promptly consigned to the wastepaper basket." British intelligence officers in Bucharest who knew Bishop's associates and life style considered his reports to be "pure drivel."

Bishop was prematurely anticommunist, tilting at the views of official Washington in the first postwar months. Kennan's Long Telegram and the agonizing reassessment that followed were still to come. Late in the summer of 1945 an official OSS assessment cited Bishop for an "extreme anti-Russian bias [which] reaches the stage of the spectacular." And the evaluator stretched to a political conclusion that conservatives could relish as evidence of leftist New Deal influence upon the OSS: "The erroneous and/or misleading information . . . contributed in some part to the reservoir of ill will against the Russians. Thus at a time in history when the future peace of the world may depend on good Anglo-American-

Russian relations, the [Bishop] reports contributed in an irresponsible way to the deterioration of such efforts."[7]

Bishop's life style in Bucharest and then in Rome allowed his critics to score credible *ad hominem* points. One of the classic pitfalls of intelligence, a factor always to be measured, is the confounding of the substance of a message with the nature and quality of the messenger. For all the political and personal eccentricities from which it came, the Bishop Traffic of 1945 proved more accurate about developments in Europe than the hopeful assessments of those who fervently expected things to work out differently.

*

The American intelligence services that picked up the pieces of the wartime OSS ran more than fourteen major operations in Romania during 1946, even without Wisner and Bishop. As the Iron Curtain descended, Washington could claim an impressive array of sources in the Romanian military staff and intelligence services, both foreign and domestic.

One valuable agent recruited by the Wisner mission was Teodore Manacatide, a staff sergeant in the intelligence section of the Romanian General Staff. Manacatide was one of those few secret "assets" retained by American intelligence after the demise of the OSS, and he provided a flow of timely data on the Soviet army maneuvers in Romania. Two officers of Schuyler's military mission, Major Thomas Hall and Lieutenant Ira Hamilton, regularly toured Transylvania and Bukovina, ignoring the watchful eyes of the communist internal security system. In February 1946 they reported that they had located "guerrilla warfare cadres to commit acts of sabotage behind enemy lines in the event of war between the Anglo-Americans and the USSR."

Some American newsmen, notably Reuben Markham of the *Christian Science Monitor*, saw no professional conflict between filing news stories for American readers and drumming up support among Romanians for the anticommunist National Peasant Party. When the Romanian government revoked Markham's press credentials, the State Department formally protested an affront to the freedom of the press, overlooking the fact that the correspondent had on occasion actually addressed election rallies with denunciations of communism and of the government in power.

Romanian security finally caught up with Sergeant Manacatide and claimed to have evidence implicating the entire American military mission in espionage. "While there may be a grain of truth in these reports," the proper General Schuyler confided to his diary, "I am certain they are much exaggerated."[8] He nonetheless recommended that Manacatide be removed from danger. The loyal spy and his family were spirited out of Romania on October 16, 1946, and granted entry to the United States as one of those special assets; he went on to take charge of anticommunist broadcasts back to his homeland.

Efforts to prevent a complete communist takeover of Romania collapsed in 1947. The surviving SSU networks switched their mission to one of "clandestine removal" of their Romanian contacts. Major Hall and Lieutenant Hamilton, both scholars of the Balkans in civilian life, attempted to evacuate two opposition leaders; the hapless politicians were arrested in July as they prepared to board an American military courier flight. Schuyler complained that the charges against them were "unfair and absurd," but when Washington asked the British to join in a formal protest, the more jaundiced Whitehall refused. The British government had concluded that the American intelligence operatives in Romania had been caught "red-handed."

Across the border in Hungary, the first Americans on the scene were also hopeful that a communist takeover could be averted. The Red Army had swept through on its way to Vienna and Nazi Germany, but the surviving government of that defeated Axis country was still noncommunist. Some five hundred Hungarian communists who had fled to Moscow during the war returned in the path of the invading army, but the Hungarian communist party gained only two ministries in a coalition. The dominant party, the Smallholders, championing a program of land reform against the large holdings of the old Hapsburg aristocracy, built up support not only among the peasantry but among urban artisans and merchants as well. The first postwar elections were held in November 1945, and correspondent John Gunther reflected Washington's assessment in calling them the freest election in Hungarian history. In a secret ballot, the Smallholders won 57 percent of the vote, the communists only 17 percent.

American intelligence access within Hungary at the war's end was no better than elsewhere in eastern Europe, and in one respect it was worse. Networks of agents were run not by the OSS or its successor SSU but by a surviving remnant of a quite different intelligence service that few in the government even knew existed. Created within the Army General Staff in 1942, separate from G-2, this secret apparatus, nick-named the Pond, was supposed to provide a source of intelligence for the military independent of the civilian OSS. It became a haven for the true-believing right-wingers of Washington, distrustful both of Roose-velt's alliance with the Soviet Union and of left-wing influence within Donovan's "hydra-headed" monstrosity.

Presiding over the Pond was a West Pointer named Colonel John V. Grombach, a no-nonsense man (he happened also to be a champion wrestler) who believed in nuts-and-bolts espionage — barroom seduc-tions, dead drops, and all the paraphernalia. He had little use for the political nuances savored by intellectuals in the OSS. Above all, Grom-bach despised communists, and to him that included socialists, neutral-ists, and New Dealers.

By chance, long after Wisner and the other OSS officers had left east-ern Europe, the man from the Pond was still hanging on under cover in Budapest. Grombach pressed the advantage. In April 1946 he engaged a new agent for Hungary, an irreverent Foreign Service officer named James McCargar. For the next two years, McCargar managed to sustain no less than three levels of secret intelligence cover.[9]

As far as his colleagues in the American legation knew, McCargar was second secretary and chief of the political section. But he presented himself to the Soviet occupation command as a military agent charged with ferreting out former Nazis and their tangible assets (the so-called SAFEHAVEN operation). At his most secret level, McCargar ran the in-telligence network built up by the Pond in the last months of the war: eight relatively well placed informants within Hungarian politics — un-fortunately, all from parties of the right wing. McCargar found the Pond to be no better informed about Soviet intentions than the SSU teams in Romania (except for Bishop).

The majority Smallholders party, attempting to capitalize on its first election triumph, brought into the streets of Budapest what they called the largest public rally in Hungarian history, the so-called Peasant Days of September 1946. The local communists, backed by the Soviet military presence, denounced the Smallholders and most other noncommunist political figures as fascists, to be summarily excluded from the political process. At the next election, in August 1947, the communist party and its coerced allies won 45 percent of the votes; the Smallholders dropped to 15 percent.

Once the omens were clear, in Hungary as in Romania, the central task for American intelligence operatives became the "clandestine removal" of politicians threatened by the communists. Among the Pond's agents inherited by McCargar was a man identified as G U Y. Sizing him up as a rank opportunist working for all paying sides, McCargar nonetheless found that G U Y had stumbled upon something useful. Through the usual intrigues, he had acquired a farm of 200 acres in the Hungarian countryside — not just any 200 acres, but a tract that squarely abutted the Austrian border. As the 1947 election approached, G U Y confided to McCargar his scheme for survival and escape: "One day, working my fields, I'll just stumble through a bush into Austria, and that will be that."

McCargar conjured up a more expansive plan; if this one agent could thus escape, perhaps G U Y could be induced — that is, paid — to offer the escape route to any "peasant" who happened one day to be working those priceless acres. McCargar sought authorization from the Pond to proceed. He was startled and encouraged by the speed of Grombach's reply: "G U Y former British agent . . . You may use him for stated purpose only provided you maintain your cover with him and provided you're satisfied he's not working with British." (The British government had by this time passed to the Labour Party — socialist, and thus deeply suspect to Grombach.)

By December 1947 the Scarlet Pimpernel of a renegade American intelligence service had managed the escape of seventy-four anticommunist Hungarians, including five scientists sought by U.S. Naval Intelligence. Almost among their number was the threatened president of Hungary, Zoltán Tildy, a founder of the Smallholders party. At the last moment, Tildy aborted his stumble through the bushes; McCargar was informed that the president needed a staff of fourteen aides to accompany him, and the cover for G U Y's escape route could accommodate no more than eight.*

---

* Tildy was forced to resign as Hungary's president after the communist takeover in 1947 and lived on in house arrest. He surfaced again in the short-lived uprising of 1956 to become a minister of state, then was rearrested in the subsequent communist crackdown. He died in Hungary in 1961.

The Pond had authorized McCargar to "extract" no more than twenty-five Hungarians, but long afterward he said he was never reproached for exceeding instructions. The escapees of 1947 became the nucleus of an émigré resistance movement that kept the idea of Hungarian democracy alive abroad for the next nine years, until the uprising of 1956.

*

Through the birch forests and placid hill villages along that porous Czechoslovak border in the summer of 1947 appeared some unusual strangers. Straggling into Germany a dozen or so at a time, they declared themselves to be nationalist partisans escaped from the Soviet Ukraine.

The border patrols of the American occupation zone were bewildered by these militant men in dark green fatigues, bearded, filthy, exhausted. Were they former Nazis on the run, freebooters seeking their fortunes from war and turmoil, or even communist agents posing as refugees, out to infiltrate the American zone and the émigré communities in the DP camps? Most ominously for immediate concern, these wild men were armed, a few with Soviet-type automatic hand pistols, mostly with captured German machine guns. They were immediately disarmed, of course, and on August 31 the United States Army ordered the occupation forces to "hold these men in internment, interrogate them, and then [we will] make up our minds as to what disposition is to be made of them."

In their "disposition," the campaigns to roll back the Iron Curtain reached their climax years later. No Americans yet knew it, but word spread swiftly among the Ukrainian émigrés in the DP camps and farther afield that the armed forces of the West had made their first contact with "the almost legendary resistance army" of Ukraine. In the following weeks of interrogation, their story emerged.[10]

Since spring, an anticommunist underground movement called in English the Ukrainian Insurgent Army, or UPA, had been locked in battle in the dense forest and isolated villages of the Carpathian Mountains where Ukraine touches on southern Poland along a ragged frontier. An estimated six thousand to eight thousand partisans had confronted division-strength Russian and Polish communist security forces armed with infantry and tanks. A Ukrainian ambush on March 27 took the life of a powerful Polish general, a revered veteran of the Spanish civil war. Reprisals terrorized the rural people; houses were pillaged and whole villages burnt down. To the local populations, the Ukrainian partisans were indeed "bandits," who brought only trouble as they went about demanding national independence.

By summer the UPA partisans saw their fate sealed by the superior forces of the communist state. They began dispersing from their fighting formations, most withdrawing back to normal village life but ready to resume combat once orders and encouragement came from outside. A small detachment decided to break out and head toward the West, where, within Ukrainian refugee communities, they hoped to reestablish their cause and seek outside support. They made their way by night through Slovakia, hiding by day in dirty bunkers, advancing by night along back trails and through obscure hamlets, under constant ambush from security forces. Most were captured; the leader of one of the breakout detachments was put on trial in Prague and executed.

On August 11 an advance guard unit reached the Bavarian border, 1,500 kilometers from their starting point. They reported twenty-two separate engagements with communist security forces across Czechoslovakia and the Soviet occupation zone of Austria. In the days following, other surviving bands of the breakout showed up and turned themselves in. American occupation authorities issued a laconic statement on September 14: "American troops disarmed and interred a detachment of 36 soldiers of the Ukrainian Insurgent Army (UPA) in the area of Passau. This UPA detachment, equipped with machine guns and automatic pistols, succeeded in forcing its way from the Carpathians through Czechoslovakia, via Linz (Austria) to Wildenraan near Passau, in four weeks' time."[11]

The Ukraine from which these men had fled was, next to Russia, the largest of the Soviet republics. During the civil war after the Bolshevik revolution, Ukrainian nationalists had declared sovereign independence, but theirs was one assertion of self-determination that failed to catch Wilson's notice in the Versailles settlement of 1919. Blessed with rich mineral resources and fertile land for agriculture, Ukraine was the envy of its neighbors; it was an early target of the Nazis as they advanced into the Soviet Union in 1939.

Intellectuals in sophisticated Ukrainian cities like Lvov and Kiev wel-

comed the Nazi invaders as liberators from Russian communist domination. The Nazi occupation held for nearly five years. As the tide of the
war turned and the Red Army moved to reoccupy Ukraine, political
commissars with the advance units were concerned that ideological cor-
ruption had contaminated the people during the years when they were
removed from communist control. The Red Army singled out for ominous "special attention" young Ukrainians who had not enjoyed a Soviet
education, who had been brought up in "bourgeois" schools. Accord-
ingly, a significant portion of the intelligentsia in western Ukraine —
students and their teachers — fled to the West with the retreating Nazis.

Among them was a nationalist functionary named Mykola Lebid,
who, under postwar interrogation, admitted that he had served the Nazis. Now, he said, he had been dispatched to the West by the revolutionary Stepan Bandera, whose checkered record emerged all too clearly
upon investigation by British and American intelligence units. Under
Polish rule before the war and then during the German occupation,
Bandera's men had mobilized partisans in the Carpathians, sometimes
collaborating, sometimes opposing the occupiers. Bandera himself had
been periodically incarcerated and released by the Nazis as local security needs dictated. In July 1944, with the Nazis in retreat, Bandera's loyalists met in a remote Carpathian village to plan the next phase of their
struggle for a Ukraine independent of both Germany and Russia.

Resistance to Soviet rule may have seemed commendable in the
West's growing mood of anticommunism, but the tactics of partisan warfare, including sneak raids upon villages to terrorize local civilians who
failed to cooperate, did not. CIC reports in 1945 and 1946 dismissed
Lebid as "a well known sadist and collaborator of the Germans."[12] Perhaps, but within a few short years American intelligence officers would
rise above such scruples.

In those first postwar years, Soviet strategists saw the implications of
nationalist resistance in eastern Europe more clearly than the Americans did. Partisan bands were gaining ground through 1946 despite the
might of the Red Army, the political commissars, and local communist
believers. And as these groups became bolder, the front-line units of
western intelligence watched in confusion, combat over turf, and impo-
tence.

As one veteran of Kremlin intrigue saw it, the last months of 1946 were when the "hostilities of the Cold War became dangerous."[13] Decades later, when Russians were allowed a measure of candor, one of Stalin's top intelligence executives, Pavel Sudoplatov, wrote proudly of the Kremlin's response. As "formerly highly successful [intelligence] activities . . . began to lose effectiveness," he euphemistically explained, the Soviet intelligence apparatus was thoroughly shaken up. Sudoplatov met that summer with the up-and-coming Nikita S. Khrushchev, Moscow's appointed officer for enforcing Soviet control over Ukraine. They analyzed the threat posed by Bandera and the Ukrainian nationalists and concluded that the traitors had to be liquidated.

At this level, however, Soviet intelligence was little better than the interrogation officers of the British and American occupation zones. The first target selected for assassination was an aging Ukrainian nationalist named Shumsky. The deed was done, a dose of poison administered in a Soviet hospital, making the man's death look like natural heart failure. But the Soviets had picked the wrong man. Western intelligence records reveal virtually nothing about anyone named Shumsky, and Sudoplatov admitted that unlike several other Ukrainians who could have been targeted, "we were never able to establish any foreign connections for Shumsky."[14]

Militant resistance to communism in eastern Europe reached its climax in the autumn of 1947, as Washington began to reload its weapons of intelligence. From Stettin to Trieste, reinvigorated communist security forces under direction from Moscow mounted massive operations to crush nationalist partisans. The Forest Brothers were decimated as a fighting force, and many of them committed suicide rather than submit. Few in the wider world noticed.

Resistance movements in the occupied nations of eastern Europe, even in Ukraine and the Baltic republics, which had been part of the Soviet Union for decades, had an ad hoc character. But refugees from the homeland of Russia could summon long memories of abortive attempts to organize an anti-Bolshevik front.

During the interwar period, White Russian and monarchist émigré communities in western Europe, Poland, and the Balkans had coalesced into shadowy political factions with grand-sounding names like Intermarium, Prometheus and, more mysteriously, the NTS. They attracted the attention of western European anti-Bolsheviks in the 1930s, and then of Nazi propagandists in the early 1940s. After World War II, British and French intelligence units, circulating within the DP camps in their occupation zones, seemed attracted to the heritage of Intermarium and Prometheus; Americans in Germany seized upon the NTS, active in the West German DP camp of Monchehof.[15]

The Narodno-Trudovoy Soyuz, called in English the National Union of Labor Solidarists, had been organized in Belgrade in the 1930s by the postrevolution generation of Russian émigrés. Their political platform adopted the ideology of the corporate state fashionable among followers of Mussolini in Italy and Salazar in Portugal. As early as 1941, Nazi commanders on the eastern front flirted with the NTS as a pliant instrument to pacify Soviet populations under German occupation. But the NTS itself was more concerned during the war with spreading its right-wing ideology — a Russian nationalist agenda that conflicted with the Nazi designs — among Russian DPs, POWs, and forced laborers. In the spring of 1944 the Gestapo arrested the NTS leaders in Berlin, where they had been conducting training schools for Russian POWs.

American occupation authorities were ready to forgive these anticommunist factions their Nazi affiliations as matters of wartime pragmatism; indeed, they were reassured by the frictions between the NTS and the Nazi leadership. They watched warily as NTS cadres launched into classic techniques of social mobilization in the DP camps, setting up schools, child-care centers, churches, even a Russian Boy Scout society. Starting in March 1947, the NTS published a newspaper, called *Possev*, which quickly attracted a wide readership among the Russian refugees. Within the year, American observers noted, the NTS had enrolled two thousand members, to become the most influential of the Russian émigré parties.

From the Monchehof base, the NTS sought to spread out. "We were convinced the German economy would never recover, so we prepared to emigrate to any country that would have us," recalled Gleb Rahr, an early NTS idealist. "We studied the languages of our destinations; it made for a flourishing amateur cultural life in the camps."[16] Rahr himself went to Morocco, where a small community of displaced Russians had started to build a new life. But soon he and many of his partisans returned to Germany, where interesting opportunities — and funds — started flowing in from unnamed outside sources.

Stalin's watchful intelligence apparatus took the anticommunist refugees far more seriously in these early years than the Americans did. After all, from the first years of the Bolshevik revolution, penetration of émigré communities had commanded high priority in the Kremlin. Scarcely was the war over in Europe before Soviet agents went to work on the reorganized émigré organizations, including the NTS; surrendering to the camps in the guise of destitute DPs and defectors, Russian agents were able to set themselves up as double agents and sustain a steady flow of reports back to Moscow.

SSU agents picked up word as early as February 1946 that Soviet intelligence was compiling lists of all Soviet citizens anywhere in sight, making them vulnerable to forced repatriation or even assassination on the spot. Should a new war break out — and that fear was alive in both East and West — the Kremlin worried that Britain and the United States would be more imaginative than the old "bourgeois" enemies of Bolshevism, including the hidebound Nazis, who had treated émigrés from the East with contempt. In a new war, the SSU source reported, the Kremlin believed that the western powers would "make better use of tens of thousands of Soviet citizens" who had fled the revolution.[17] In this expectation, and knowing of thousands of other refugees from the satellites, the Russians appreciated better than the Americans what was to come. Kennan and his colleagues were only starting to notice the émigrés; Moscow already understood full well their potential for anti-Soviet agitation.

Far from these scenes of intelligence and espionage, the United States signed formal treaties of peace with various governments of eastern Europe on February 10, 1947. C. L. Sulzberger, the wise and worldly diplomatic columnist of the *New York Times*, witnessed the ceremony at the Quai d'Orsay. He reported "strangely little joy either in the room or in Paris itself, which greeted the event with supreme indifference."

Secretary of State James F. Byrnes remarked upon the ambivalence of American attitudes toward the nations of eastern Europe, now that the presidency had passed to Truman and the wartime alliance with Soviet

Russia was crumbling. In his last speech before leaving office Byrnes gave a succinct and understated depiction of the political transformation taking place as the midpoint of the century approached: "During the year or more that these treaties were under discussion it was inevitable that the differences between the Allies should be emphasized, and at times exaggerated. On the other hand, during the war some of these differences were minimized and overlooked."[18]

Indeed they were, and had been for a much longer time than the war years that Byrnes chose to address.

PART II
Washington at Peace

3

Liberals and Conservatives

ONCE UPON A TIME, Washington was a sleepy southern town on the tidewater Potomac. But in the fourth decade of the twentieth century, the placid atmosphere over the District of Columbia ripened into the air of a national capital in ferment.

Armies of enthusiastic social reformers from across the country had moved in with Roosevelt's New Deal to staff the burgeoning agencies of an activist government. From 1933 to 1938 the rolls of federal employees grew by 50 percent, and the demands of World War II only intensified the transformation. Settling into the comfortable life of a booming civil service, the reformers sought each other out and shared their zeal in study groups, after-hours discussion circles, and meetings with kindred souls around town. Acting on their passion to lift the United States from depression and make the world better, they became fascinated with the social experiments of communist Russia, even as they feared the rise of fascism in Europe.

More sedate and remote from the mainsprings of New Deal power were the conservative civil servants, military officers, diplomats, and intellectuals who, while offended by fascism, nonetheless considered the excesses of Hitler a transitory distraction from the longer-term threat to democracy posed by Stalin's communism. They chafed at the realization that their warnings were not heeded in New Deal Washington.

The phenomenon of Bolshevism had puzzled Americans from the start. Woodrow Wilson, president at the time of the Russian Revolution in 1917, saw in Bolshevism "a curious policy, . . . a protest against the way in which the world had worked." At the same time his secretary of state,

5 3

Robert Lansing, had made up his mind that Bolshevism was "the most hideous and monstrous thing that the human mind has ever conceived." If the New Deal reformers tended to be tolerant of Bolshevik missteps along the path toward what would surely be a more just society, the professional diplomatic service concurred with Lansing's attitude. The austere diplomat Joseph C. Grew, who had served in America's embassy to the tsar before the revolution, found attempts to do business with Bolsheviks "profoundly disgusting."[1]

Outside the corridors of government, fundamentalist Christians across the land saw their faith in conflict with communism; Lenin had closed the churches of Russia and executed thousands of priests and active believers. If the voices of evangelical Christians were not widely respected in the Washington of the New Deal, no lawmaker could ignore the resounding presence in the capital of Edmund A. Walsh, founder of the School of Foreign Service at Georgetown University. This articulate Jesuit scholar of Russian history had managed a relief mission to Russia in the early 1920s, and upon his return home he entered upon a long and illustrious career of outspoken anticommunism. Even further from the favors of the New Deal than the conservative diplomats, Walsh's students were nonetheless dispersed through the church and government, including military officers' training schools where the revered father regularly taught courses on "godless and materialistic" Marxism.[2]

From far-distant New York came constant feudings of the restive and contentious intelligentsia, a group enlarged by émigrés who had fled from Stalin's power before the war, now huddled together on the Lower East Side. Many were partisans of Stalin's archrival, Leon Trotsky, languishing in exile in Mexico City; others had become disenchanted, well before the New Deal, with the failed promise of Bolshevism. Intellectuals like Sidney Hook, professor of philosophy at New York University, pursued nasty and vocal vendettas against academic colleagues who clung to the Marxist dream. Though Hook's sentiments may have matched the views of the Washington conservatives, they were endlessly expressed in the tiresome fury that only academic communities can muster. In that era New York intellectuals lived a world away from the civil servants of the capital.

Two public forces that would later stir up national zeal for a strategy to roll back the tide of communism in eastern Europe did not really count in this prewar intellectual ferment: the Federal Bureau of Investigation under its domineering director, J. Edgar Hoover, and the House of Representatives Select Committee on Un-American Activities, chaired by the conservative Democrat Martin Dies of Texas. Dies was not inhibited by pretensions to intellect, but he was ever sensitive to the predispositions of his conservative constituents. Conceding at one point that the New Dealers running all those new Washington agencies might not actually be communists, he claimed they were certainly "irresponsible, unrepresentative, radical and crackpot." One of them, he charged, was even a nudist![3]

Hoover was of a different cut. Riding on his well-publicized success against gangsters, he found it prudent to tolerate New Deal sympathies for Soviet Russia. The manipulative FBI director was not yet ready to make his break with the presidency.

The New Deal got off to a bad start with the conservatives of Washington. One of President Roosevelt's early foreign policy decisions, to the dismay of Walsh, Grew, and others, was to open diplomatic relations with the Soviet Union, sixteen years after the Bolshevik Revolution. In that interim State Department experience with Soviet affairs came primarily through the American legation at Riga, capital of (briefly) independent Latvia. There George Kennan, Loy Henderson, and their generation of professional diplomats first encountered the realities of Marxist-Leninist-Stalinist power. The veterans of Riga built the institutional memory of the East European Division of the State Department, and it was not at all sympathetic to the social experiment of communism that so intrigued the New Deal zealots.

Picking up the mood of the White House, Undersecretary of State Sumner Welles abolished the East European Division in 1937, folding it into a broader European section. When Henderson returned home from Moscow in October 1938, he found himself covering Soviet affairs from one of two desks in a lower-floor office; his colleague at the other desk kept watch over Poland and the Baltic states. Neither had a secretary. Kennan was one who suspected that this seemingly efficient reorganization "was the result, if not of direct communist penetration, then at least of an unhealthy degree of communist influence in higher counsels of the Roosevelt administration."[4]

The diplomats from Riga, the émigrés in New York, and the ideological anticommunists of Jesuit Georgetown were about the only Americans who noticed the arrival in the United States of a mysterious defector from Stalin's power on November 10, 1938.

*

When the French luxury liner *Normandie* docked that day in New York Harbor, newsmen and photographers with boxy flash cameras converged on the arriving celebrities in first class; Noel Coward and Laurence Olivier, on their way to the Broadway theaters, were judged newsworthy. No headline-hunting journalist would have deigned to notice an obscure passenger disembarking from steerage, a stateless thirty-eight-year-old Jew from Polish Galicia.

At birth his name was Shmelka Ginsberg; to his secret comrades in adulthood he was revered as Walter G. Krivitsky, veteran of a career in espionage for Soviet Russia. "The things in which Krivitsky was embroiled cast a long, unpleasant shadow that has not yet blurred painlessly with history" — that judgment came from the *Washington Post* in the mid-1960s, fully twenty-five years after the man's death.[5] The suspicion and discomfort provoked by Krivitsky reached their final resolutions only in the 1990s, as the intelligence secrets of the former Soviet Union began unraveling.

Deception as a way of life must have been endemic in the Galician shtetl of Podvolochiska: Shmelka Ginsberg was one of six village schoolmates at the turn of the century who rose to responsible careers in the Kremlin's secret network. This remarkable apparatus was able to undermine the conspiracies of the émigrés who fled the revolutions of 1917, even turning some of their leaders into double agents. Stalin's intelligence officers led combat in Spain against Franco's fascist movement. In Britain the comrades scored a success that Stalin never fully appreciated, stitching together a web of operatives among disaffected young gentlemen at Cambridge University — Burgess, Maclean, Philby, Blunt were names of men exposed in the headlines years later. Efforts toward the same end were just getting started in Washington when, in 1936, the Soviet dictator himself botched the whole secret mission.

Stalin unleashed an orgy of purges against loyalists who he thought threatened his rule; show trials, executions, and terror took hold of his Communist Party. Agents serving abroad, such as Krivitsky, were particularly vulnerable, for in Stalin's eyes they had been corrupted by years of living under sinful capitalism. Espionage networks built up over years were abandoned; comrades were summoned to Moscow for consultations, never to return to their foreign bases. Among those who managed to stay on post, a few assassinations sent an eloquent message. In 1937 alone, three thousand professionals of the Soviet foreign intelligence apparatus were liquidated. Four of Krivitsky's schoolmates were among that number. Then a fifth, the most formidable of all, Ignace Reiss, was found machine-gunned to death in a ditch outside Geneva, the Kremlin's reward for his secret life of dedication on the underside of the world revolution.

Krivitsky, the last survivor of the Podvolochiska boys, disappeared into Paris over the 1937–38 winter into the circles of motley émigrés, his own agents and agents of others. Living furtively in the gray zone between discipline and defection, he had no trouble making contact with Trotskyists and former adversaries in French intelligence; the cat-and-mouse game familiar to all clandestine operators began in earnest.

The Russian agent had knowledge of plots and networks that the French wanted to penetrate; the French were able to offer some degree of personal security until the dust settled. Twice, Krivitsky believed, he was the subject of assassination attempts; twice his French protectors saved him. In return he submitted to interrogations by the French counterintelligence services. Records of these debriefings have not come to light and, given the tenacious secrecy of counterespionage, probably never will. But other contemporary records show tidbits of proffered information that reached the highest levels of the French government. Some months after Krivitsky started talking, for instance, Premier Edouard Daladier learned of alarming clues about Soviet espionage networks at work in Washington. Over breakfast one day early in 1938, Daladier told the American ambassador, William C. Bullitt, that the Russians were in regular contact with left-wing sympathizers in the State Department. He dropped a name that was unknown to him or Bullitt: Hiss.

Intelligence services, even those of friendly governments, often play games with each other to smoke out information, to assert an advantage in ongoing operations, or even just to make mischief. Bullitt thought little of the premier's tip, but he sent a casual note to a State Department friend, Stanley K. Hornbeck of the Far Eastern Division, where the up-and-coming Alger Hiss was serving. Hornbeck considered the identification to be gossip, and far-fetched at that. Hiss was, after all, a personal friend, and Washington was full of people intrigued by the Soviet experiment. Bullitt, nonetheless, had picked up enough information about this mysterious man Krivitsky to deem him worthy of a hearing in Washington. He arranged a temporary visa allowing entry into the United States, and the apostate Soviet agent debarked unnoticed from the lower decks of the *Normandie*.

A defector from Soviet Russia was an alien being in the America of the late 1930s. None of the usual mechanisms of counterintelligence — the interrogations, safe houses, and identity changes — were yet in place. Nor was the intellectual climate particularly welcoming to an undercover conspirator like Krivitsky. He arrived at the high point of the fashionable campaign called the Popular Front Against Fascism, an operation of the Comintern, which ordered comrades to cooperate with other political activists — even the class enemy — to combat the Nazi threat. Comintern agents were making their way into New Deal discussion circles, stimulating and nurturing the growth of study groups and turning them into purposeful cells and networks. Government officials, never questioning their own patriotism, were subtly enticed in the interests of social justice to provide useful information to agents of a foreign power. "Seldom if ever have individuals who prided themselves on rationality and humanity been so impervious to evidence or so indifferent to mass inhumanity," wrote a conservative critic years later.[6] Idealistic Americans did not fully grasp it at the time, but internal Comintern documents exposed decades after the fact leave no doubt that espionage was from the start Stalin's purpose in promoting the Popular Front.[7]

Krivitsky was not the sort to be welcomed by earnest New Dealers like Alger Hiss, but on Ambassador Bullitt's advisory a few lonely officials on the lower floors of the State Department were willing to give him a hearing.

*

Settling in to his new Washington posting after leaving Riga, Loy Henderson called an old contact in New York with whom he had often compared notes about the Bolshevik phenomenon, a journalist and publicist named Isaac Don Levine. Henderson asked if Levine could help him get in touch with this secretive man Krivitsky. Could he indeed!

Levine, then forty-six, had launched himself as a freelance journalist covering the Russian Revolution of 1917. Fluent in the language, gregarious, and self-promoting, he made it his business to know everyone who knew anything about the Bolsheviks. From his Russian émigré contacts in New York, he learned about the arrival of a stateless Russian with a background in conspiracy. Above all, Levine was after the Big Story, and in Krivitsky he thought he had it. Krivitsky spoke no English; Levine was warm and welcoming to him those first weeks in America.[8]

Levine took Krivitsky to meet Henderson on January 10, 1939.[9] The spy and the diplomat had a pleasant introductory chat, the sort that spies and diplomats engage in while they make up their minds about each other. Neither man knew exactly whom he was meeting. For all his experience with Russian matters, Henderson was not accustomed to conversing with Soviet intelligence agents, at least knowingly. Krivitsky, inevitably suspicious, had no way of knowing whether this courteous man Henderson was part of the underground network of Russian contacts within the State Department (the cells he had already described to French counterintelligence) or the opposite.

The problem for a defector is always deciding how much to tell. Revealing too little invites the loss of attention; too much too soon may waste valuable counterintelligence secrets — the defector's only major asset — and poses the risk of confiding in the wrong person. Krivitsky did not want to reveal what he knew about Soviet espionage in Washington; on this occasion he never mentioned Hiss's name. But he did make bold to drop word of spy cells in the British Foreign Office, mentioning specifically a minor civil servant with access to highly secret dispatches. Henderson, impressed, promptly alerted the British embassy, which checked out the evidence and eventually apprehended the obscure offender.

Krivitsky correctly saw in Henderson a conventional high-minded diplomat to whom the tradecraft of counterintelligence was an unsavory matter to be handled by others. He proceeded to switch his candor to a matter of state policy, which he was certain would get Henderson's full attention: Stalin, he warned, was on the verge of making a deal, a nonaggression pact, with Hitler. The implications were clear to both men; at a stroke the Soviet dictator would undermine the entire Popular Front just as surely as he had sabotaged the Soviet intelligence service. Cautious and punctilious, Henderson noted Krivitsky's information, but he regarded it as too incredible to be taken seriously.

Krivitsky's final ploy was to tell Henderson how easy it was for the Soviet intelligence services to infiltrate agents into the United States. The diplomat arranged for the defector to step downstairs to meet Ruth Shipley, dutiful director of the State Department's passport office, who made it her business to keep undesirables out of the country — and, not incidentally, to enhance her own power within the department bureaucracy. Krivitsky found in Shipley a kindred spirit in the nuts and bolts of undercover activity. In years to come, Shipley and J. Edgar Hoover became partners in detecting and rooting out communist influences, but at this early time she saw no reason to inform the FBI of all she learned from Krivitsky about the individuals and techniques of Soviet intelligence.

Krivitsky's professional paranoia led him to fear that the Stalinist apparatus that had found his friend Ignace Reiss would find him too. He reported to Henderson on March 15 a chance encounter he had had at a quick-lunch stand at Times Square with a Soviet undercover agent he had known long before in Moscow. Krivitsky took refuge in a lobby of the *New York Times* building nearby, then sneaked out a back door to fade into the crowds on Broadway. Henderson was alarmed by the suspicious encounter but, despairing of attracting high-level attention to instances of Soviet perfidy, he wearily wrote up Krivitsky's story in a secret memorandum for the files. It finally came to light only in 1986.

Over the next months Levine complained to Henderson and everyone else he could snag that no one in government was listening to Krivitsky. The journalist/publicist spread the story about an imminent Nazi-Soviet pact, to the scorn of the Popular Front enthusiasts and the disbelief of everyone else. In desperation, he persuaded the defector to go public with a series of exposés of Soviet espionage to be published in the then-influential *Saturday Evening Post* (contracted and ghost-written, of course, by Don Levine). The first article appeared on April 5, 1939. Taken aback by this unfavorable publicity, Hoover's FBI challenged the defector's credibility, and the propagandists of the Popular Front swung into action with denunciations of this audacious — indeed, outrageous — Russian apostate who was exploiting American hospitality. Krivitsky endured four months of public contempt, until the day in August when Hitler's Germany and Stalin's Soviet Union announced their nonaggression pact.

The Popular Front imploded overnight. The House Committee on Un-American Activities was finally roused to listen to the Soviet defector who had first warned of the astonishing development; Krivitsky testified before the committee on October 11.[10] For the eager anti-Stalinists of New York and Washington, it was a thoroughly wasted opportunity. William Hood, a latter-day American intelligence professional, wrote that Krivitsky had "managed to disclose some important information, [but] the committee squandered his time with primitive questions. . . . For Krivitsky this was far from the counter-intelligence wringer through which he would have put a senior officer who had defected from a hostile intelligence service."[11]

But among Krivitsky's tidbits was an authoritative depiction of how the Comintern intelligence service recruited members of the American Communist Party — not all 100,000 of them, of course, only those who could pass a rigorous screening for propensity in undercover work. "Often for a particular job it was more advantageous to use a person who was actually not a member of the party," Krivitsky explained. Buried midway through the twenty-five-page transcript of his congressional testimony in October 1939 was a single sentence, which Krivitsky volunteered, about Soviet manipulation of their sympathetic contacts in New Deal Washington:

> It very often happens that a member of the party furnishes information . . . to individuals whose identity he does not know, without realizing that he is thereby engaged in espionage.[12]

Too subtle for the bemused congressmen of the Un-American Activities Committee that day, the remark was left dangling, without followup. In the following decades the lives and professional well-being of countless American liberals and New Dealers would have been spared if anyone had remembered this explicit explanation from a serious Soviet undercover agent.

Krivitsky made one public appearance, on October 13, at a forum in New York's Town Hall.[13] The passions of the academics and the émigré intellectuals were still running strong, but Krivitsky's style was sullen, his attempts at English incomprehensible; his presence conveyed none of the import of his substance.

Too visible now to be deported, as the spokesmen of the left demanded, he was ignored by all except the likes of Levine and others on the ineffectual fringe. Early in 1941, on a visit to some well-meaning friends in Virginia, he said he wanted to set up an anticommunist research center. And he bought a handgun for protection, he said, against lurking enemies. On February 9, he left for an overnight stop at a modest hotel in Washington. The chambermaid found him the next morning, shot and killed instantly with a bullet from his new handgun.

Krivitsky's death became the first great unsolved mystery of the Cold War. The District of Columbia police inquiry turned in a verdict of suicide, and the supporting evidence was strong. The FBI issued a dismissive statement, declaring that the obscure defector had provided nothing of value to the United States.[14] But the conservatives in Washington and New York never doubted that Walter G. Krivitsky had been assassinated by the long reach of Stalin's secret service — the fate of Trotsky in Mexico a few months before, and of Ignace Reiss and the others from Podvolochiska.

Four decades later, in the 1990s, the American writers Jerrold and Leona Schechter reviewed the Krivitsky case with Pavel Sudoplatov. By this time, agents of the defunct Soviet Union found that their conspiratorial habits were irrelevant. Sudoplatov, who still took pride in having masterminded the murder of Trotsky and a dozen other enemies of Stalin, claimed no "credit" for this one. He stated unhesitatingly: "There was an . . . order issued to look for Krivitsky, but this was routine for all defectors. We were not sorry to see him go, but it was not through our efforts that he died. We believed he shot himself in despair as a result of a nervous breakdown."[15]

The case of Shmelka Ginsberg, a.k.a. Walter Krivitsky, might have seemed to be closed in 1941, but the suspicions and unease he brought to America grew into a political movement of anticommunism that dominated the political agenda for generations to come.

*

One American found himself jolted to immediate action by the news of Krivitsky's defection. Jay Vivian Chambers (his name at birth in 1901), son of a dysfunctional Long Island family, had worked his way into the bohemian literary circles of New York. One beneficial quirk of his muddled upbringing gave him entrée: he was fluent in German, thanks to the ministrations of a kind aunt who cared for the boy when his parents failed him. That fluency, combined with a genuine stylistic flair, got him an assignment to translate a modest whimsy by an Austrian poet, Felix Salten, about a little fawn named Bambi. For this project, the translator took the professional name of Whittaker Chambers; his depiction of the fantasy of *Bambi* brought joy and sorrow to children of all ages across the English-speaking world.*

Chambers had been a member of the American Communist Party since 1925, and he had advanced to be one of those who passed the screening for undercover work.[16] He became a secret and trusted courier for Soviet spy rings in Washington. He had never met European comrades like Reiss or Krivitsky, of course, but their names and dedication to the cause inspired him.

As news of the purges and the breaks with Stalin reached comrades in the United States, Chambers joined the murky realm of the defectors. Building a new life for himself outside the party cells, he sought out others who might share his interest in communism and Russian history, without the dedication and discipline he had just escaped. He became acquainted with Isaac Don Levine, and when Chambers was hired as a writer at *Time*, Levine called on him at his new office. Krivitsky's *Saturday Evening Post* series was then in galleys, and Levine thought it might be interesting, certainly a good story, to get Chambers and Krivitsky together.

The two undercover apostates from communism were suspicious, wary of contact with any branch of the apparatus they had defied. After initial sparring, each accepted an invitation to Levine's Manhattan apartment at 38 East Sixty-fourth Street, for a late evening in May 1939. For a few moments they sat in silence, then Krivitsky spoke in German (once again, Chambers could only thank his kind aunt). Small talk led to big talk; names, dates, and circumstances were exchanged as tests of

* In later decades, as anticommunist paranoia took hold of American society, eager investigators were tempted to find a subliminal communist message in the verses of *Bambi*, which may have been contaminating American youth. By and large, they failed. Perhaps critics in the postmodern era of deconstructionism will have better luck.

bona fides. Warming to the occasion, Krivitsky helped fill gaps in Chambers's knowledge of what had been going on in the purges, so little understood to a foot soldier at the end of the line across the Atlantic. Levine went up to bed; when he came back down a few hours later, the two conspirators were still talking of their former ideals, their despair at what Stalin was doing to the socialist dream and, more to the immediate point, what the two of them could do about it.

Levine had already found the ready answer for Krivitsky in publicity and the *Saturday Evening Post* exposés. For Chambers, however, this course was not the answer; he had a promising career and an influential job at *Time*, where discretion about his political past seemed necessary. But Levine knew that Chambers could corroborate much of what Krivitsky had told disbelieving ears about Soviet networks in Washington. Never shrinking at presumption, Levine requested an appointment for Chambers with President Roosevelt; the White House appointments staff arranged for Chambers to meet and present his story to an aide whom Roosevelt often consulted on matters of intelligence and internal security, Assistant Secretary of State Adolf A. Berle.

Berle was not engaged with the Washington conservatives, but because the White House wanted him to meet Chambers, he invited him and Levine to his Washington estate, Woodley, on Saturday, September 2, 1939. Berle's wife served dinner; the table talk was dominated by the Nazi invasion of Poland the previous day, which all knew meant the beginning of a European war. After dessert and coffee the men talked business on the terrace. Berle took careful notes of Chambers's report and, after leaving Woodley, Levine wrote up his own recollection of the meeting. Both sets of notes have survived, and in all important respects they coincide.[17]

Berle's four-page memo, entitled "Underground Espionage Agent," outlined systematically Chambers's stories about individuals and activities in the government and public organizations, proceeding name by name. The contacts cited by Chambers from his years as a courier for Soviet intelligence later became headlines: [Laurence] Duggan, John Abt, Lauchlin Currie [Berle spelled it Lockwood Curry], Alger Hiss. Some, Chambers said, were Communist Party members; with others the relationship was "more casual." But all had passed him secret documents and paraphrased reports for the use of Soviet intelligence. Furthermore, Chambers said, these American officials fully understood what they were doing.

What happened next remains an embarrassment to the cause of American right-wing anticommunism. For the simple fact is that after writing his memo, Berle did nothing. The notes of his meeting with Whittaker Chambers went into a memory hole, not to reappear during the next two years, when he was preoccupied with matters of more importance to President Roosevelt. Levine heard later that Berle raised the matter of communist penetration of the government in a private meeting with Roosevelt, naming Alger Hiss, but was brushed aside. Berle made no notation of such a conversation, and, like the others in the State Department hierarchy, he went on enjoying social contacts with the popular and promising Hiss. Spruille Braden, a well-placed career diplomat, claimed that he knew of three different occasions when Hiss's name was raised with Roosevelt, including once by someone outside of the government with no access to secret files — apparently the liberal columnist Dorothy Thompson. "Each time they were completely ignored," Braden said.[18] The notion of a high State Department official spying for Soviet Russia languished in inattention — except within the ineffectual and ignored circles of Washington right-wingers.

Two years later the death of Krivitsky jogged Berle's memory of that late-night conversation at Woodley. On the last day of February 1941, he called the FBI to ask that responsible agents contact him about a person named Whittaker Chambers. Two of Hoover's men met with Berle the next day, and afterward an agent named Foxworth gave Hoover a routine briefing. "We are not conducting any investigation and I have appropriately informed Mr. Berle," Foxworth reported.[19] Not inclined to let the matter rest, Berle called Agent Foxworth a week later to warn that Chambers might need protection against the same assassination plots suspected in the Krivitsky case. "This matter was not followed up," Hoover's aide conceded, "and the memorandum concerning it was merely filed." Hoover later told his men that he had no recollection of any requests for an immunity guarantee for a Soviet intelligence agent willing to come forward.

Only on May 13, 1942, did the FBI approach Chambers, two and a half years after the renegade communist had told his story to Roosevelt's designated contact. Such was the low esteem endured by Hoover's agency that before proceeding any further, Chambers insisted that Berle authorize him to repeat his information to the FBI. Berle later informed Hoover that Chambers had specifically asked that the FBI not be brought into the picture, "particularly if the source was to be revealed." Whatever Chambers's reasons for reticence at that time, his lack of confidence in the FBI seemed justified: Hoover dismissed the eight-page memorandum of the May 1942 interview with Chambers as "either history, hypothesis or deduction."

At the end of 1948, when Whittaker Chambers had become a public icon for conservatives in their charges against Roosevelt and Truman, Hoover expressed incredulity about his bureau's cavalier attitude. An internal memo revealed his exasperation: "Do I understand correctly that Chambers talked to Berle in 1939; we interviewed him first in May 1942; and Berle gave us information first in June 1943? How did we come to contact Chambers in 1942 and did we take any investigative action then? What did we do in the year from May 1942 to June 1943 about the data received from Chambers? H."[20]

Hoover's queries brought a lame response. "The Bureau did not press Mr. Berle for information which he might have had concerning Whittaker Chambers," a hapless aide informed the director. "The files do not indicate a definite explanation, but if one exists it might be that the Bureau did not feel that it was desirable to press the Assistant Secretary of State for information which he did not see fit to volunteer concerning a subject which had been raised by him." Those were years when the FBI was actually respectful of the State Department.

Hoover's written response to this explanation was uncharacteristically restrained. "Of course hindsight is better than fore-sight but we should learn from this incident and not have any recurrence in other cases and situations. H."[21]

*

The FBI later cultivated a reputation for diligence in protecting American democracy from the threat of communism. But the unexploited contact with Whittaker Chambers was not the last of the bureau's lapses. On August 7, 1943, three months after the Chambers debriefing, a strange anonymous letter, in Russian, postmarked 2 A.M. in Washington, arrived at FBI headquarters.[22] "Mr. Hoover," it began. "Exceptional circumstances impel us to inform you of the activities of the so-called director of the Soviet intelligence in this country. . . . He personally deals with getting agents into and out of the USA illegally, organizes secret radio stations and manufactures forged documents. His closest associates are: . . ."

Over two single-spaced pages the unnamed informant cited names and details of Soviet penetration into the government of the United States in 1943, a time when the two countries were allies in the war against Hitler. Hoover's analysts promptly concluded that the letter was genuine, even though the identity of the writer could not be discerned. The FBI increased surveillance of the persons named, even managing to turn two of the agents recruited by the Russians into FBI informers. But the FBI chose not to engage any other responsible security systems of the government in the search for communist fifth columns.

No community of trust held in those years among the diverse American intelligence agencies: the FBI for internal security, the OSS for foreign intelligence, the intelligence staffs of the uniformed services at war. Though the anonymous letter clearly pointed to foreign intelligence — the activities of Soviet citizens as well as Americans — the FBI kept the tipoffs to itself until after World War II had ended.

To be fair, the FBI was not alone in jealously guarding its counterintelligence secrets. A few months earlier, in February 1943, a far more secret intelligence service, the army's Signals Security Agency, had started looking systematically at a cache of intercepted radio signals from Soviet offices in the United States, addressed to Moscow.[23] They were in Russian and encrypted, apparently, through several layers of inscrutable codes. The data of counterintelligence is naturally not made public, nor, given its fragmentary nature, would it have much meaning standing alone. Successive triangulations of analysis are necessary before the fragments become comprehensible to policymakers who are the consumers of intelligence and even to the intelligence professionals. And President Roosevelt for one, and thus many of his faithful, had no interest in evidence that might undermine the antifascist alliance with the Soviet Union. If he would not respond to information presented by a loyal lieutenant like Adolf Berle, he would certainly not be impressed with mysterious indications pieced together by technicians deep within a secret bureaucracy.

But in February 1945, as Roosevelt was preparing to meet Stalin at Yalta, a tangible break in counterintelligence came into the open. An alert OSS officer in Washington noted an ominous coincidence in the pages of an academic left-wing journal of modest readership called *Amerasia*.[24] A few paragraphs corresponded verbatim to the text of a secret OSS report from overseas. While the information in those paragraphs was innocuous, the obvious fear was that other, more sensitive parts of the same cable might also have been leaked to unauthorized persons. For once, cooperation among intelligence services worked. Alerted by the OSS, FBI agents launched a surveillance of the *Amerasia* office in New York. By chance there came an opportunity for what cops call "surreptitious entry"; without a warrant, Hoover's special agents went in. They found hundreds of photocopies of sensitive government papers, apparently leaked from within the State Department and Naval Intelligence.

The evidence of a security breach, clear in itself, was legally tainted by the improper means of acquiring it; government prosecutors were thwarted in building a case that could be presented in public. To the dismay of conservative militants, such as Levine, Henderson, and Chambers, the Department of Justice accepted plea bargains with the editors of *Amerasia*. Nothing had to be said in open court about solid evidence of communist espionage against the United States. American citizens, reading in their newspapers cryptic little dispatches about a legal case against an obscure academic journal, remained unwitting about the coming Cold War.

"Did I Do Right?"

IN THE HIGHER REALMS of strategy and statecraft, as well as in the lower reaches of espionage, the White House and the Kremlin were sinking toward enmity in the first months of 1945, exposing the mutual suspicions that had been stifled during their alliance against Hitler. The United States, Britain, and the Soviet Union had been guided through the war by charismatic leaders with a common strategy. Then, in each of the three powers in turn, domestic politics, mortality, and paranoia took hold. Winston Churchill, Britain's unity prime minister during war, was summarily defeated at the polls two months after V-E Day. Franklin D. Roosevelt, the only man in American history to be elected president four times, succumbed to a massive brain hemorrhage on April 12, just five weeks after meeting Stalin at Yalta.

Roosevelt and Stalin had developed a guarded respect for each other during the war years. Intimate records trickling out of the Kremlin five decades later revealed an otherwise paranoid dictator who was strangely comfortable with Roosevelt and, to a lesser extent, with Churchill. Con-temptuous of all his own underlings, politicians, generals, and diplomats alike, Stalin showed himself impressed by his alliance partners; they were men of power and destiny, whom he considered to be of his own stature in history.

Stalin's shock on hearing of Roosevelt's death was visible, deep and even sincere. Ambassador Harriman telephoned the news flash to the Kremlin shortly after midnight on April 13 (Moscow time) and asked to meet Stalin personally. The dour foreign minister, Vyacheslav Molotov, immediately ordered his chauffeur to drive him to the ambassador's residence, Spaso House, at three A.M., for a solemn and, Harriman reported, heartfelt call of condolence. Stalin received Harriman as his first visitor later in the day. The Soviet dictator "held my hand for perhaps thirty seconds in silence before asking me to sit down," Harriman reported to Washington. Stalin promised to honor the late president by continuing his wartime cooperation with the man Roosevelt had chosen as his successor.[1]

Like most people the world over, even the few Russian officials attuned to the outside world knew little about this Harry Truman. Kremlin archives opened for examination in the 1990s reveal that Soviet intelligence assigned highest priority to an urgent assessment of "Truman's surroundings" in the first weeks of his presidency. "Besides studying political, social and military figures of interest to us," Moscow instructed the New York station chief, "you must direct the [agents] to study Truman himself, his intentions, politics, etc. . . . [based] on conversations with high-ranking officials."[2]

First indications from the intelligence card files were not propitious. The obscure senator from Missouri had been quoted in June 1941, for instance, as the Wehrmacht attacked the Soviet Union, that he wished Hitler no success, but "if we see that Germany is winning we ought to help Russia and if Russia is winning we ought to help Germany and that way kill as many as possible. . . . Neither of them think anything of breaking their pledged word."[3]

Senator Truman's language was careless (as it so often continued to be when he became president), but the sentiment of nonalignment between dictators was not the quirk of a know-nothing. As the Nazis attacked Russia, the American intelligentsia was torn asunder by debates about intervening, or not, in power struggles that seemed peculiarly European. The pro-Soviet Popular Front sprang back into life, but gaining at least an equal voice was the America First movement, arising from the isolationism of the interwar decades. Was there really a meaningful difference between fascism and communism? asked intellectuals who later thought better about the question; both were incompatible with the American way of life.

For all the maudlin reverence they expressed in the first hours after Roosevelt's death, Stalin and Molotov did not think Truman would last very long among statesmen. Years later Molotov confided his first impression of the new American president: "a bit half-witted . . . far behind Roosevelt in intellect."[4]

As senator and then briefly vice president, Truman had not been privy to all the negotiations at Yalta and the summit conferences before that. As is commonly the fate of a deputy under a strong chief executive, he felt patronized by Roosevelt's inner circle, and he distrusted many of those who had been advising the fourth-term president. Truman had never met Stalin or Molotov, nor would there have been any occasion for him to do so. Only on becoming president did he read the secret telegrams exchanged between Roosevelt and Stalin in the last week of Roosevelt's life, which deplored the reciprocal suspicions that threatened to tarnish the imminent Nazi surrender but promised to set things right for the new postwar era.

On April 23, having been president for just eleven days, Truman received Molotov at the White House. This was only the second time the Soviet diplomat had set foot in the United States and, ever nervous about straying too far from the presence of Josef Vissarionovich, he came reluctantly. A conference was about to begin in San Francisco to establish the United Nations organization; Stalin had been hesitant about committing the Soviet Union too generously to this international venture. But Harriman had presumed on his own initiative to suggest that Molotov's personal participation in the founding conference would be a fine gesture to the memory and aspirations of the late president. The sincerity of the Kremlin's bereavement thus put to the test, Stalin sent his foreign minister off to the United States.

The Soviet diplomat's first meeting with the new American president proceeded about as badly as any official encounter ever could. Roosevelt's senior foreign policy team had briefed Truman about the state of relations with Russia; in particular the army chief of staff, General George C. Marshall, had warned against saying anything untoward that would interfere with the Soviets' readiness to enter the continuing war against Japan. But the State Department experts, including Harriman (rushing home from Moscow) and the up-and-coming Charles Bohlen, seized upon the new president's inexperience to press a hard anti-Soviet line that, as they well knew to their frustration in years past, Roosevelt had always brushed aside.

Truman later fumed over what he considered the State Department's patronizing manner, but on this early occasion he welcomed the starkly simple way in which his diplomats explained Soviet-American relations. They warned of a new "barbarian invasion of Europe." Eliding all the nuances that Roosevelt had treasured, they drew for Truman (in historian William Taubman's artful phrase) the formulas of arithmetic, not algebra.[5]

Face to face with the envoy from the Kremlin, Truman let loose in a style that had always gone down well with Missouri county politicos, but it grated on diplomatic ears, even those as callused as Molotov's. The Soviet government had failed to live up to the agreements it made at Yalta, Truman said; it was attempting to impose its will on eastern Europe without any pretense of the promised democratic procedures. Molotov "turned a little ashy," recalled Bohlen, who acted as interpreter for the remarkable exchange. The Soviet visitor tried to shift the conversation onto the war against Japan, a matter on which he apparently knew Truman could not afford to be rude. (Knowing, half a century later, of the access Soviet intelligence enjoyed in the upper reaches of the Democratic administrations, it is interesting to see that Moscow understood American priorities at the highest level.) Truman, however, would have none of it. He curtly dismissed his Russian guest with the words "That will be all, Mr. Molotov; I would appreciate it if you would transmit my views to Marshal Stalin." Molotov left the Oval Office in a huff.[6]

Among the many Cold War uncertainties scholars explored when the Soviet diplomatic archives were selectively opened in the 1990s was the report Molotov himself filed about his first meeting with Truman. The memorandum conveyed the exchange of differing points of view; Molotov faithfully transmitted the substance of Truman's views, just as the president had directed.[7] But there was not a hint of what Molotov knew Stalin would not like: harsh words as two officers of state started feeling their way into new circumstances and a new power relationship.

For all the satisfaction Truman drew from shooting his mouth off at an unattractive communist visitor, cooler minds immediately worried that the Truman-Stalin relationship was off to a bad start. Marshall and the secretary of war, Henry L. Stimson, were appalled; even Harriman, who had helped put Truman in a belligerent mood, confided later, "I was a little taken aback, frankly, when the President attacked Molotov so vigorously." Just after Molotov left the White House, Truman met privately with Joseph E. Davies, the former ambassador to the Soviet Union. Still puffed up with the bluster that came naturally to him, the new president told Davies he had just given Molotov "the old one-two to the jaw." He sensed in the diplomat a certain hesitancy. Turning suddenly contrite, a more sheepish Truman asked, "Did I do right?" Davies delicately warned the new president that, in general, Russians did not respond well to bullying.[8] So successive generations of American diplomats would learn in the decades to come.

Harriman and Bohlen, knowing the official Russian mind as well as anyone in Washington, set out to repair the mischief that they had inadvertently let loose. During a recess in the San Francisco conference, Bohlen raised a bold suggestion with Harriman, tentatively, for the ambassador had an authority and an ego far greater than his own. Could the president be persuaded to send a personal envoy to meet Stalin, a gesture of respect from a new player in summit diplomacy as well as a way to open a candid and direct dialogue? To Bohlen's relief, Harriman jumped on the idea. The junior diplomat pressed on to suggest for this sensitive mission the person of Harry Hopkins.

At first breath, the choice was ludicrous. No man had been closer to the late president (and thus aloof from the vice president) than Hopkins, a former social worker and pioneer of New Deal welfare policies. For months he had actually lived with Roosevelt in the White House. Moreover, though only fifty-five, Hopkins had long suffered from a stomach ailment. Early 1945 found him confined to the Mayo Clinic; he was discharged temporarily upon the news of Roosevelt's death, to help in the difficult days of the presidential transition. Even for that task he remained bedridden in Washington. Was this the man to make the long and arduous flight to Moscow to negotiate with Stalin?

It was, nonetheless, well known to Washington insiders that the Soviet dictator held Harry Hopkins in higher esteem than any other American official — for reasons that became fully understandable only half a century later. Hopkins had flown once before to Moscow, in July 1941, within a month of the Nazi attack on the Soviet Union, to offer American Lend-Lease military aid even before the United States entered the war. He went on to establish a channel for confidential exchanges with successive Soviet ambassadors in Washington, presumably with Roosevelt's authorization and encouragement. Decoded intercepts of Soviet intelligence cables, declassified in 1996, pointed to Hopkins as a person the Kremlin might have considered a secret source of information.[9] In May 1943 a mysterious "Source 19" had sent word to Stalin of details of the Anglo-American plans for the invasion of France the next year, the most sensitive military secret of World War II. Through subtle and painstaking triangulation of the evidence, the American historian Eduard Mark argues that "Source 19" was indeed Hopkins.

When the leaders of the anti-Hitler coalition met at Teheran later in 1943, alert diplomats noted an unusual gesture by the Soviet dictator. Stalin normally stood aloof at official receptions and let others approach him; this time he spotted Hopkins among the American delegation and walked over to greet him. "Stalin showed Hopkins a degree of personal consideration which I had never seen him show anyone except Roosevelt and Churchill," a bemused Harriman recorded at the time.[10] No mere ambassador would have known about Source 19 and, given the secrecy about the identity of sensitive sources that intelligence professionals sustain even with their political superiors, it cannot be assumed that Stalin knew Hopkins to be Source 19. What he surely would have known was that Harry Hopkins had been extraordinarily helpful to the Soviet war effort.

Hopkins, the primordial New Dealer, was openly contemptuous of the anti-Soviet diplomats in the State Department. Yet, as the Soviet intelligence cables noted, he seemed to be on close working terms with at least one official there, the minor but promising young Alger Hiss. Russian intelligence had long since identified Hiss as sympathetic and even responsive, though the senior spy master Sudoplatov said long afterward, "There was no indication that [Hiss] was a paid or controlled agent."[11] In later years, right-wing critics of Roosevelt and Truman, hot on the trail of Hiss as a traitor, tried to denounce Hopkins as well as a "Soviet spy" within the New Deal, a cavalier charge that went nowhere. Hopkins was engaged in the confidential diplomacy that all governments are known to practice, not to be confused with the espionage that all governments are assumed to practice.

Returning to Washington in the San Francisco conference recess, Harriman and Bohlen wasted no time in pursuing their little strategem, stopping on their way from the airport at Hopkins's rented Georgetown house to see if the New Deal veteran was up to a new mission to Moscow. Hopkins rose from his sickbed, and the fire of his old activism returned to his eyes. Seeing his vivid resolve, Harriman put the suggestion to Truman.

The new president had already shown his tendency toward impulsive decisions, some of which he later regretted. But Truman asked for two or three days to think over this idea from two of his Soviet experts. He could readily understand that Hopkins's intimacy with Roosevelt would give him special authority in approaching Stalin, something that might normally be a minus in the eyes of a successor. But Truman had actually known Hopkins since 1933 through New Deal relief programs. Moreover, given his frail health, Hopkins was in no position to patronize or threaten the new president's self-esteem.

A more political matter gave Truman pause. Friendship with Stalin was an obvious asset on one level, but might he be too friendly? Truman had no knowledge at that time of Soviet intelligence activities in Washington, of course, but his suspicions of Soviet Russia far exceeded Roosevelt's. The 1944 Republican challenger for the presidency, Governor Thomas E. Dewey of New York, had made expansive charges against the Roosevelt administration for "coddling communists" within the government. Though he lost the election, Dewey's campaign point stirred the energies of the Republican opposition, and even Truman seemed a little wary of some on the left wing of his party, including the late president's widow, who might be inclined to carry sympathy for the Soviet war effort to excess in the uncertain postwar world.

As he was thinking it over, Truman floated the idea of a Hopkins mission to Moscow with several confidantes whose opinions he respected: James F. Byrnes of South Carolina, whom he intended to name as his own secretary of state, and Cordell Hull, who had served Roosevelt in that office from the start of the New Deal. Hull of Tennessee was no left-winger; like Truman, he was a border-state Democrat and, also like Truman, he had been held at arm's length by the Roosevelt coterie. Without hesitation, Hull assured Truman that Hopkins's rapport with the Soviet Union was that of a wartime ally against Hitler, and not that of a communist sympathizer; Hopkins was solid in loyalty and reliability. That was what Truman needed to hear.

On May 19, 1945, a cable marked "Personal and top secret from the President for Marshal Stalin" went off to the American naval attaché in Moscow (at the time, navy communications channels were considered the most secure from prying eyes on any side). Remarking on the "difficulty of dealing by exchange of messages with the complicated and important questions" before them, Truman proposed that Hopkins fly to Moscow as his personal emissary, to talk things out directly with Stalin. He suggested a starting date of May 26, "if this time is convenient for you." A reply came back the same day, a promising sign. "Personal and secret from Premier J. V. Stalin to President H. S. Truman: I readily accept your proposal. . . . May 26 is quite convenient for me."[12]

Whether the Mayo Clinic approved or not, Hopkins and his caring wife, Louise, left Washington on May 23. They paused in Paris for a working lunch with Eisenhower, then flew over the wreckage of Germany to the capital of the Soviet Union. Stalin received his favored American in the Kremlin on May 26 at eight P.M. (given Stalin's idiosyncratic schedule, it was probably his first working appointment of the day). Over the next twelve days the Soviet dictator cleared his schedule for six long meetings, at a pace set by whatever stamina Hopkins could muster. As Stalin noted, in an arch reminder of the ordeals through which *his* country, at least, had passed, with the European war over he had "more time at his disposal."

Hopkins's conversations opened a new dialogue between the United States and the Soviet Union in the postwar era, analogous to the dialogue he had started on his original visit in 1941. But instead of a great-power alliance in war, the 1945 dialogue led to distrust and rivalry. Courteous and respectful of each other, Stalin and Hopkins nonetheless found themselves quibbling, with no common cause or shared vision to transcend the disputes of the moment.

Hopkins opened with the same ploy that Roosevelt had used in Teheran and Yalta: the pressure of public opinion bearing down upon the president. Perhaps in those faraway years American leaders honestly believed that such talk would mean something to Stalin. Americans were losing sympathy for Soviet Russia, Hopkins said, not just the usual Roosevelt-haters and right-wingers but even "the millions of Americans who believed that despite [the] different political and economic ideology of the two countries, the United States and the Soviet Union could work together in order to bring about a secure peace for humanity." That sort of tone may have gone down well in a presidential fireside chat, but as an opener with the dictator of communism it fell flat. Stalin retorted, when it came his turn to speak, that he "would not attempt to use Soviet public opinion as a screen." He regretted the remark, which he knew hurt his friend Mr. Hopkins "to the quick," and he apologized at their next meeting.

On the underlying reality they agreed: the two allies were falling out. Each argued that it was the other's fault. Stalin's list of grievances seemed petty to Hopkins, for all they revealed about the paranoia of the Kremlin: the abrupt termination of Lend-Lease aid after V-E Day, Washington's support for Argentina's membership in the United Nations despite that country's semifascist stance during the war. Stalin complained that decisions of the major powers should not be overturned by UN "votes of Honduras and Puerto Rico" (actually, no one had ever suggested Puerto Rican membership; perhaps Stalin or his interpreter confused it with Costa Rica).[13] He railed about the status of the German navy and merchant marine, competition for reparations from occupied Germany and, most insulting of all to Stalin, the western Allies' decision to let France share in the reparations negotiations. France had collaborated with Nazi Germany, Stalin declared, and "to attempt to place France on the same footing as the Soviet Union looked like an attempt to humiliate the Russians."

When he had spoken for Roosevelt, Hopkins knew well how to maneuver. But now he spoke for Truman, whose interest was not in learning details but in assessing the integrity of the people with whom he was dealing. Truman expected all men — Soviet dictators included — to keep their promises. The night Hopkins left for Moscow, the president wrote in his diary: "Uncle Joe should make some sort of gesture . . . that he intends to keep his word. Any smart political boss will do that."[14] Instead came more deception, with Poland the flashpoint. The American side believed that Stalin had promised free and democratic elections once the Nazis were routed. But communist authorities, acting behind the occupying Red Army, seemed determined to impose a Polish regime dominated by their own partisans, after "free" elections that excluded every anticommunist faction.

Keeping a promise was Truman's measure of a man and, for all

Hopkins's efforts to keep the alliance alive, Stalin was failing to measure up. The most revealing moment in the dialogue showed up not in the official records of either side but, as is so often the case, in the instant notes of the interpreters.

Hopkins asked if the Soviet Union was "prepared to honor the Yalta agreement on entering the Far Eastern war." Stalin replied impatiently, "The Soviet Union always honors its word," and his voice drifted off into mumbles. Bohlen, interpreting for Hopkins, noted that his Soviet counterpart, named Pavlov, faithfully translated the first phrase, then stopped. "When I said to him in English, 'I believe there is a little more, Pavlov,' and the Russian hurriedly mumbled Stalin's qualification: 'except in case of extreme necessity.'"[15]

Hopkins's energies were dwindling, and such weaseling did not help to restore his spirits. Between Kremlin meetings he let Louise take him to the ballet school of the Bolshoi Theater. To break the ice that evening with Stalin, he raved about the children and their art. Hopkins's biographer, playwright Robert Sherwood, wrote that, like the New Yorker who has never gotten around to visiting the Statue of Liberty, Stalin replied that for all his twenty-eight years in Moscow he had never been to the Bolshoi ballet school.[16]

Stalin gave the obligatory formal reception for the American envoy the night of June 1, with forty guests seated for dinner at one long table in the Kremlin ballroom of Catherine the Great. Hopkins seized upon an informal moment to remind Stalin of the powerful Polish-American community in Roosevelt's electoral constituency, one of "the many minority groups in America who were not sympathetic to the Soviet Union." No record survives of Stalin's reply.

After the talks ended, Harriman cabled his summation to Truman:

> I am afraid Stalin does not, and never will, fully understand our interest in a free Poland as a matter of principle. He is a realist in all of his actions, and it is hard for him to appreciate our faith in abstract principles. It is difficult for him to understand why we should want to interfere with Soviet policy in a country like Poland, which he considers too important to Russia's security, unless we have some ulterior motive.[17]

If Truman had no such ulterior motive, other Americans did. The imposition of communism upon Poland and eastern Europe was a danger signal to, among many others, George Kennan, Harriman's journeyman deputy, who had been managing the embassy while this high-level discourse was going on.

Hopkins left Moscow on June 7, lunched in Berlin, and prowled through the wreckage of Hitler's bunker behind the Wilhelmstrasse. (Stalin had warned him that Hitler might be alive still.) Over breakfast at his familiar White House on June 13, he gave Truman a personal report, amplifying the cables he had dutifully sent each night from Moscow. The president asked him to join the delegation to the summit meeting of the Allies in Potsdam in July, but Hopkins demurred, fully aware that his work was done, that Stalin (and Truman) now had to deal with new men. Hopkins died seven months later, when the era of straight talk with Uncle Joe Stalin was over.

For all the illusions and trappings of power, leaders like Truman and Stalin, to say nothing of Hopkins, Harriman, and Kennan, were hostages to events far below their notice. Politics, particularly international politics, proceeds at many levels, and the moments when disconnected events suddenly fit together come when least expected.

That April, as official Washington was consumed by the presidential transition, a secret American source in the Nazi foreign ministry sent out a huge cache of documents revealing sentiment within the Wehrmacht to stop the war against the western allies and mobilize all resources for a one-front offensive against the menacing Red Army to the east. The news did not come out of the blue: American and British ground forces had achieved an unanticipated breakthrough a month before, crossing the Rhine into the German heartland on March 7 by the one bridge, at Remagen, that retreating German forces had inexplicably failed to demolish. Strategists among the western allies, and suspicious Russians as well, wondered if this fortuitous maneuver had came about simply by chance; or could it have been a subtle signal from German field commanders that they were ready to give the western allies a military advantage?

The Berlin agent further reported hearing of a general of the intelligence staff, named Gehlen, who was stashing the records of his spy networks behind Russian lines to make them available to the victorious

Americans once they turned their energies to war against communism. This notion was too far-fetched in April 1945 to be taken seriously in Washington. The tip was not even reported to the American occupation forces, and the commanders of the POW camps were therefore unprepared when General Gehlen turned himself in.

Even less noticed by the men making policy was a chance discovery by an American field intelligence officer in the last days of the war. When Lieutenant Colonel Paul Neff wandered into a hastily abandoned castle in Saxony, a part of eastern Germany slated for occupation by the Red Army, he found stacks of Berlin foreign ministry archives that had been sent south for safekeeping. Amid the heaps of documents, the alert officer spotted a sheaf of partially burned papers, which he recognized as a Soviet military intelligence codebook that the Nazis had somehow managed to capture, perhaps years before. Neff grabbed the charred papers and rushed back behind American lines the day before the Russians arrived.[18] Too many were the spoils of war in those first days after V-E Day, and too arcane the paraphernalia of cryptology to make the codebook a priority; it languished unstudied for fully eight years. When it was finally noticed, the codebook turned out to be a missing link that helped confirm what a number of Americans had feared about an unsavory underside of the New Deal and the Soviet-American wartime alliance.

As events unfolded, Stalin was often better informed than Truman about undercover operations proceeding in eastern Europe. He caught Hopkins and Harriman unawares with a story about a Polish anticommunist activist who had managed to smuggle himself out of Warsaw in the uniform of an American officer. Who had arranged that? Soviet security forces in the occupied Baltic republics detected anticommunist partisans making radio contact with British intelligence. American officers had flown into Bucharest led by some lawyer in naval uniform named Frank Wisner, a name neither Stalin nor Truman would have recognized at this early stage. But Stalin saw that Wisner's OSS mission was interfering with the Red Army's efforts to impose communism upon Romania.

Such matters were beyond Truman's awareness. He had told Hopkins to impress upon Stalin that the United States had no interest in east European politics. "Poland, Romania, Bulgaria, Czechoslovakia, Austria,

Yugoslavia, Latvia, Lithuania, Estonia *et al* made no difference to U.S. interests," Truman wrote as Hopkins set off — unless they threatened the prospects for world peace.[19] But, armed with reports of incidents Truman knew nothing about, Stalin was inclined to doubt these protestations from Washington.

Soon, however, Truman began hearing reports that fed his own suspicions. From Canada's prime minister, Mackenzie King, who called at the White House in September 1945 for his first meeting with the new president, Truman learned that a Russian code clerk (and, it emerged, a lieutenant in Soviet military intelligence) named Igor Gouzenko had just defected from the Soviet embassy in Ottawa. Interrogations were turning up evidence of Soviet spy networks in Canada and the United States. A month later, a woman from Connecticut named Elizabeth Bentley walked into an FBI field office to tell of Soviet agents she knew to be at work in Washington. Hoover, at last liberated from Roosevelt's disinterest, started bombarding the Truman White House with FBI reports. Was any of this intelligence credible? The names of Gouzenko or Bentley meant nothing to the president, his administration, or the public — yet.

Truman and his countrymen had little time to savor the victories of World War II; the triumphant allies were falling into dispute over the shape of the peace. Revelations of espionage were trickling in. Even if the evidence was never introduced in court, the *Amerasia* case stirred suspicions, not only about sympathies for communism within the New Deal but about actual espionage by government officials.

What did break into the open were the inevitable American partisan rivalries that had been muffled during the war. The Republican drumbeat was mounting against the Democrats' "coddling of communists." In May, even as Hopkins set out on his last-ditch mission to Stalin, Republican senator Arthur Vandenberg of Michigan began a series of jeremiads against communist influences on America's postwar foreign policy. James Forrestal, secretary of the navy, weighed in with memos to the White House arguing that communists were up to no good inside the U.S. government. The politically active Polish-American community, already disillusioned by the accords at Yalta, found their worst fears confirmed as they saw Stalin turning Poland into a satellite. The six million Polish Americans were predominantly Catholic, and the old arguments of Father Walsh and his students came up for new attention. Other ideological anticommunists were roused from long obscurity. Professor Hook in New York saw his moment for pursuing long-standing vendettas against fellow academics who had supported the Comintern-inspired Popular Front; he enlisted the venerable progressive educator John Dewey to agitate against the communist threat to American society. The indefatigable publicist Isaac Don Levine raised funds to start a magazine, *Plain Talk*, that would present the anticommunist case to a broad public under his own name, without having to invoke a front like the difficult old defector Walter Krivitsky. Right-wing anticommunists, in public and in government, had not learned how to distinguish intelligence from tittle-tattle; Levine's journal was full of both, served up indiscriminately.

Even Hoover's advisories to the White House often seemed gossipy, ill grounded, and incoherent, difficult for any responsible executive to take seriously. As official diplomatic dispatches discerned undefined strains within the Kremlin in October 1945, Hoover did the diplomats one better with the report passed to the White House that Stalin had actually been deposed! Some months later he was impolitic enough to forward an airy report on Soviet espionage that seemed to implicate two of the long-serving American officials whom Truman was coming to accept within his own circle, Dean Acheson and John J. McCloy.[20]

Stymied in the courts by the difficulties in assembling and presenting evidence acquired by irregular means, right-wing spokesmen had to swallow hard as their left-wing adversaries taunted them for never making espionage charges stick. To build their case of a communist danger to America, they turned to the device of the Washington leak. Republicans on Capitol Hill were ever ready to seize upon issues to combat the New Deal after its leader had passed; the obvious partisanship of the charges made it all the easier for the Democrats to dismiss them.

Outside the arena of party politics, however, more serious research was under way within the academic community. A diligent student of Father Walsh, John Cronin of Baltimore, was fired up to expand his studies of communism in the American labor movement and to explore subversive penetration of government agencies. Cronin developed a friendship with William Sullivan, Hoover's deputy at the FBI, who supported the scholar's inquiries with counterespionage data from the bureau's files — clues that Hoover, cautious under Roosevelt, had chosen not to develop. From his research post at the National Catholic Welfare Conference, Cronin used FBI sources and his own analytical incisiveness to develop a flow of editorials and commentaries that were far more informed and nuanced than anything heard on Capitol Hill. The danger was not that America would "go communist," Cronin wrote as Truman became president. "The question is not so much that of direct communist control, but rather a question of pressure, confusion, deception, and general misleading of the public and public opinion . . . It is probable that the communist groups would create sufficient confusion to lead to a do-nothing policy."[21] Cronin later became a speechwriter and adviser on the communist threat to senator, vice president, and president Richard M. Nixon.

With this sort of warning to the new administration, the perceived dangers of communism became relevant to ever wider circles of Americans. Three years later, when the names of Whittaker Chambers, Igor Gouzenko, and Elizabeth Bentley became known to the public, the sullen cause of anticommunism had gained respectability, and communism itself was no longer an abstraction. It had become a reality, if not in the United States, in the faraway countries of which Americans knew so little.

PART III
Political Warfare

5

Kennan's Design

"SOVIET PROPAGANDA against the U.S. and U.K. has reached the highest pitch of violence," Truman learned from a Top Secret intelligence memo in August 1946. Perhaps it was a step toward "preparing the Russian people for Soviet military action." Or perhaps it was a response to alarming internal threats only dimly perceived: "discontent in the Ukraine, . . . Murmansk and other areas," a cautious and highly tentative rendering of the data on partisans and resistance networks that had been mounting at the field outposts of American intelligence. Playing it safe, the sober analysts in Washington conceded, "We have no real basis for evaluating the extent and seriousness of such discontent or its potentialities for effective resistance to the present [Soviet] regime."[1]

Such advisories, to Truman's thinking, were mere waffling — and from hard-boiled professionals who were supposed to do better. A chief executive under stress likes to be told things in clear declarative fashion; here were senior intelligence officers hedging their bets just like the diplomats. Early in his presidency Truman had hit upon the tactic of bypassing officials to seek out firsthand reports from individuals he trusted. Thus, in December 1945, he dispatched to eastern Europe an otherwise unversed friend from Kentucky, Mark Ethridge, publisher of the Louisville *Courier Journal*. Ethridge minced no words in denouncing Soviet actions in Romania and Bulgaria, the only two countries he visited, and his report hit home with Truman.

Others around the president were scornful of both the substance and provenance of such sweeping judgments. His new secretary of state, James Byrnes, for one, was clinging to the Rooseveltian notion that cooperation with Moscow was still an option in eastern Europe. Then, as Ethridge was roaming around, word came from Moscow that Stalin had refused to receive Harriman on a routine call; using the line that Roosevelt had so often invoked, the Soviet dictator pleaded the demands on his time of an upcoming election campaign. The Soviet nomenklatura recognized the rebuff as the end of the American ambassador's high-level access. Harriman left his post in the Soviet Union the third week of January 1946, leaving Kennan in charge.

Not only was intelligence from the field becoming too elusive and fragmentary for the kind of clear judgments Truman sought, in Washington the endemic competition among intelligence services continued to fester. As one ploy to resolve the problem, Truman created a Central Intelligence Group to perform the functions of a news desk, to keep the president informed and to filter out the gossip and rumor. The new CIG may have managed to coordinate intelligence coming in from abroad, but Hoover's FBI, nurturing its own networks, was not about to share anything with any upstart competing agency.

Anti-Soviet circles within government moved swiftly to try satisfying a curiosity long absent at the highest level. Many in the State Department had little sympathy for Byrnes's notions of reasoning with the Russians. The specialists on communist affairs, having long languished under presidential inattention and the open scorn of White House aides like Harry Hopkins, started pushing upon the new president long scholarly analyses of the subversive designs of international communism — long, that is, on dire judgments, short on relevant facts.

Neither the FBI nor the State Department yet knew about certain stunning developments in the arcane realm of cryptography, the tedious and subtle art pursued by sophisticated analysts under tightest security to build and break the codes of secret government communications. Off in suburban Virginia, at the army signals center in the converted private girls' school, Arlington Hall, were the files of wartime Soviet telegrams that had languished unread. There, on July 31, 1946, a civilian scholar of linguistics named Meredith Gardner managed finally to extract in clear English a phrase from a coded Soviet report sent from New York during the war; the message happened to be a discussion of Soviet intelligence activity in Latin America, but the cryptographic breakthrough led, after years of tedious effort, to a vivid record of Soviet espionage in the United States.[2]

The middle months of 1946 were in fact a season of secret jousting between codebreakers on all sides. Obviously priceless for decrypting a code system is an uncoded text of the same message. Opportunity for such a comparison came about, seemingly by accident, on September 20, with an innocuous British embassy dispatch transmitted to London *en clair* and thus readable by any interested eavesdroppers. Whitehall promptly reprimanded its Washington embassy for such carelessness, and the responsible British diplomat replied in gentlemanly dismay: "We were indeed aghast when we saw what had happened."[3] No overly suspicious nature is required to suppose that the "carelessness" may not have been all that accidental. The offending diplomat was Donald Maclean, first secretary of the embassy and one of the best-placed Soviet spies in London and Washington.

"I'm tired of babying the Soviets," the president told Byrnes after his first eight months in office. "Unless Russia is faced with an iron fist and strong language, another war is in the making."[4] Presidential petulance aside, official Washington remained confused and divided at the turn of 1946. The question was put: Did the Soviet Union present a real threat to the United States? And, if so, what should the United States do about it?

This was the setting in which Kennan's Long Telegram landed. The newly emboldened chargé d'affaires pulled together in that message the fears of competing intelligence agencies (though he knew nothing and, at that time, cared less about motley defectors and bureaucratic infighting) and of a generation of Soviet specialists in the State Department. The Soviet Union, Kennan declared, "has an elaborate and far flung apparatus for exertion of its influence in other countries, an apparatus of amazing flexibility and versatility, managed by people whose experience and skill in underground methods are presumably without parallel in history."

The threat was far more than espionage.

We have here a political force committed fanatically to the belief that with US there can be no permanent modus vivendi, that it is desirable and necessary that the internal harmony of our society be disrupted, our traditional way of life be destroyed, the international authority of our state be broken, if Soviet power is to be secure.

This political force ... is seemingly inaccessible to considerations of reality in its basic reactions. For it, the vast fund of objective fact about human society is not, as with us, the measure against which outlook is constantly being tested and re-formed, but a grab bag from which individual items are selected arbitrarily and tendentiously to bolster an outlook already preconceived.
This is admittedly not a pleasant picture.[5]

Nor was this, admittedly, a routine State Department dispatch from an ordinary diplomat serving *ad interim*.

Four decades later the world outside the Kremlin learned that the Soviet Union was also conducting a global assessment that dangerous year of 1946. The Russian ambassador to the United States, Nikolai Novikov, sent his own "long telegram" to Moscow a few months later, casting similarly thoughtful scrutiny upon attitudes within the United States that seemed, from the Kremlin's perspective, equally ominous.

Like Kennan, Novikov was a caretaker for his embassy, a journeyman careerist of the Commissariat of Foreign Affairs who had arrived in Washington early in 1945 as deputy to Ambassador Andrei Gromyko. Though he lacked Kennan's literary style, he did not shrink from the long look. He reported "a decline in the influence on foreign policy of those who follow Roosevelt's course for cooperation among peace-loving countries." (Molotov, his own suspicions confirmed, underlined this phrase on his copy of the cable, with a vertical line in the margin and the word "cooperation" underlined a second time.)

The ascendance to power of President Truman, a politically unstable person but with certain conservative tendencies, ... meant a strengthening of the influence on U.S. foreign policy of the most reactionary circles of the Democratic party [Molotov underlined this phrase as well]. The constantly increasing reactionary nature of the foreign policy course of the United States, which consequently approached the policy advocated by the Republican party, laid the groundwork for close cooperation in this field between the far right wing of the Democratic party and the Republican party. ... This is the source of what is called, even in official statements, "bipartisan" foreign policy.[6]

Moscow's assessment of Washington at the dawn of the Cold War was no more pleasant a picture than Kennan's of Moscow.

Fearful of the jolt his ambassador's analysis might cause within the

Soviet nomenklatura, Molotov ordered that Novikov's "long telegram" of September 27 be held in his own private files, without circulation. The records do not show whether Stalin ever saw it. Soviet historians produced the document, complete with Molotov's personal annotations, at an academic conference in the summer of 1990; it was the first time even knowledgeable Russian officials had heard of it.

If Kennan's Long Telegram found a receptive readership among visceral anticommunists in Washington, the new president had also to cope with the New Deal's lingering left wing and the hopes for continuing cooperation with the Soviet Union. This idealism coalesced in the person of Henry Wallace, a cabinet secretary under Roosevelt, held over by Truman. More to the point, Wallace was the man who might actually have been the president — he had been a near choice for the vice presidency in 1944 when Roosevelt chose the senator from Missouri instead. (Wallace broke with Truman in 1948, ran a quixotic campaign for the presidency with support from the American Communist Party, and carried the left wing of the New Deal into an exile comparable to what conservatives had endured under Roosevelt.)

To sort out the conflicting advice coming in from all sides, Truman characteristically turned to one person he trusted, Clark Clifford, also of Missouri. The thirty-nine-year-old special counsel on the White House staff had no experience or expertise in matters of foreign policy, but he had the street smarts of a political aide and, from hours at late-night poker games with Truman, he knew what the boss wanted to be told and how he wanted to be told it. Truman's assignment to Clifford revealed his own way of looking at things: describe all the times the Soviet Union had violated international agreements, had broken its word. Clifford turned for help to a White House staff aide named George Elsey, who had worked for the last four years in Roosevelt's Map Room, the equivalent in that era of the later National Security Council staff. Warming to the task, Clifford expanded the presidential assignment to assess the overall prospects for relations with the Soviet Union.

For two months Clifford and Elsey canvassed officials across Washington and assembled their collective views into one 26,000-word report that attempted to answer Truman's underlying questions. Yes, the Soviet Union represents a threat; here, in conclusion, is what we can do about it.

As long as the Soviet Union adheres to its present policy, the United States should maintain military forces powerful enough to restrain the Soviet Union and to confine Soviet influence to its present area.

All nations not now within the Soviet sphere should be given generous economic assistance and political support in their opposition to Soviet penetration. Economic aid may also be given to the Soviet Union [as well as] private trade with the U.S.S.R. . . .

Even though Soviet leaders profess to believe that the conflict between Capitalism and Communism is irreconcilable and must eventually be resolved by the triumph of the latter, it is our hope that they will change their minds and work out with us a fair and equitable settlement when they realize that we are too strong to be beaten and too determined to be frightened.[7]

This was good Missouri language that Truman could appreciate; no longer would he worry about whether he had done right in talking tough to the Russians. As a classified internal history years later stated, Clifford and Elsey produced "an important state paper [which] charted the postwar prospect with startling prescience, outlining the shape and thrust of Truman's subsequent programs."[8]

Clifford handed the report to Truman on September 24, 1946, by chance the day the president finally dismissed Wallace from his administration.* At seven the next morning, Truman called Clifford at his home and asked how many copies of the memorandum had been run off and whether anyone else had yet seen them. Assured that all twenty copies were locked in Clifford's office safe, Truman ordered him into the office immediately: "Get all twenty copies . . . I want them delivered to me at once." As Clifford deposited the unwieldy stack of papers on Truman's desk, the president explained that he had read the entire memo late into the night. "It is very valuable to me — but if it leaked it would blow the roof off the White House, it would blow the roof off the Kremlin. We'd have the most serious situation on our hands that has yet occurred in my administration," Clifford recalled the president's words. "The president took the reports from me, and neither I nor Elsey, nor anyone else, ever saw them again."[9]

Like Molotov with his telegram from Ambassador Novikov, Truman

* It was about this situation that Maclean of the British Embassy "accidentally" cabled London *en clair*. Maclean's Kremlin masters would perhaps have been much more interested in learning about the Clifford-Elsey report the same day.

understood that a premature statement of an unpleasant world view would preclude sound preparation of policies and instruments to serve the evolving national interests. The American president also had the mood of the electorate to consider, and the midterm congressional elections were just six weeks away. The time was too short to make a credible case for confrontation with the Kremlin, even as the Republican opposition was campaigning on an angry anti-Soviet stance that had not scored with the public during the New Deal and war years. In November 1946 the Republican Party won control of Congress for the first time in thirteen years.

*

We [Americans] have been handicapped . . . by a tendency to view war as a sort of sporting context outside of all political context, by a national tendency to seek for a political cure-all, and by a reluctance to recognize the realities of international relations — the perpetual rhythm of struggle, in and out of war.[10]

George Kennan, holding forth on the Big Picture, had come a long way from the journeyman diplomat who waited until his political superior went away before speaking up on his own. Established in the higher reaches of the State Department at the start of 1947, he set upon his new responsibility, to assemble and manage a team of thoughtful professionals, freed from operational tasks, to engage in long-term policy planning. With neither energy nor inclination to respond to all the critics of Mr. X, Kennan set his staff to work on the design of the "counterforce" necessary to contain communism.

The last pretenses of Soviet-American cooperation ended with the acrimonious conference of foreign ministers in April. It was this conference, held in Moscow, that "really rang down the iron curtain," wrote the tough-minded diplomat Robert Murphy.[11] In public came the Truman Doctrine and the Marshall Plan, foundation stones of American Cold War policy to support democratic governments in resisting Soviet communism.

Other developments deep inside the government were not noticed by the public, or even by Kennan. Alger Hiss was eased out of the Foreign Service. The head of State Department research and analysis, a holdover from the OSS, resigned in April, threatened by charges of "strong

Soviet leanings." The patient codebreakers at Arlington Hall, building on Meredith Gardner's breakthrough, finally figured out that late in the past war "someone inside the War Department General Staff [had been] providing highly classified information to the Soviets." They had deciphered hundreds of cover names for apparent Soviet informants. Army intelligence broke out of its classified confines to inform the FBI of tangible new evidence of a "massive Soviet espionage effort in the US."[12]

Kennan had no interest in such matters. On his arrival back in the State Department, among the more intriguing classified documents to cross his desk were advisories about a new source of personnel, the refugees pouring out of Soviet control into the West. A Top Secret intelligence summary of January 1947 stated the situation in tantalizing terms: "The [Red Army] occupation has furnished a large number of Soviet citizens with their first opportunity to view the outside world. The 'bourgeois fleshpots' of Germany, Austria, and the Balkans have produced disillusionment, a reluctance to return to the USSR, and a substantial number of desertions."[13] Defectors, disillusioned intellectuals, stateless refugees who survived through all manner of conspiracy may have been an irritant to the military occupation authorities in Germany and Austria. But to Kennan in Washington, this formless mass began to take the shape of an asset, human weapons for a campaign with grand goals.

Two OSS veterans back in private life but consulting for the State Department, Frank Lindsay and Charles Thayer, submitted a plan in September, and Kennan sent it over to Forrestal at the Pentagon. In language appropriate to bureaucracy but formidable in its implications, Lindsay and Thayer proposed "to extract for U.S. advantage disaffected foreign nationals from Soviet-dominated areas." Kennan wondered if the Joint Chiefs of Staff might consider establishing a guerrilla warfare school to provide Americans and selected "extracted" foreigners with "training in air support, communications, local security, counter-intelligence, foraging, sabotage, guerrilla tactics, field medicine, and propaganda."[14]

A month later, another military intelligence report landed in Kennan's in-box. It seemed that some two thousand anti-Russian Finnish refugees had informally organized themselves into military units and were offering to engage in guerrilla war against the Soviet Union. Kennan would have had no occasion to know it, but Finns held a special place of honor in the annals of American intelligence. Huddled up against Russia in the Arctic north, they had fought the Soviet Union before any of the western democracies; their secret services were in possession of invaluable counterintelligence data. (The Finns were the likely original source of the charred codebook that Lieutenant Colonel Neff discovered in the abandoned Saxon castle.) These Finns had probably been considered Nazi collaborators on the German eastern front once World War II was joined in earnest; in 1945 they had fled to Sweden, then to Venezuela and Canada, then entered the United States and were ready to enlist in the U.S. army.

The Joint Chiefs were scornful of Kennan's bold ventures, guerrilla schools, and anti-Soviet brigades. The officers in Europe had had their fill of refugees, émigrés, "bandits," and partisans. They informed the State Department that these cadres and DPs might well include "a large sprinkling of free-booters, criminals and petty racketeers." Facing cutbacks in budgets for its own core purposes, the Pentagon was not eager to assume new and troublesome missions. But Kennan's imagination was fired up. He retorted that the State Department saw merit in the concept of guerrilla warfare; "a beginning should be made to carry it out. . . . It would seem advisable to start the project with these men and gradually to build it up as a top-secret undertaking."[15] Top secret indeed, for the dispatch of thousands of anticommunist partisans behind the Iron Curtain would amount to quite a "counterforce," implying a policy considerably more aggressive than merely "containing" communism.

Discouraged by the military's reluctance to get engaged, Kennan hoped for better from the new Central Intelligence Agency, which had been established the previous July. The CIA had looked into the record of the émigrés and concluded that "these groups are highly unstable and undependable. . . . They are almost exclusively interested in obtaining maximum support (usually from the U.S.) for their own propaganda activities and insist upon the provision of substantial financial, communications, propaganda, movement and personal assistance in return for vague and unrealistic promises of future service."[16] Enthusiasm for action was also dulled by bureaucratic caution. The CIA's general counsel ruled that while intelligence could properly be collected from the various refugees factions, the agency could not engage in active missions against Soviet power without specific congressional authorization — and, given the need for secrecy, that seemed unworkable.

Just before Christmas of 1947, the National Security Council secretly but formally designated a major component in the foreign policy of the United States as "psychological warfare"; that was the first bureaucratic euphemism for covert action. Truman, reacting to the Clifford-Elsey report, was ready to try something. Without delving too deeply into the implications of organizing resistance armies behind the Iron Curtain, the so-called psychological warfare decision was explained in terms of generating credit and praise for Marshall Plan aid then on its way to western Europe. But no one in the inner circles of the Truman White House could have been in any doubt that they had embarked upon a significant and sensitive initiative: the decision, called NSC 4-a, was typed out in only three copies, one for the White House files, one for the CIA, and one for the personal attention of George Kennan.[17]

Over the first four months of 1948, Kennan and his Policy Planning Staff started fashioning specific projects to undermine communist power or, in the rhetoric of the 1950s, to roll back the Iron Curtain through a variety of operations "in which the originating role of the United States Government will always be kept concealed," as the NSC directed. They presented the overall campaign to the National Security Council on May 4 under the title "Organized Political Warfare."[18]

Even when writing an operational plan for tightly restricted consideration by policymakers and bureaucrats, Kennan could not resist the occasional rhetorical flourish.

> Political warfare is the logical application of Clausewitz's doctrine in time of peace, . . . employment of all the means at a nation's command, short of war, to achieve its national objectives.
>
> Such operations are both overt and covert. They range from such overt actions as political alliances, economic measures, . . . and "white" propaganda, to such covert operations as clandestine support of "friendly" foreign elements, "black" psychological warfare and even encouragement of underground resistance in hostile states.

His program comprised four broad categories, parts of which were overt and visible to the public, others clandestine. Their interconnections were always to remain secret and "deniable" by responsible government leaders — and so they remained for decades, until the effort unraveled through mishaps and selective disclosures years later. Only in the 1990s was the existence of a coherent plan made known to the public, when declassified planning documents laid out the full scope of the secret initiative, discrete operations that practitioners, legislators, and historians came to call Rollback.

As the first step, Kennan proposed to encourage "trusted private American citizens" to come forward as a public committee to mobilize interest and support for carefully selected émigré factions in the United States and Europe, who could be supplied with "access to printing presses and microphones" — as long as they served American interests as well as their own.

"This is primarily an overt operation," Kennan told the NSC, "which, however, should receive covert guidance and possibly assistance from the Government. . . . The American Committee should be so selected and organized as to cooperate closely with this Government." Thus the model of the old "front organizations" of Comintern days seemed newly attractive in Washington. But Kennan was careful to couch the notion in a patriotic American context:

What is proposed here is an operation in the traditional American form: organized public support of resistance to tyranny in foreign countries. Throughout our history, private American citizens have banded together to champion the cause of freedom for people suffering under oppression. Our proposal is that this tradition be revived specifically to further American national interests in the present crisis.

Second, the action plan called for clandestine assistance to anticommunist factions in countries outside the Soviet orbit where local communists might gain power through the democratic process. (Kennan specifically cited France; Italy was also a concern at the time.) "This is a covert operation again utilizing private intermediaries," Kennan explained. "To insure cover, the private American organizations conducting this operation should be separate" from the public committee. This was a delicate distinction, and Kennan's rationale was still withheld by government censorship nearly fifty years later. The obvious point was that the Americans leading the public committee for émigré nationalists could be distinguished persons of stature, but tangible support for anticommunist forces in western Europe would be more effective if it came from less august quarters, such as labor unions and similar affinity groups with local organizations and networks.

The plan of political warfare then turned distinctly nonpolitical, advocating "resort to direct action" to protect "vital installations, other material or personnel from being (1) sabotaged or liquidated, or (2) captured intact by Kremlin agents or agencies." Some indication of what this euphemistic language really meant came in hypothetical examples of "direct action": deliberate American sabotage of Middle Eastern oil installations if they were "on the verge of Soviet capture"; "control over anti-sabotage activities in the Venezuelan oil fields"; "designation of key individuals threatened by the Kremlin who should be protected or removed elsewhere" — just as early intelligence field officers had done in Hungary and Romania the year before.

Finally and most boldly, Kennan's counterforce against Soviet power was to include outright paramilitary actions: guerrilla units, sabotage forces, all kinds of subversive operations and localized rebellions behind the Iron Curtain. Here was Rollback at its most militant.

> In contrast to CIA [intelligence collection] operations, involving the American Government directly with underground activities, this project would follow a principle which has been basic in British and Soviet political warfare: remote and deeply concealed official control of clandestine operations so that governmental responsibility cannot be shown. . . .
>
> General direction and financial support would come from the Government; guidance and funds would pass to a private American organization or organizations (perhaps "business" enterprises) composed of private citizens of the approximate caliber of Allen Dulles; these organizations, through their field offices in Europe and Asia, would establish contact with the various national underground representatives in free countries and through these intermediaries pass on assistance and guidance to the resistance movements behind the iron curtain.[19]

The Truman administration gave its Top Secret approval to Kennan's action plan on June 18, 1948, as NSC Directive 10/2.

Kennan seemed to be seeking refuge in selective memory when American covert operations behind and around the Iron Curtain later turned sour and publicly embarrassing. "The political warfare initiative was the greatest mistake I ever made," he told a Senate committee in the 1970s, speaking by then as an aloof elder statesman and before Congress had seen the working documents. "It did not work out at all the way I had conceived it."

> We had thought that this would be a facility which could be used when and if an occasion arose when it might be needed. There might be years

when we wouldn't have to do anything like this. But if the occasion arose we wanted somebody in the government who would have the funds, the experience, the expertise to do these things and to do them in a proper way.[20]

That may be the way he wanted to remember it; in May of 1948 Kennan showed no such restraint. "Time is running out on us," he warned Secretary of State George Marshall. "If we are to get into operation in this field before the end of summer, Congress must be approached immediately with a request for the necessary funds." The NSC, the State and Defense departments, even the president, were all enthusiastic about the concept of political warfare, but its implementation "is not working out well," Kennan complained. "If the Executive Branch does not act soon to firm up its ideas as to what should be done along these lines, the possibility of getting secret funds out of Congress for covert operations will be lost."[21]

For the original problem remained: Kennan and his State Department planners, heirs to a tradition that had started in the Riga legation in the 1930s, could conjure up the ideas to contain communism, even to roll back the Iron Curtain. But who in Washington in 1948 could summon up the will, the expertise, and the audacity to carry them out "in a proper way"?

The Secret Game

A QUARTER-CENTURY after the decision of 1948, a veteran of the American clandestine services named Gerald Miller began writing down all he could learn from the secret CIA files about an obscure command headquarters for political warfare hidden within the United States government. Miller knew firsthand about some of what he found in the files. Starting out on a career in banking in Detroit after World War II, he had changed course and signed on to America's new intelligence service in the summer of 1949; he rose over two decades of anonymity to become chief of CIA political operations in western Europe.

The story Miller uncovered was strange to the new generation of intelligence professionals for whom he was writing. By the 1970s America's sense of purpose in confronting international communism was taken for granted; so also was the sprawling Central Intelligence Agency and its affiliated technical services, which had inherited the functions of that hidden headquarters. Even ordinary Americans had grown accustomed to the notion of covert operations conducted routinely around the globe. Miller nonetheless stamped the classification Secret on his researches, for the time had not come for Washington to admit that from the start, the American public was to be kept totally in the dark about this enterprise.

Had there been public discussion, even in closed congressional hearings, voices might have been raised against the wisdom or propriety of the American government engaging in clandestine subversion, paramilitary operations, and acts of sabotage in peacetime. Arthur Darling, revered as a teacher of history at Phillips Academy and Yale, and the CIA's first official historian, wrote in his own classified narrative that some of the public believed that "the 'national security' would be better served if the United States never marred professions of truth with actions that belie it."[1]

As it is, one can pore over the most secret policy transcripts of 1947 and 1948 without finding any debate about whether an action plan like Kennan's was a right and proper function of constitutional government. To responsible officers of state in that era, the danger of communist aggression was so great and obvious that a parallel counteroffensive, however irregular in its tactics, was only prudent. As Miller described the scene, people in Europe and elsewhere who opposed communism had few resources to advance their cause.

> They would need a strong source of secret support, financial, material and moral. It had to be secret to allay possible charges of foreign political meddling which might defeat the very purpose of the support. If covert aid of this sort were not forthcoming from the United States, it appeared that [the Kremlin] might proceed unhampered in its program to envelop the world with communist ideology.[2]

Secure against inconvenient public scrutiny, even hard-nosed policymakers of the Truman administration exhibited some uneasiness about the course on which they were embarking. Both the State Department and the Joint Chiefs of Staff wanted to call the shots, Miller wrote, "without actually playing in the secret political and psychological warfare game." That much was easily grasped by hardened intelligence professionals of the 1970s, who knew all too well the risks of their chosen careers. Miller's readers were probably more amazed to learn that their own CIA harbored even greater inhibitions against expansive subversive activities.

Established in 1947, the civilian Central Intelligence Agency was still the domain of military officers. Its director was a genial rear admiral, Roscoe K. Hillenkoetter, who had built impressive intelligence credentials as military attaché in Ambassador Bullitt's Moscow embassy and later in Paris. ("Military attaché" was a polite title, recognized as such by all governments, for an officer who collected intelligence by overt and, if possible, covert means.) Hillenkoetter knew and respected the traditional business and, like his successor, General Walter Bedell Smith, he regarded collection and assessment as the real function of intelligence.

Settling in at the CIA, he asked the agency's legal counsel, Lawrence

R. Houston, whether novel operations of political warfare were within the new agency's mandate. Houston replied on September 25, 1947, that activities such as "ranger and commando raids, behind-the-lines sabotage, and support of guerrilla warfare . . . would be an unwarranted extension of the functions authorized. . . . We do not believe that there was any thought in the minds of Congress that the Central Intelligence Agency under this authority would take positive action for subversion and sabotage."[3] Though Houston was later persuaded to change his mind and support the clandestine operations of later years, the CIA's first lawyer delineated a fundamental distinction in modern intelligence.

Well established and understood was the secret collection of information about a given situation; a quite different mode of operation, it seemed, were activities aimed at altering that situation to better serve the interests of the people carrying them out. It is one thing, according to this reasoning, to dispatch an agent to sketch the pilings and struts of a strategic bridge but something else to have the agent plant an explosive charge under those pilings and struts. The distinction has practical implications beyond the intellectual logic. The development of agent networks to penetrate closed situations and report back useful intelligence often involves years of patient nurturing, and an intelligence headquarters will go to extravagant lengths of deception to protect the continuing security of its networks. A positive act of sabotage, by contrast, becomes obvious immediately, putting at risk an agent who otherwise could serve as a valuable long-term asset. Hillenkoetter and the early CIA leaders were ever mindful of this problem.

The contrary view was taken by some intelligence professionals who had had experience running agent networks in World War II and had found that the same agent could indeed do double duty; if he could get into position to observe the bridge, he could also plant the explosives to destroy it. And, if the operation was clever enough in its design, he could escape apprehension or identification.

One American of unquestioned expertise who took this view was "Wild Bill" Donovan, retired director of the defunct OSS. Agitating from his out-of-office loneliness in New York and eager to get back into the Washington power game, Donovan peppered his friends in government with ideas for expansive and aggressive tactics to combat communism: the OSS had fought a good war against Hitler; now it was time to do the same against Stalin. Beginning to hear gossip about something they were calling political warfare, and with the instincts of a seasoned empire builder, Donovan saw the opening for the new CIA to enhance its reach and authority. "This is a great opportunity for your organization," he wrote Hillenkoetter.[4]

The amiable admiral would have none of it. His CIA was perfectly ready to run clandestine networks to collect intelligence and even run so-called morale operations, like dropping propaganda leaflets into enemy territory from free-floating balloons, as the military had done during the war. But subversive activities were always to stop short, as Hillenkoetter regularly put it, "of the physical" — sabotage or paramilitary operations.

Kennan grew exasperated with these distinctions drawn by jaded military officers. He complained of the intellectual limitations of lieutenants and colonels, contemptuous of their inability to see that political warfare involved much more than the tired notions of "black propaganda" — so petty compared to the great American crusade for freedom that he envisaged. At one point in the summer of 1948, when Kennan was trying to implement his action plan, he felt his vision stymied by military deadwood and advised his State Department superiors that it might be better to abandon the whole idea. Getting wind of this, Hillenkoetter wrote a friend at the White House that "since State evidently will not go along with CIA operating this political warfare thing in any sane or sound manner, . . . let State run it and let it have no connection at all with us."[5] The expansive Donovan would not have been amused.

Bureaucratic petulance thus aired and spent, Kennan calmed down and steered his Policy Planning Staff on a different tack. "The CIA set-up in respect both to personalities and organization is not favorable," he advised. "We therefore reluctantly decided to let the CIA sleeping dog lie and recommend a separate organization which might at a later date be incorporated into CIA.[6]

Thus emerged the secret agency that Gerald Miller tried twenty-five years later to explain to a bemused new generation of intelligence professionals.

✻

Its name was the Office of Policy Coordination (OPC), sounding reasonable (perhaps) on a bureaucratic chart of organization; opaque (certainly) about its actual purpose. Its official creation attracted no attention; its functions were known only to the inner circle of Truman administration policymakers who approved the Kennan action plan in NSC Directive 10/2. Outside those rarefied circles, said one calloused OPC veteran, "no one ever heard of it."

The founders were under no illusions that deliberate obscurity would endure forever. A "fable" was formulated, Miller explained, "to substitute vagueness for any strenuous effort at total secrecy that might not long be sustained." Here was the cover story: "In explaining the OPC role to persons with a legitimate interest, no mention was to be made of action programs; only its planning, intelligence coordinating, and defensive aspects were to be stressed. To the greatest extent possible, contacts were to be arranged through secure cutouts, with no reference whatsoever to OPC."*

The OPC operated under the fable through its four years of independent existence. It was not officially under the skittish CIA and certainly not part of the State Department; it hovered, with little accountability, in between. In the 1970s, when stories of illicit subsidies, bribes, and arms stockpiling began coming out in the American media, defenders of the intelligence agency could assert that CIA had not done these things — which may have been literally, though deceptively, true. It was the OPC that did them. And the OPC was always under orders to ensure that responsible officers of the United States, from the president on down, could plausibly deny any role in whatever this peculiar intelligence agency chose to do.

Just as Kennan's vision for political warfare was threatened with bureaucratic stillbirth, an unexpected savior appeared. A lawyer in private life, he had no confirmed government position and was not cleared for access to the most secret planning documents. Officially he was an outsider to political Washington; in reality, he was a force to be reckoned with in matters of foreign policy and secret intelligence. His name, invoked by Kennan in the planning meetings, was Allen Dulles.

* One of OPC's most effective (though not fully witting) field operatives, the American editor Melvin J. Lasky, told me he had never even heard a reference to the OPC during the years he was active.

Dulles had a formidable, if shadowy, reputation for his undercover work as the OSS representative in neutral Switzerland during the war. There he had built networks — he called them chains — of agents within the resistance movements of occupied Europe, even within Hitler's Third Reich itself. A cheerful youth from Watertown, New York, he had apprenticed in the trade of Old World intelligence as a diplomat during World War I and at the Paris Peace Conference of 1919.

Though he returned to his law practice after the war, Dulles maintained contact with agents and colleagues both foreign and American. When army intelligence officers were trying to figure out what to make of the former Nazi general Reinhard Gehlen, for instance, they visited Dulles in his comfortable New York townhouse late in 1946 for confidential counsel. Dulles remembered Gehlen's name from the secret reports of his Berlin agent that came to him in the last weeks of the war. He reviewed Gehlen's plans to activate anticommunist networks in eastern Europe (for security, Gehlen's group had disguised their proposed organizational structure to look like the electrical system of a large house), and gave his blessings to the German general's proposal.

Like other OSS veterans, Dulles was dismayed at the postwar disarray of American intelligence. As a lifelong Republican and a friend of Governor Dewey's, he was disturbed by the seeming nonchalance of Truman's Democratic administration about the threat of communist subversion. At Forrestal's initiative, he was summoned in February 1948 as one of three outside consultants — the other two were William H. Jackson and Mathias F. Correa, both experienced in intelligence but neither having Dulles's political stature — to assess the new CIA's ability to meet the Soviet threat to democratic institutions. Arriving in Washington in the midst of bureaucratic turf wars, these outsiders knew nothing of the National Security Council's secret decision the previous December to embark on "psychological warfare." But Dulles quickly picked up signals that something big was afoot and that the CIA was not showing initiative or imagination in confronting the problem.

The disaffected émigrés from eastern Europe caught his special attention. In 1942, before leaving for his posting in Switzerland, Dulles had been active in both the New York Republican Party and the OSS in mobilizing foreign-nationality communities in the United States for the war effort in Europe. Opposed to the Nazis at the time, these refugee activists were also hostile to communists. Independently of Kennan and his policy planners, Dulles saw that this group was ripe for exploitation.

Outside consultants had no mandate to initiate covert operations; they were not even cleared for access to secret policy discussions. But Dulles was an old hand at extracting information from closed quarters; he craftily arranged his own network of informants in Washington to keep him abreast of discussions to which he was not officially privy. Forrestal helped his consultants along by shrewdly assigning his trusted special assistant, Robert Blum, as staff aide for the CIA assessment panel. Blum was cleared for everything, and he knew what his boss wanted passed on. With Blum's help, Dulles fleshed out his intuitions about the CIA's nervousness in conducting political subversion and sabotage operations alongside its task of collecting intelligence. And Blum steered Dulles toward the point man for a new and expansive intelligence mandate.

Dulles knew George Kennan as Mr. X. As a director of the Council on Foreign Relations in New York, Dulles was proud that the council's journal, *Foreign Affairs*, had presented the doctrine of containment. Only from his informal network in Washington did he learn of Kennan's parallel secret role as a champion of aggressive political warfare, and that pleased him even more. Blum arranged for Dulles and Kennan to meet off the record on April 30, 1948. Accompanied by his Policy Planning assistant, John Paton Davies, Kennan briefed the "outside consultant" on both the emerging action plan for political warfare and the CIA's reluctance to take on the job.

This meeting had three major consequences. First, it gave Dulles the opening to weigh in, far more effectively than the outcast Donovan could ever have managed, on the inefficacy of dividing covert actions between two competing networks, one for information, the other for action. It also reassured the Wall Street Republican that the Truman administration was not as nonchalant about the communist threat as he had feared. And it persuaded Kennan that, given Hillenkoetter's maddening reluctance, Allen Dulles was the man to take on the direction of aggressive covert operations, of political warfare.

Thirteen days after the Kennan-Dulles meeting, the outside consultants submitted an unsolicited brief to the NSC, "Relations between Secret Operations and Secret Intelligence." They labeled it an interim report.

"We have been informed that a plan for developing certain other covert operations is being submitted to the NSC," they began, and if that was the case, the views of some disinterested but highly qualified intelligence professionals might be germane.

> It would be dangerous to have several unrelated and uncorrelated clandestine operations carried out in such sensitive areas as those behind the Iron Curtain. There would be duplication of effort, crossing of wires in the use of clandestine agents, and serious risk for the chains and agents used in the respective operations. . . .
>
> Secret operations, particularly through support of resistance groups, provide one of the most important sources of secret intelligence, and the information gained from secret intelligence must immediately be put to use in guiding and directing secret operations. . . . We recommend that a Director . . . should be made responsible for all forms of covert activities, including secret intelligence, secret operations, clandestine psychological work and such other covert operations as may be assigned.[7]

Allen Dulles's views on matters of covert operations were too seasoned by experience for policymakers of the Truman administration to ignore; they coincided, moreover, with what George Kennan was advocating. But there was another reason why this Republican lawyer argued so strongly for a powerful centralized command over America's secret tactics in the Cold War.

In May 1948, Truman looked like a lame-duck president, unelected, patronized, endured. His opponent in the forthcoming November election would be the worldly and elegant Tom Dewey, defeated in 1944, but only by the overpowering President Roosevelt in wartime. Dewey looked like a sure thing for the Republicans, and his supporters were already making their plans.

Dulles's older brother, John Foster, was the leading foreign policy spokesman for the Republicans, and Allen was ready to serve the campaign as soon as he finished his job as consultant to Truman's intelligence community; his professional stature and his connections assured that he would be President Dewey's likely choice to head the CIA. Naturally, he wanted this position to be a powerful one, with authority to oversee all the clandestine weaponry for the battles ahead.

Kennan, a career diplomat with neither taste for nor experience of domestic politics, would not admit to calculation of electoral matters; what he knew was that Allen Dulles was the man to do the job he wanted done. Within days Kennan commended the interim report to his State Department superiors. "Dulles hit the organizational problem head on," he wrote Undersecretary Robert A. Lovett, who handled managerial matters for the regal Secretary of State Marshall. "I have high regard for Dulles' experience and knowledge in the field and, therefore, attach great weight to his recommendations." He proposed that Dulles be named to replace Hillenkoetter at the CIA or, at least, to be the responsible officer for the new agency that would implement the action plan. Dulles would be in Washington the next week, Kennan noted; perhaps Lovett should sound him out for his availability. For extra impact, Kennan added that Forrestal felt so strongly on the matter that he would be willing to drive over from the Pentagon to meet with Lovett and Dulles personally.[8]

Less than a month had passed since Kennan's briefing to Dulles. On May 28 the meeting suggested by Kennan convened in Forrestal's office (sparing the defense secretary the indignity of driving over to meet an undersecretary of state). Allen Dulles and Robert Blum were in attendance; Hillenkoetter and General Alfred M. Gruenther from the Joint Chiefs of Staff reviewed the plans for covert operations, then discreetly left the room when the issue came down to the personality of the man to be put in charge.

Forrestal and Lovett jointly asked Dulles if he would accept the post of director of clandestine political warfare, to serve under the present CIA director. From the official minutes of the meeting: "[Dulles] replied that he did not think so, but that he would give his final decision in a few days. Names of other persons who might fill the new post were considered."[9] Forrestal and Lovett, unlike Kennan, were men of politics; they were not surprised at the intimations that Dulles would surely have a better offer just a few months hence. Accepting a secret post under an ineffectual superior was not Allen Dulles's style.

✳

Among the comrades in arms of intelligence with whom Dulles maintained close contact after the war was Frank Wisner, veteran of the high-living OSS mission in Romania at the end of the war. Like Dulles, Wisner was chafing at Washington's nonchalance as the Soviet Union imposed communism in eastern Europe and even made inroads in the western European democracies. Since V-E Day he had been struggling to turn the target sights of intelligence onto the Soviet Union, without success. In a huff, he left the OSS's successor agency, the SSU, to return, also like Dulles, to a comfortable New York law practice.

Over lunch one day early in 1947 at the watering place of the legal establishment, the Down Town Association, Wisner and Dulles commiserated over the sorry state of the great intelligence arm of government they had both served, which they considered essential for the looming battle against communism. The worldly Dulles tried to calm his younger protégé and advised that if he really wanted to serve his country (and, incidentally, get back into the action), the best course would be to find an obscure post in the Washington bureaucracy. From there he could work to restore the clandestine services to their rightful role. Wisner took Dulles's suggestion, said his good-byes to his law firm, and accepted the relatively modest post of deputy to an assistant secretary of state in the Office of Occupied Territories.

Wisner, hailing from an old southern family of Laurel, Mississippi, and a graduate of the gentlemanly University of Virginia, had naturally fallen in with the ancien regime of eastern Europe during his brief stint with the OSS in Bucharest. After the war, the charming young American had been welcomed into the elite circles that had always managed to endure alien occupations — Nazis, communists, even Hungarians — collaborating or resisting as their survival instincts guided. Many of Wisner's Romanian friends went into exile to escape the emerging communist power; indeed, his own agents had helped some of them escape. At home and at his office, Wisner's doors were always open to them. Like Dulles, he was impressed with the potential of the displaced anticommunists.

Settling into his modest State Department post, Wisner formed a group to study what he called "Utilization of Refugees from USSR in US National Interests." The intent coincided neatly with the emerging interests of Kennan's Policy Planning Staff, but Kennan was not sure that this energetic young man downstairs should be encouraged. In February 1948, as his own staff was looking into the potential value of anticommunist émigré communities, Kennan urged Undersecretary Lovett to rein in Wisner's study group and, indeed, to keep him at arm's length. "Because of security considerations, Mr. Wisner should not be informed of the reasons lying behind your instructions, but he can be told that this is in response to higher level decision," Kennan advised.[10]

Four months later, when Kennan saw that Allen Dulles would not be available to carry out his grand design of secret political warfare, he turned to some other candidates, including Mathias Correa, another of the outside consultants; but, as Kennan wrote Lovett, "I am told there is little likelihood of getting Correa." Another possibility was Irving Brown, the Paris representative of the American Federation of Labor, who had played a key role in the Americans' ad hoc effort to prevent the Italian Communist Party from winning in the Italian elections of April 1948. Brown was "a very able and active citizen," Kennan observed, but added the (to him) damning verdict that "this would have to be considered a political appointment."

All else failing, "I have placed Wisner at the head of the list on the recommendations of people who know him," Kennan concluded. "I personally have no knowledge of his ability, but his qualifications seem reasonably good, and I should think that it would be relatively easy to spare him for this purpose."[11]

George Kennan, who knew what it was like to be patronized by Averell Harriman, thus bestowed about the most lukewarm blessing imaginable on the obscure deputy assistant in the State Department. Allen Dulles had vouched for Wisner; Kennan had no one better to suggest. On August 19, 1948, the NSC confirmed the appointment of Frank G. Wisner as director of the Office of Policy Coordination, to fight America's political war with communism.

Wisner led the OPC through almost its entire four years until, in 1951, he became the CIA's deputy director in charge of the clandestine operations that the OPC had pioneered. The presidential election of 1948 did not turn up the expected result, of course, and Allen Dulles found himself out in the cold as his protégé took command of political warfare.

Wisner sought to assert his authority even before assuming office. He called a meeting on August 6 with White House and Pentagon representatives, Kennan, Hillenkoetter, and Blum. Kennan took immediate charge. "Political warfare is essentially an instrument of foreign policy," he declared, meaning that the State Department, and not CIA or OPC, would call the shots. Underlining the point, Kennan added that he personally "would want to have specific knowledge of the objectives of every operation and also of the procedures and methods employed."[12]

When it came his turn to speak, Wisner smoothly concurred with Kennan; his position would require, he said, "continuing and direct access to the State Department and the various elements of the military establishment without having to proceed through the CIA administrative hierarchy in each case." Hillenkoetter reluctantly agreed, and thus Wisner eased himself out from under CIA control.

As for Kennan's threatened heavy hand, Wisner said the head of the new agency "would require broad latitude in selecting his methods of operations — for example, as to whether he would use large numbers of Americans working abroad or whether he would work primarily through foreign groups." Above all, Wisner stressed, the new chief should not be "committed to any existing methods of operations." Kennan let this potentially ominous assertion of authority pass. Then, in a move familiar to every bureaucrat staking out a dominant position, Wisner generously offered to write up the memorandum of the meeting, thus making sure that his own points were recorded just as he wanted them to be.

Full of ideas and energy, Wisner appropriated for his own purposes the wasting assets of the postwar intelligence apparatus: a small staff of holdovers from the OSS and SSU, some two million dollars in funds authorized but never spent; a stock of high-altitude balloons for spreading propaganda leaflets behind the Iron Curtain (one of the less unimaginative ideas of the military intelligence officers), and a modest radio transmitter acquired in 1947 but sitting around while the officers tried to figure out a use for it.

On the critical matter of new personnel, Wisner was blessed with a marked shift of mood within the American elite. The events of early 1948 — the communist coup in Czechoslovakia, the Truman Doctrine promising material aid to potential victims of communist aggression, and, above all, the Marshall Plan to rebuild Europe in democratic capitalism — had shown the nation that it could not settle into a complacent era of peace. Anticommunism captured the imaginations of young Americans eager for public service.

Dulles and Wisner were not the only OSS veterans yearning to be active in the new national interest, and the old OSS recruiters on the faculties of Ivy League universities went to work. The notion of "political warfare," though the recruits did not yet know enough to call it by that name, became a noble cause among young elitists. Word spread of exciting job opportunities, even if no one could say exactly what the work would be. Wisner created "the atmosphere of an order of Knights Templars," in the words of William Colby, "to save Western freedom from communist darkness." Colby was one youth who eagerly signed up; he rose to become director of Central Intelligence in 1973.[13]

Civil servants already embarked on their careers, particularly in the diplomatic service, were less enthusiastic. As Kennan saw Wisner's operation moving out of his control, he wrote Undersecretary Lovett that "while this Department should take no responsibility for his operations, we should nevertheless maintain a firm guiding hand." He proposed that "a small body of personnel — perhaps no more than five men — who have Foreign Service and Department experience must be designated to guide Wisner's operation. . . . But we have met with stubborn resistance from our own personnel people." The problem, Kennan noted in frustration, was the high secrecy in which the OPC had been established. Foreign Service careerists "do not understand the overriding importance of the assignments which we request. . . . With no sense of proportion they resist the release of officers who are assigned to functions of relatively minor importance and their appointment to the job which Wisner and I wish them to take. Because of the high security classification of NSC 10/2, it is impossible for me to reason with our personnel people on this score."[14]

In his first year on the job, Wisner attracted a grand total of 302 people to his secret agency, a complement scarcely worth noting in the federal bureaucracy. Some, like Gerald Miller, came from private business; others, such as Colby, were OSS veterans; there were even a few idiosyncratic Foreign Service officers who did not share the inhibitions that so frustrated Kennan. James McCargar, for instance, the "Scarlet Pimpernel" of Hungary, bitten by the lure of undercover operations, found the diplomatic service too confining and his army intelligence network, the Pond of "Frenchie" Grombach, too crude for the new era.

One of Wisner's first hires eventually brought the OPC grief as well as value. Carmel Offie, the son of Italian immigrants who worked the coal mines of Pennsylvania, was one of the more colorful and bizarre figures in the diplomatic establishment. As an entry-level clerk in the prewar Moscow embassy, Offie lacked the intellectual graces customary to the diplomatic corps, but he had built a singular reputation as a "fixer," a modern-day court jester who knew how to humor the moods of his seniors. Those whom he amused called him "Offlet," and they relied on him to accomplish the multifarious, perhaps even unsavory, little tasks that polite diplomats pretended not to notice.

In London just before the war, Ambassador Joseph Kennedy so valued Offie's pluck that he tried to hire him as a personal assistant at several times his Foreign Service salary. Then, serving as counselor to an old mentor, Ambassador Bullitt in Paris, Offie made his flat in the rue de Rivoli available to Kennedy's young sons, Joseph, Jr., and John, over the summer of 1938. The Kennedy boys "did not learn much French," Bullitt cheerfully informed President Roosevelt in one of their regular exchanges of gossip, "but we got them invited to various parties where they could meet young ladies." Offie became a favorite bridge partner to the Duchess of Windsor. "He was a man of all work . . . more lines out than the phone company," said Louise Page Morris, who found her way into undercover operations from the upper reaches of the Social Register. "Everybody used Offie, he was funny as the dickens, always had the latest gossip. He looked like a monkey but his drollness made up for his ugliness."[15]

Like any good court jester, Offie loved intrigue. He was ever busy collecting and maintaining private networks of friends and fellow fixers of every nationality. For Wisner's purposes, he seemed an ideal recruiter, someone who could reach down into the lower levels of a dozen political and diplomatic circuits. "I presume that after you and Frank work on [a certain junior officer] in Washington he will agree to anything," wrote another mentor, Robert Murphy in Germany. (Offie had alerted Murphy that the man was about to be transferred to Paris: "He would, of course, be in the Embassy but actually would be doing very little real embassy work . . . doing certain other thing also!" This was the modus vivendi of Wisner's emerging apparatus.)[16]

Offie lasted only two years in the OPC. For all Offie's "highly sociable nature," Kennan primly found in him "a certain lack of measure and discretion," indeed, a lack of "a well-rounded educational background." Such traits Wisner, if not Kennan, could have tolerated, but it came out that the gregarious fixer had, a few years before, fallen afoul of the District of Columbia police for soliciting young men in a public convenience. As Senator Joseph R. McCarthy lambasted the Democratic administrations for harboring a practicing homosexual (and thus, it was assumed in those days, a security risk), Wisner had to move Offie to a private-sector job with the international bureau of the American

Federation of Labor. From that perch he continued to run helpful errands for his contacts and networks.*

By 1952 the OPC payroll numbered 2,812, plus an important 3,142 personnel under contract overseas. From seven overseas offices in his first year — "stations," in intelligence jargon — Wisner had extended his agency's reach to forty-seven. "OPC was to learn by doing," Miller explained in his internal history. "The conduct of political and psychological warfare in peacetime was a new art. Some of the techniques were known but doctrine and experience were lacking. . . . The secret war provided an immediate area of confrontation and, as a consequence, there was much governmental pressure to 'get on with it.'" Starting with only skeletal staffs and capabilities, Miller went on, the OPC overseas stations performed a crucial role as the Cold War gathered: "Their very presence was a cogent factor. Local individuals, groups, and intelligence services quickly came to understand that there was a force abroad in the world around which they could rally and gain support in their own opposition to communism."[17]

"The heart and soul of covert operations," advised the top lawyer of the intelligence services, Lawrence Houston, is "provision of unvouchered funds, and the inviolability of such funds from outside inspection."[18]

Recruiting personnel, Wisner had to pay their salaries. "Unvouchered funds," cash for which no formal accounting was required, was the time-honored device for evading budget lines and signed receipts. The OPC started with a modest budget of $4.7 million, plus whatever Wisner could scrounge up from other government departments. Three years later the OPC was spending $82 million, three times the CIA budget for traditional intelligence collection. In 1952 the OPC budget was nearly $200 million, half of which was spent on Rollback operations in eastern Europe alone.

---

* Offie died in 1972 at the age of sixty-three, in a plane crash on a routine flight from London to Brussels, where the American ambassador, Douglas MacArthur II, awaited his arrival. In retrospect, Carmel Offie deserves some place of honor in the Gay Liberation movement; he was out of the closet long before the phrase gained currency. He cheerfully called his bedroom "the playing fields of Eton" and, when confronted with the charge that he might be a security risk, replied that he was not at all vulnerable to blackmail, that he had never made any secret of his sexual preferences.

Over the centuries, as every graduate student of history knows, presidents and potentates have had slush funds to carry out discreet activities of statecraft that they would prefer not to explain in public. In the United States the practice started with George Washington himself. The tab run up by the political warriors of OPC, however, mounted far beyond a defensible slush fund.

A traditional device is to bury appropriations for intelligence and secret operations on innocuous lines of other agencies' budgets. The semblance of legal accountability is preserved without wide disclosure of exactly how these funds are to be used. Early CIA administrators liked to contemplate what they supposed to be the practice in the British House of Commons: folders containing budget breakdowns for secret operations were placed at each member's bench, where they sat unopened, by revered tradition, as the House voted to approve the secret budget. In fact, that was not quite how it was done in Westminster, but something close to the principle held in the United States Congress.

Congressional scrutiny of intelligence was both circumspect and casual during the early Cold War years; no voices were raised, in or out of Congress, to have it otherwise. From 1946 until 1952, only one person on Capitol Hill knew the amount and hidden locations of the American intelligence budget. This was George Harvey, nonpartisan chief clerk of the House Appropriations Committee. Harvey would share general knowledge with the successive committee chairmen but not with other members. In that era senators and congressmen seemed to prefer not to inquire into the details of secret operations. By 1951, however, Harvey had to alert his CIA liaison officer that the CIA budget (which included that of the OPC) had "reached a magnitude which makes camouflage difficult." Sooner or later, he warned, "this situation might lead to extremely embarrassing questions from other members."[19]

In 1948, Wisner could not wait for a congressional appropriation procedure, however circumspect, to take shape. "While covert political warfare must be controlled by the [State] Department," Kennan advised from the start, "the operation must find [funding] cover elsewhere."[20] Wisner cobbled together what Miller called "tenuous understandings" with key members of Congress, the General Accounting Office, and other government departments, setting up obscure accounts that his agency could draw upon without having to answer for them in public.

The first tempting target was an extraordinary and little-noted account in the Treasury Department. Established in 1934, the Exchange Stabilization Fund (ESF) had provided the then-extravagant sum of $2 billion in working capital before World War II for short-term currency trading to stabilize the value of the dollar in world trade. Then in 1941, war powers legislation designated this convenient accounting device as the holding pool for captured enemy assets and other monies being smuggled out of Europe. After the war the bulk of the ESF was transferred to the new International Monetary Fund as America's capital contribution. But a relatively small portion, $200 million, was retained in the Treasury to help in unspecified ways in the "reconstruction and rehabilitation of war-torn countries" — as Congress was later told.[21]

Wisner's financial officers and their counterparts in the White House spotted the ESF as a promising source of seed money. Most enticingly, from its origin it had been endowed with a special provision, which was well suited to the funding of secret operations that were never contemplated when the measure was enacted. Currency trading and hedging tactics required "a high degree of flexibility and discretion," Congress noted in setting up the fund. "Operations for the account of the ESF are likely to be highly sensitive, requiring a substantial degree of confidentiality." Thus Congress placed the fund "under the exclusive control of the Secretary of the Treasury, with the approval of the President, whose decisions shall be final and not be subject to review by any other official." For Wisner and his OPC, this extravagant freedom from scrutiny, enshrined in law, was nothing short of ideal.

A reported $10 million from the ESF was quickly made available to the OPC for its first year, above and beyond the authorized budget; no official accounting was required or made. Lest the legality of this old loophole ever be challenged, Wisner sought the sanction of the NSC in December 1949, saying that undefined financial measures could "jolt" the communist bloc, with repercussions "bound to be felt in the political, military and cultural spheres."[22] Use of the ESF was thus brought within the OPC's purview. Since Congress had already stated that ESF disbursals were not proper subjects for scrutiny, neither the Senate nor the House of Representatives held any hearings in the early Cold War years on the confidential accounts of the Exchange Stabilization Fund.

Then there opened a cornucopia that gave promise of providing much more than seed money for political warfare against communism

George F. Kennan in 1947, a moody, intellectual diplomat known to the public only as "Mr. X," as he argued for the strategy of "containing" Soviet communism. At the same time, in secret, he was pressing an aggressive and militant strategy to "roll back" the Iron Curtain in Europe with covert action, sabotage, and insurrection. *UPI/Corbis-Bettmann*

Frank Wisner of the OSS, just emerging from his "glory days" of resisting communists in Romania at the end of World War II. He exchanged his navy lieutenant commander's uniform for a secret position in American intelligence, in charge of the program of subverting communism by clandestine, "plausibly deniable" operations by the United States government.

Carmel Offie (left), the irrepressible "Offlet," who served Wisner and a whole generation of American diplomats and spymasters as embassy fixer, court jester, and builder of anticommunist networks. This rare photograph survives from pre-World War II days, when he was just beginning his secretive career, with an early mentor, William C. Bullitt, then ambassador to Moscow. *UPI/Corbis-Bettmann*

Michael Burke, Irish-schooled adventurer and deft manager of spies and saboteurs. After he turned away from his covert career with American intelligence,
he became an entrepreneur in the entertainment business, with Ringling
Brothers Barnum and Bailey Circus, CBS, and Madison Square Garden. This
photo was taken for his ID card at CBS in 1956, as he transformed himself
from undercover agent to corporate executive. *CBS Photo Archive*

Frank Lindsay, who parachuted behind the lines as an OSS agent in wartime Yugoslavia, became Wisner's first director of operations for undercover missions in eastern Europe. One of the first to declare Rollback a failure, Lindsay went public as head of a defense company that developed classified technology for the intelligence community.

(Left) Bill Coffin, a Yale man from Oyster Bay, New York, who left divinity school in 1950 for a secret assignment in American intelligence. His job was to mobilize and train Soviet refugees for penetration missions behind the Iron Curtain, where they were expected to incite popular uprisings in the communist satellite nations. This photo is from his undergraduate class book at Yale, where the OPC/CIA first tried to recruit him. *Courtesy of Yale Picture Collecton, Manuscripts and Archives, Yale University Library*

(Right) The Reverend William Sloan Coffin, fiery chaplain of Yale University, who became a national symbol for the American civil rights campaign and the Vietnam war protests in the 1960s and 1970s. His past in anticommunist covert action a decade earlier went unnoticed. *UPI/Corbis-Bettmann*

Across the American and British occupation zones of western Germany after World War II, camps of displaced persons dotted the countryside. Under the direction of American intelligence officers like Burke and Coffin, the camps became recruiting centers for tough fighters who were ready to try rolling back the Iron Curtain. *UPI/Corbis-Bettmann*

Michael Josselson (right), worldly link between intelligence and the intelligentsia, was director of the Paris-based Congress for Cultural Freedom until 1967, when his cover as a senior intelligence officer was blown. Behind this snapshot lies an untold story. One night in the early 1960s, the plaque of the Congress disappeared from the façade of its headquarters on Boulevard Haussmann; Josselson and his CIA managers feared that radical students would brandish it at some protest rally. After a search by the police, the plaque turned up innocently on the wall of a café in Switzerland. Josselson rushed to the scene with some colleagues to celebrate its recovery and, contrary to his usual wariness, allowed himself to be photographed.

Revered elder statesman George F. Kennan celebrating his ninetieth birthday in 1994, his ill-starred role in promoting insurrection behind the Iron Curtain long forgotten. With him is Madeline Albright, who later became secretary of state. *Council on Foreign Relations, photo by Elsa Ruiz*

in Europe. Among the terms for Marshall Plan aid to postwar European economies was the provision that a small portion — 5 percent — of the payment for imports from the United States could be made in local currencies; these so-called counterpart funds could be spent only in the countries of origin, for purposes unspecified. Publicly, it was said that they would support the costs of maintaining embassies and other official facilities in each country. (They could also defray the costs of congressional and other official junkets, so that these would not be charged to the taxpayers, a point that eased passage of the European Recovery Program through Congress.)

Scarcely was the Marshall Plan under way when Wisner sought out Averell Harriman and Paul Hoffman, directors of the recovery program in Europe. On November 16 they offered Wisner access to the counterpart funds as they accumulated, to be used for his own unspecified programs. Wisner promptly accepted.[23] At first the agreement applied only to France and Italy, where local communists were making such headway that the entire Marshall Plan program was in danger; subsidies to anticommunist political parties and labor unions seemed a reasonable means for strengthening the effects of American economic aid. In short order, according to a report in October 1949 by Wisner's financial officer, the OPC started using the counterpart funds for more specific forms of political warfare: direct propaganda, purchase of a newspaper for a labor group, conferences to counter the parallel activities of the old Comintern (by then renamed the Cominform). Inevitably, disbursals came to include what were described as "entertainment and developmental expenses incurred in dealing with principals of foreign political and labor groups."[24] When detailed accounts and receipts are not required, money tends to flow freely to helpful individuals.

The exact amount of counterpart funds channeled into anticommunist political operations is buried in the obfuscations and classifications of confidential government accounting. It probably was only a fraction, a large one, of the hundreds of millions that accumulated in the four years when western Europe was recovering from the war. But for Wisner and the OPC, the monies returned to American use from Marshall Plan aid served as a lavish and unvouchered base of support. Speaking as a member of what passed in those innocent days as the congressional oversight committee for intelligence, the moderate Republican Senator Leverett Saltonstall of Massachusetts, said:

It is not a question of reluctance on the part of CIA officials to speak to us. Instead, it is a question of our reluctance, if you will, to seek information and knowledge on subjects which I personally, as a member of Congress and as a citizen, would rather not have, unless I believed it to be my responsibility to have it because it might involve the lives of American citizens.[25]

One official responsible for the management of the Marshall Plan, Richard M. Bissell, said long afterward, when it was safe to talk openly about such things, "Wisner came for the funds but said I didn't have to know what for. My feeling was that we needed this procedure because we needed a political action arm."[26] Bissell, an academic economist, later became deputy director of CIA.

PART IV
Guerrillas, Sabotage, and Subversion

7

Starting with Intellectuals

THE OPC AND ITS PLANS for political warfare to roll back the Iron Curtain may have been the American government's biggest secret of the era, but Soviet intelligence learned about it within a week.

On August 22, 1948 — Wisner's appointment had come through just three days before — the Soviet press agency, Tass, sent out a small dispatch that was promptly conveyed to the party faithful by *Pravda* in Moscow and major newspapers in the other communist capitals. The United States was setting up a special office "for sabotage and terrorism in eastern Europe," the official party line warned. Indeed, America was setting out to "organize political and economic sabotage in the whole world, . . . diversions and every sort of provocation directed against the USSR and the countries of the people's democracy."[1] The tone was set for a stream of jeremiads for years to come.

To the nugget of their hard intelligence, the Soviet analysts added some fanciful details. They supposed that the head of the new subversion apparatus would be none other than Wild Bill Donovan and that Allen Dulles would direct its European operations from a base in Switzerland, just as he had during the war. On seeing the Soviet speculation, the ever-genial Hillenkoetter could not resist twitting Dulles, in spite of the tensions between them. "I see you are being fixed up with a new job in Switzerland," the CIA director wrote in congratulation. "This will move you up on the Soviet list to a place right near the top!" The Soviet reports added that front-line espionage bureaus were being set up in Berlin and Istanbul; on this, the Russian spies were confused by the opening of parallel but legitimate offices of the United States Information Agency.

Soviet intelligence was accurate on one final point: the new secret agency had a mysterious name that revealed nothing of its purpose. Lacking specificity, *Pravda* referred to the American sabotage plan as "Organization X."

Given all the secrecy within the United States government about NSC Directive 10/2 and the OPC itself, how did this intelligence leak to the Kremlin? A clue came in the original Tass dispatch, which cited British intelligence reports as a source. The British Embassy in Washington was closer to Top Secret planning than most of the American government; it would not have been at all exceptional if word of Kennan's political warfare planning had been shared unofficially with trusted colleagues in the American-British "special relationship." Of all those colleagues, none was more attuned to matters of confronting communism than the embassy's senior political officer, Donald Maclean, the yet-unmasked Soviet spy who had been so "aghast" at having allowed a diplomatic cable to be sent out uncoded two years before. Within a fortnight of the leak about OPC in 1948, Maclean left his Washington post, apparently worried that his life of betrayal was about to be exposed.

Maclean may have supplied the hard intelligence, but Soviet listening posts in the United States would have had no difficulty in picking up loose talk coursing through the newly invigorated conservative circles of Washington. Late in 1947, before knowing he would have any personal role to play in the matter, Kennan himself had mused, to an academic seminar at the National War College — off the record but freely shared by the participants with like-minded associates — about the possibilities of "psychological dissolution of Soviet power in eastern Europe."[2]

On Capitol Hill a leading conservative, Republican Senator Styles Bridges of New Hampshire, liked the idea of using the same tactics of subversion and propaganda that the Kremlin was employing against the western democracies. As chairman of the powerful Appropriations Committee, he let it be known that as much as $30 million could be found somewhere in the budget as a starter if the administration asked for it — a hint that Kennan pressed, ineffectually, upon his superiors in the State Department and the White House, who were not yet ready to ask for anything.

In April 1948, alert reporting by an upstart newsweekly catering to conservative businessmen, *U.S. News & World Report*, came perilously close to revealing the secret discussions then reaching their climax among State and Defense, CIA, and the White House. The magazine wrote with seeming authority of a plan to "adopt some of Russia's own tactics in Europe."[3] It spoke of proposals to "finance underground movements in Russia's satellite states" and went even further with another idea it said was under consideration: "American agents, parachuted into eastern Europe, . . . would be used to coordinate anticommunist action. Volunteers for such work, many of them veterans of the undergrounds of World War II, already are turning up in Washington to look for jobs." However, wary of alarming an American public unprepared for such aggressive policies, the editors of *U.S. News* assured readers that "outright sabotage behind the Iron Curtain is not an immediate prospect" — and a dangerous journalistic scoop disappeared.

On one small point, the emboldened conservatives of Washington, the editors, and the Soviet intelligence agents paid an unwitting tribute to the driving force behind the incipient American policy. *U.S. News* called the sabotage program then being considered "Organization X," and *Pravda* picked up the titillating label. Surely none knew how close they had come to identifying the man behind the plan, Mr. X himself.

As far as the public knew, the Truman administration was reluctantly turning against the Soviet Union as a matter of moral principle, without any thought of aggression to penetrate the Iron Curtain. The president staked his expectations for long-run western success on the Marshall Plan and the economic progress it would generate. A week after the belligerent *U.S. News* article, he declared that the European aid program would raise the Iron Curtain in peace. "Eastern Europe and western Europe are so integrated that if western Europe is prosperous, eastern Europe will have to come in."[4] In the event, Truman's vision was not all that faulty — it just took longer than he or anyone else could imagine at the time.

Even before his appointment became official, Wisner hitched a ride with the undersecretary of the army, William Draper, for a swing around the capitals of western Europe. To anyone who asked, he explained that he was investigating procedures for distributing relief supplies among the war-ravaged needy; after all, he was still only a deputy assistant in the State Department concerned with the postwar occupation. Anyone curious enough to note his schedule would have found that he met with British Foreign Secretary Ernest Bevin, French Foreign Minister Georges Bidault, the American military commander in Germany, Lucius D. Clay, and his political adviser, Robert Murphy — none of whom normally received minor State Department officials. Wisner was obviously introducing himself at the high levels appropriate to his new assignment.

By the end of October, Wisner was ready with a full agenda for the OPC. He contemplated no less than seventeen distinct programs of clandestine political warfare, in four categories.

• Psychological warfare: "direct mail, poison pen, rumors, etc."

• Political warfare: "support of resistance (underground), support of DPs and refugees, support of anticommunists in free countries, encouragement of defection."

• Economic warfare (thus justifying access to the Exchange Stabilization Fund): "commodity operations (clandestine preclusive buying, market manipulation and black market operations" and "fiscal operations (currency speculation, counterfeiting, etc.)."

• "Preventive Direct Action: support of guerrillas, sabotage, countersabotage and demolition, evacuation and stay-behind[s].[5]

Kennan looked over Wisner's agenda, which neatly matched his own action plan, and called it "the minimum of what is required."[6]

A few ventures that even Wisner took on only reluctantly were holdovers from feints at political warfare in more naïve days: distributing propaganda from high-altitude balloons, for instance. Military intelligence planners, recalling what they called "morale operations" on the World War II battlefields, had stockpiled large polyethylene balloons capable of rising to 30,000–40,000 feet. The prevailing winds would carry them above the Iron Curtain; they would break open at predetermined coordinates and shower the communist lands below with their payload of propaganda leaflets. Amazingly enough, this operation went on until 1956, spreading some four hundred tons of reading matter upon the earth.

Of course, prevailing winds did not always behave. On the very first launch, the balloons suddenly reversed direction and hovered over West

Germany instead of their targets in Czechoslovakia; another time they were wafted as far west as Scotland, where puzzled farmers collected the leaflets and wrote angry letters to the British press.[7] General Walter Bedell Smith, a hardened soldier who later became director of the CIA, once vented his scorn for such tactics, recalling a leaflet drop on labor camps in Nazi Germany during the war. "The bundle of leaflets had failed to open. It struck and sank a barge in the Rhine." That, the ascerbic Smith said, "was the greatest achievement of psychological warfare in Europe."[8]

Wisner took far more seriously "Preventive Direct Action": infiltrations of guerrillas, sabotage missions, and "stay-behind" cadres to serve the West under cover in areas that might be taken over in a feared Soviet invasion. The preparations for such missions, organizing of manpower and assembly of materiel, required the cooperation of the Department of Defense. Wisner faced an unforeseen problem when the enthusiastic defense secretary, James Forrestal, resigned in March 1949.* Replacing the pioneer Cold Warrior at the Pentagon was a fundraiser for the Democratic Party, Louis Johnson. All through 1949 Wisner and Johnson negotiated fitfully over the facilities the OPC could expect from the military services. They reached a pact only on October 6, nineteen months after the OPC started operations.

The OPC, Johnson insisted, "must assume autonomous responsibility and be so effectively obscured as to assure that neither the president nor the Secretaries of State or Defense will be placed in a position of having to answer publicly for its activities." That much Wisner could take. But Johnson specified that military materiel and facilities bearing "markings which would indicate the Department of Defense as their source will not be transferred unless such markings can be altered or obliterated to prevent such identification."[9] Pettifogging of this nature only mounted. Wisner's — and Kennan's — designs for paramilitary operations were inhibited by the self-protective caution, if not deliberate delaying tactics, of a skeptical military establishment.

Wisner sought more immediate results from nationalist political movements organized by eastern European refugees. The OPC's chosen ve-

---

* Depressed and paranoid, Forrestal committed suicide on May 22.

hicle for clandestine support was a private corporation chartered by New York State, the National Committee for a Free Europe.

Kennan's original vision of Rollback had included "a public American organization which will sponsor selected political refugee committees so that they may act as foci of national hope and revive a sense of purpose among political refugees from the Soviet world; provide an inspiration for continuing popular resistance with the countries of the Soviet world; and serve as a potential nucleus for all-out liberation movements in the event of war."[10]

Allen Dulles was Kennan's kindred spirit in the endeavor; even before Wisner got started, Dulles worked on his own to mobilize the New York legal and corporate establishment for the coming battle against communism. Diplomatic elders such as Joseph Grew, who had served in the United States mission to the Russian tsar before the Bolshevik revolution, and DeWitt C. Poole, a former OSS officer, were among his early recruits. It fell to Poole to rent office space on his own account in the Empire State Building in March 1949; nine months later the lease was assumed by a more mysterious funding source. On May 11 a certificate of incorporation was issued; Dulles's firm, Sullivan and Cromwell, drew up the papers. A week later Allen Dulles was named president of the private corporation. But it quickly became apparent that Dulles's intelligence connections would be awkward for the cover, so he turned over the presidency to the faithful Poole; Grew became chairman of the board.

At a press conference on June 1, Grew gave not the slightest hint that funding for the organization of émigré nationalists would come from anywhere in the United States government. An eager young diplomat, John Foster Leich, who had served his Foreign Service apprenticeship in eastern European postings, said long afterward: "When I joined the staff [of the committee], I was made aware — after an appropriate probation period — that government funds were involved, but that this was officially to be denied; the precise origin, means of transmission, or obligations which this funding imposed upon the Committee were never discussed with any staff member who did not have a direct 'need to know' and had not been 'cleared' for that purpose."[11]

Yet internal memoranda of the committee were stamped with government classification codes, strange for a private organization. The committee's top executives would refer cryptically, whenever budget matters came up for discussion, to "our friends in the south." A later president of the committee, Sig Mickelson, wrote that "memos regarding organizational disputes or controversies also went to 'our friends in the south,' and the first set of initials on the documents was almost invariably 'F.W.' It does not require skill in cryptography to interpret the name behind the initials."[12]

Only seven months after its foundation did the committee's board of directors resolve, as an apparent afterthought, to organize a nationwide fundraising campaign. A public relations consultant, Abbott Washburn, another OSS veteran brought in from the corporate world, paid his first call at what he assumed would be "the barren loft suitable for a struggling young organization of European refugees," and instead found himself at a comfortable headquarters suite in the Empire State Building.[13]

Over the centuries, political exiles have formed peculiar communities, restive and nostalgic for their homelands yet cut off from the political realities they fled. Too often they find themselves dependent for survival on fluctuating degrees of welcome provided by foreign governments. "In the absence of an electoral mandate, the political exile can only emphasize his differences with his fellow exiles," wrote Leich after many years of experience. "He begins to see victory in terms of favors or concessions he has extracted from the protecting power."[14]

The early activists of the OPC looked upon intellectuals from eastern Europe as an undifferentiated mass of refugees, sharing wholeheartedly American concerns about communism and ready to combat the Kremlin's occupation of their homelands. They were quickly disabused of such simple-minded portrayals.

Even — perhaps especially — in exile, Czechs feuded with Slovaks and Romanians harbored a century of grievances against Hungarians. Bulgarians had for generations been buffeted by Russia and Germany. Poles and Lithuanians had been trying to define their respective identities since 1386. Ukraine had first rebelled against Poland and Lithuania in 1648. More recent history offered even less solace. Hungarians sought to distance themselves from their pro-Nazi wartime regime. The Romanian exiles, having fought on both sides during World War II, were split between partisans of the pro-Nazi King Carol and the anti-Nazi King Michael. Polish émigrés, the largest and most dispersed of the émigré communities, were divided into three factions, which were often more hostile to and suspicious of each other than of Soviet Russia. Between Poles and Ukrainians, even though both were under communist rule, lingered the bitter residue of the "ethnic cleansing" of 1943, when Ukrainian nationalists had sought to clear their land of Polish residents and influences.

Upon this troubled tapestry the OPC attempted to impose a coherent front against communism. Ultimately a dozen or so "national councils" were formed, each with ten to fifteen members — bureaucrats, ex-ambassadors, political party leaders — to provide cover for the anticommunist propaganda and resistance generated by the OPC. That modest old radio transmitter preserved by the military staff suddenly looked promising; the vision grew of a bold new broadcasting service, to be called Radio Free Europe, that would allow the émigré councils to address their compatriots languishing behind the Iron Curtain.

Overall direction came from New York (or, rather, Washington), but the national councils' organizational and propaganda work was carried out in the German DP camps and nearby villages where refugees were trying to build new lives for themselves. If operations to collect intelligence were afoot, these were matters into which the New York front committee deliberately "did not pry," in Leich's carefully measured words. "It was my impression that such intelligence services as the committees undertook were delivered directly to interested American governmental agencies."[15] Even decades after the fact, a loyalist like John Foster Leich could not bring himself to identify the OPC.

Financial support for this network of national councils varied. Emigrés from the three Baltic republics could draw upon substantial funds sent to western banks by the respective governments during their brief independence before the Nazi and then Soviet occupations. The Romanian national council continued operating in its time-honored lavish style with the monies sent overseas by wealthy Romanians determined to protect their interests against Soviet (or, earlier, Nazi) occupation. All else failing, the national councils could readily draw upon the Marshall Plan counterpart funds, at least in their German base-camp operations of propaganda and social outreach. Wisner had taken care to gain concurrence from the incoming American high commissioner, "Jack" Mc-Cloy (because Germany was not yet sovereign, McCloy was not yet an ambassador), for the special financial arrangements he had already established.[16]

For all the secrecy and dissembling imposed by skittish Americans, émigré activists seemed never in doubt about the source of their funding — indeed, they were proud to hint at official U.S. government sponsorship. In a candid moment with Leich, one worldly ex-ambassador from Romania dismissed the ruse as just "a Punch and Judy show."

The OPC's National Committee for a Free Europe could assert some legitimacy among exiles from the nations of eastern Europe newly fallen under Soviet domination. But it had no standing whatever among spokesmen for the diverse nationalities of the Soviet Union itself — Ukrainians, Belorussians, the peoples of the Caucasus. These defectors from Kremlin power were not experienced in the interplay of parliamentary politics; with few exceptions they were not even intellectuals. Sincere (perhaps), idealistic (perhaps), they required tighter managerial controls than the Free Europe Committee could ever provide.

As Kennan had proposed, Wisner and the OPC quietly set up a separate front organization that came to be called the American Committee for the Liberation of the Peoples of the USSR. Shunning the bother of Allen Dulles's illustrious boards of directors or public fundraising campaigns, the American Committee became the OPC's first major covert operation, under tight control. For three years it led the secret campaign of political warfare on a dilatory, frustrating course.

✻

The Russian emigration was a dramatic and durable fixture in European capitals throughout the twentieth century. Fractious and conspiratorial, these émigrés were often snobbish beyond measure, both toward their host societies in western Europe and toward each other. At the top of their social order were the so-called Old Immigrants, survivors and heirs of refugees from tsarist autocracy and the White Russian aristocrats who fled the Bolshevik revolution of 1917. To their number in the 1940s were added recent defectors from communism, the New Immigrants, prisoners of war and, though it was considered impolitic to say it, collaborators with the Nazis against Stalinist rule. These people were not of the same social class as those who came before. Throughout were communist infiltrators, secret agents sent by Stalin to root out his enemies. Cohesion and mutual sympathy were in short supply within the Russian emigration.

Among the hundreds of thousands of Soviet nationals holding on in western Europe after the war, western intelligence sought immediate contacts with promising individuals who might help in a future confrontation with Soviet power. The early intelligence files are full of indiscriminate depictions of the activities of Russian émigrés, mainly in Paris but also in Munich and the surrounding DP camps. Military minds in Washington grew impatient with this kind of intelligence, as indeed did most outsiders to the murky and self-important worlds of émigré politics. In August 1946, SSU headquarters cabled Munich in exasperation:

> Most of the contacts which we are cultivating in Munich are not worth the time and effort spent on them. *Our main target should be to (1) locate and identify Soviet intelligence personnel, and (2) try to penetrate their organizations and neutralize the effectiveness of their work* . . . In concentrating as much as we have on doubtful and low level White Russian sources of information, we are getting away more and more from arriving at the primary aim.[17]

Three years later, however, Wisner defined the "primary aim" more broadly than had the military intelligence staffs. Through his American Committee, the OPC turned to the émigré politicians to forge an anticommunist front — just as Stalin had long feared. And the émigrés quickly learned that the Americans would back up their new interest with *valuta* — hard currency.[18]

Early in the autumn of 1950, the American Committee dispatched a representative to sound out four groups that the inventive Carmel Offie and his scouts supposed would be like-minded. They were a disparate crowd, ranging from recent veterans of General Vlassov's ill-starred Russian Liberation Army to loyalists of old anti-Bolsheviks like Alexander Kerensky, Boris Nikolaevsky, and David Dallin. More to the right was the venerable NTS, slowly recovering from its Nazi affiliations during the war, and a small but influential group of intellectuals in Paris under the leadership of an Old Emigrant and former Duma parliamentarian named Sergei P. Melgunov. Like-minded or not, several of the Russian factions tried to steal a march by setting up their own front in advance to meet the American delegate and accept his fabled largesse. Their preemptive ploy failed; they informed their followers that they had not received "the necessary support from the American Committee."

The American Committee sent a former journalist named Spencer Williams to meet with the Russians; he convened a more controlled planning conference in January 1951. As his first earnest, he wrote a check to rent comfortable living and meeting quarters in the Bavarian inn Zum Hirsch on the outskirts of Füssen, which he reported would be far enough from Munich that their deliberations would not be interrupted or subjected to unspecified outside pressures — except, of course, his own. (Williams tried to manage his own participation discreetly, staying forty miles away in the pleasant town of Garmisch-Partenkirchen, and actually met with the émigré delegates only once, hosting a cheerful but contentious tea party.)

The Füssen conference went badly. The NTS representatives withdrew when they saw they would not be in charge. Professor Melgunov challenged the rights of "outsiders" to interfere with the "unity of the [Russian] peoples." Williams canceled the reservations at the Zum Hirsch after one week and let the delegates find their own ways home. David Dallin took to the pages of the *New Leader*, a small but articulate anti-Bolshevik journal in New York, to blast the effort under the headline "The Wrong Russians Again." The American Committee had treated the Russians as "subordinates," Dallin charged; "it tried to give orders by cable on how to conduct the Conference, what to do and what not to do, interfering in the smallest details." The American Committee and its sponsors in the south headed by "F.W." had intended the whole organizing project to be secret; now they found their effort blasted in public. So began the OPC's education in the perils of dealings with Russian émigrés.

The American Committee reluctantly established itself a month later as a private corporation based in New York. In May the founders elected a new member introduced by Offie: none other than Isaac Don Levine, the publicity-minded sponsor of the Soviet apostate Krivitsky before the war. Levine flew immediately to Europe, armed with plenty of disposable cash.

He found a cauldron of competing interests; beyond the formidable personal egos there was a fundamental conflict between émigré generations and, more significantly, between nationalities. Ethnic Russians regarded Moscow as the legitimate political center; other nationalities of the USSR — Ukrainians, Belorussians, Armenians, Georgians, Azerbaijanis, and more — entertained separatist visions and memories of long-distant eras when they were not under Russian domination. The American grand plan allowed for little differentiation; they were all Soviet citizens, and they should all be ready to march against communism.

From the moment of his arrival Levine insisted that the ethnic Russian factions hold the door open for the other Soviet nationalities in the proposed anticommunist front. Putting the wrong foot forward from the Russian viewpoint, he contacted Ukrainian separatists on his own. More clumsily, he actually disbursed some of his bounty to Armenian nationalists who had promoted their cause from the shortwave news desks of Nazi Berlin. Even the words bandied about by the American Committee, "liberation" from "Bolshevism," made more democratic émigrés wince, for they were just the words used by the Nazis during the disastrous German occupation of the western Soviet Union.

Flush with Marshall Plan counterpart funds, Levine organized his first conference in August 1951 in Stuttgart. He made no pretense of secrecy or discretion; he ran the show. The attendance of the seventy-year-old Kerensky, briefly prime minister in 1917 before Lenin's Bolsheviks overthrew him, attracted wide attention; the London *Economist* adapted the famous Marxist image to accuse the American Committee of foolishly "lifting Kerensky from the dustbin of history." Old Professor Melgunov thundered his opposition to dealing with the non-Russian nationalities, but even he eventually succumbed to Levine's money-backed persuasion. "If we didn't consider those who want to help us, we could do much more," he told his proud followers, "but consider them we must."

By agreeing to let Ukrainians, Armenians, and other nationalities drink from the cornucopia served up by the American Committee, the four Russian factions made what they felt was an epic concession. The pathetic declaration of the wizened Kerensky revealed the dimness of their vision: "Never before has one ruling nation voluntarily, and on its own initiative, conceded so much on the national independence question." Never mind whose initiative, the fact was that the "ruling nation" making the concession actually ruled nothing.

After his Stuttgart meeting, Levine pressed the momentum sought by his friends in the south. He paid the hotel bills for a rump gathering of Ukrainian nationalists early in October at the Bavarian village of Fürstenfeldbruck; though for only two nights, the accommodations at the inn were more comfortable than the DP camps, and this group of Ukrainians became thoroughly pliable to American interests — to the disgust of the more legitimate Ukrainian factions. One of the rump group's leaders, the aging Cossack Diomid Gulay, was physically assaulted when he returned to the Schleissheim camp, rescued only by the timely intervention of a fellow refugee in the next room.

Representatives of the Russian and the other-nationality émigrés then came together in a Wiesbaden hotel to sign on to the anti-Soviet platform sought by the American Committee. Will Cates, in-house historian of the American Committee, called this the first meeting of Russians and non-Russians in the history of the emigration. No mere tea party would suffice; Levine hosted a festive dinner. The Wiesbaden conference of November 1951 marked the high-water line of the American Committee's effort to organize the émigré community in western Europe. Levine showed what could be done with determination and money — and what could not.

After five days of heated debate the delegates signed a common document declaring their unity in the fight against communism, but after heading home they realized that they could not deliver on anything they had promised. Even Kerensky, for all his pleasure at being taken seriously as a statesman again, denounced Levine. "The American Committee may succeed in calling a new conference," Kerensky wrote afterward in the newspaper of the New York émigrés, *Novoye Russkoye Slovo*, "but I am sure there will be no Russian people at the [next] conference who value their good name and the honor of Russia." From Paris Professor Melgunov weighed in: "If the American Committee had not interfered in the Russian community, alien to it, and had not attempted to dictate, we would undoubtedly have been able to come to terms with the nationality minorities (at any rate with some of them), and we would have avoided internal division." The NTS flatly demanded that Levine be fired.

Passing through Munich a few months later, even Carmel Offie turned against his OPC protégés (he called them the Fizz Kids). From his quarters at the luxurious Vier Jahreszeiten hotel, he wrote the American labor union leader Jay Lovestone (his latest mentor): "At one time I made something of a defense for the Fizz Kids. I take it all back. After listening first hand to the facts, I was shocked and outraged by what I heard here about the whole performance."[19]

To the friends in the south, the common front of Soviet émigrés was becoming a chimera, and it was no longer essential to Wisner's plan of establishing an effective propaganda platform. The American Committee sent an advance team of broadcasting technicians to Munich to design a sophisticated radio station that would beam its messages into the Soviet Union. Levine invited any émigré faction that wished to cooperate, Russians and non-Russians alike, to yet another comfortable conference in the nearby town of Starnberg and announced the American Committee's plan in June 1952. "We will give you an excellent and powerful radio station," Levine told the wary delegates, "if the emigration will meet us halfway." Then he left the room, letting the factions pursue their feuding without him. When Levine returned home after spending fifteen months in Europe, he left ill feeling among the Russian and non-Russian émigrés but also a frail cover to give Wisner and the OPC a vehicle for waging political warfare over the airwaves of Radio Liberty.

Jon Lodeesen, a latter-day official of Radio Liberty/Radio Free Europe, reviewed the work of the American Committee from a safe distance:

> The objective of the Russians, liberation from communism, was not necessarily synonymous with the objective of most of the others, liberation from the Russians. . . .
> The Americans had made the decisions to treat the various émigré organizations as though they were political parties, whereas they were apt to be debating clubs or mutual protection associations or the instruments of individuals or small groups. They are practised in discussing and opposing but, with few exceptions, having no constituency, authority or responsibilities, they were not very good at doing.[20]

By the end of 1952 the ranks of Soviet émigrés in Europe were thinning; the most motivated and talented among them had found their way out of the DP camps to new lives in the United States, South America, or any country that would accept them. Left behind was an unpromising hard core, as Cates described them — too old, infirm or tainted by past crimes and discredited politics to emigrate. Though the American chronicler chose not to admit it, some of those who remained were deliberate plants from Moscow, Soviet agents up to their old practice of penetrating the émigré organizations to serve the interests of the Soviet state. For all these dubious remnants, the prospect of a paying job at the American Committee's Radio Liberty, poor cousin to the more respected and dynamic Radio Free Europe, became the only goal in sight.

On the other side, the Kremlin fired the opening shots of political warfare from a formidable advantage over the western democracies. The Soviet state had been at work, after all, building undercover networks of sympathizers and agents since 1923 — January 11, to be precise, according to records of the Soviet Foreign Intelligence Service. "A special bureau for disinformation" was created on that day under the control of the Communist Party Central Committee and tasked "to break up the counterrevolutionary plans and schemes of the enemy." By 1947, well before "Organization X" was established in Washington, Moscow's KI (Committee of Information) was already at work in small unmarked offices on Gogolevsky Boulevard, running undercover operations to "unmask the anti-Soviet activity of foreign circles, influence the public opinion of other countries, and compromise anti-Soviet officials and public figures of foreign governments."[21]

A specific mission known as Service 2, later Service D, sought to "create agent networks in influential press and propaganda organs" of the West; this work was kept secret even from comrades in KI. This branch would scrutinize incoming intelligence (perhaps including the report about "Organization X"), polish it up for disinformation value, and pass it to the foreign press through trusted channels as a way of "exposing and compromising" anti-Soviet programs and plans. Other branches of Soviet intelligence were also far ahead of the West in building agent networks, which were targeted on Germany and western Europe. Pavel Sudoplatov, an old hand at "wet" operations (kidnappings, assassinations, sabotage, and the like) set up shop under cover of an import-export business in Prague late in 1947.

For the American public, the Cold War was engaged initially as a battle of minds and ideology, and in this realm, too, the Kremlin had a head start, through the expansive networks of the prewar Common Front. Ideology was a battlefield for political warfare as much as sabotage and subversion were, and for the wars of ideology, the most visible weapons are mass meetings, flashy conferences of the like-minded, where eloquent zealots from around the world speak to the converted and promote an image of mass popular support.

As the OPC's American Committee was convening its secret planning sessions among the displaced persons and émigrés of Europe, the Cominform took to the hustings in time-honored fashion. In October 1947, with the rubble of war still cluttering the streets of Berlin, it launched its "peace offensive" with a writers' conference; on that success it convened a broader conference a year later in Wroclaw, formerly German Breslau. Cominform propagandists generated momentum among intellectuals in western Europe, mainly in France and Italy, where local communist parties could mobilize enthusiasm for the party line.[22]

In March 1949 the Kremlin made bold to take the "peace" campaign across the Atlantic to New York City, choosing as its audacious venue the symbol of American capitalism, the Waldorf Astoria hotel on Park Avenue. On this occasion and in this setting, the familiar charges of "U.S. warmongering" would be aired, and in the ensuing confrontation, Wisner and his OPC found a target of opportunity. In fits and starts, they mounted a controversial operation that would build an intellectual force as impressive as their parallel effort to mobilize anti-Soviet émigrés was pathetic.

This time the initiative came honestly from private citizens, New York anti-Stalinist intellectuals still smarting from their relegation to obscurity during the wartime alliance with Soviet Russia. The indefatigable Sidney Hook of New York University drew colleagues like Dwight Macdonald and Mary McCarthy into an effort to organize a simultaneous counterconference to raise their own rhetoric and drown out the declarations of the fellow travelers. They demanded meeting and working space at the same famous hotel. Running into resistance from the Waldorf management, which claimed to be fully booked, Hook's cadres found a devious but effective resource to deploy.

One of their number was a committed journalist of the labor movement named Arnold Beichman, who nurtured useful contacts among anticommunist union leaders. On being refused a suite at the Waldorf, Beichman (no man to be trifled with) warned the wary management that his union friends would mount a job action to close the hotel down. A three-room suite suddenly materialized, and members of a telephone workers' union came in to install ten special phone lines — on a Sunday morning! Hook's activists worked their way into the disciplined panel discussions of the pro-Soviet conference; they put pugnacious questions to the speakers spouting the party line, and in triumph staged their own outdoor rally.

In Washington, where officials were not inclined to pay much heed to the fractious New York intelligentsia, Wisner and his staff read news reports of the confrontation, and it occurred to them that this spontaneous energy could be harnessed for the OPC's purposes. Most enthusiastic was Offie, who made bold to ask his former colleagues in the State Department how they intended to respond to the communist "peace offensive." Traditional diplomats tended not to notice propaganda shows and certainly did not bother to answer them; nor were the brainstorms of this uncouth man Offie taken very seriously. But a few diplomats in junior slots were interested. One, Raymond Murphy, warned that the communist theme "is that the United States and the Western democracies are the war-mongers and Fascists, and the Kremlin and its stooges the peace-loving democracies. And there is a better-than-even chance that by constant repetition the Commies can persuade innocents to follow this line. . . . This phony peace movement actually embraces far more than intellectuals."

Wisner found here an opening to show, as he had warned Kennan, that his freewheeling OPC would not be "committed to any existing methods of operations." A few days after the Waldorf conference and counterconference ended, Wisner cabled Harriman at the Marshall Plan office in Paris requesting five million francs (about $16,000) in counterpart funds to generate another counterdemonstration when the Cominform loyalists next convened, in Paris the following month. Irving Brown, Paris representative of the American Federation of Labor and always one of Offie's more useful contacts, mobilized his friends in French unions to prepare for the conference. Covertly the OPC covered the travel expenses to Paris for friendly delegates from Germany, Italy, and the United States; among the Americans were Hook and novelist James T. Farrell, neither of whom knew at the time who had bought their plane tickets.

The April 30 anti-Cominform demonstration in Paris disappointed its OPC sponsors and the reason was one that would plague Wisner's political warfare among intellectuals for a decade to come. In their zeal to assemble an impressive slate of anti-Stalinist intellectuals, the French organizers invited speakers who had less than nice things to say about the United States; indeed, they came across as anti-American. This, to Wisner, was not what his governing directive from the NSC had in mind. He vented his frustration in an internal OPC memo: "We are concerned lest this type of leadership . . . would result in the degeneration of the entire idea (of having a little 'DEM-INFORM') into a nuts folly of miscellaneous goats and monkeys whose antics would completely discredit the work and statements of the serious and responsible liberals."

One brief encounter that April in Paris proved portentous for the OPC and the anti-Stalinist intelligentsia of Europe. Lobbying to promote his idea for a continuing campaign of anticommunist intellectuals, Sidney Hook chanced upon a young American journalist named Melvin Jonah Lasky, a graduate of City College of New York, which was a hothouse of combat between Stalinists and anti-Stalinists in the 1930s. Lasky had worked on the New Leader, then was drafted into service as a combat historian for the U.S. Seventh Army. Demobilized in Berlin, he quickly fell in with the same left-wing but anti-Stalinist intellectuals he had known at City College, future luminaries such as the Anglicized Hungarian Arthur Koestler and the English writer George Orwell. They all despaired at the naïveté of American liberals who failed to recognize the evils of Stalinism. Lasky's skills as a reporter and editor caught the attention of the American commander in occupied Germany, General Lucius Clay, who offered Lasky the sponsorship and funding to create a sophisticated journal for German intellectuals striving toward a post-Nazi democracy, to be called Der Monat.

Hook commended the promising young editor for service in the anti-Stalinist cause, but Wisner remained skeptical. From what little he knew of Lasky, he thought this radical fellow would be just another of the "goats and monkeys," too bohemian in thought and life to front for the OPC. Lasky rose a notch in Wisner's estimation, however, when a Soviet propagandist depicted him as "a cheap Hollywood imitation of Trotsky."[23]

After the unimpressive show at the Paris counterconference, Lasky lobbied his left-wing intellectual crowd to set up a conference of their own. They scheduled it for Berlin the next year, 1950, and decided to call it the Congress for Cultural Freedom. As one of the organizers described it to a skeptical friend in the American diplomatic service: "It should be a gathering of all ex-communists, plus a good representative group of anti-Stalinist American, English and European intellectuals, declaring its sympathy for . . . the silent opposition in Russia and the satellite states, and giving the Politburo hell right at the gates of their own hell." Notes about the plan went into the diplomatic pouch to Washington; they hit Offie's desk at OPC in mid-September. Passing the idea along, even Offie could not shake Wisner's contempt for a "nuts folly" of ex-communists claiming to wave the American flag of freedom.

Soon came another chance encounter, of Lasky with a minor cultural officer on General Clay's staff, a naturalized American from Estonia who had studied in prewar Berlin and Freiburg and had landed a job as a buyer for Gimbels/Saks in Paris in the 1930s; Michael Josselson was fluent in English, French, Russian, and German. Lasky and Josselson became buddies in the fight against communism.

When Josselson died in 1978, none of the world's major newspapers printed an obituary, much less a tribute. There was no way editors could have known of his achievements, or who he really was. Holding a polite post in a public arena, he was nonetheless the quintessential undercover operative. He enjoyed his life and was proud of his accomplishments, but he always shunned public recognition. In Mike Josselson, Wisner and the OPC stumbled upon a master at manipulating the subtleties of political warfare upon the realities of postwar Europe. His role became that of matchmaker for the stormy partnership of intelligence and the intelligentsia.

❋

Lasky unveiled his scheme for an anticommunist intellectual offensive to this forty-one-year-old cultural attaché in the American military government (a legitimate position; Josselson was not yet under any intelligence cover). "The drama and intrigue of postwar Berlin awakened something in Josselson and gave him scope to exercise his considerable talents as an operator, administrator, and innovator," noted the CIA's classified internal history. "His enthusiasm was boundless, his energy immense." Daniel Bell, a Harvard professor of sociology who became Josselson's close friend, called him "a Prussian by day," for his organizational rigor, but "a Russian by night," for his love of ideas and argumentation.[24]

He was also a realist. However worthy the cause, financial backing from the American government in those first postwar years would have been self-defeating, giving party-lining critics unanswerable charges to denounce an imperialist charade. Yet nothing could get started without ample funding. Arthur Schlesinger, Jr., also of Harvard, later defined the dilemma: "Organizations of the Right in most countries get financial support from the local business communities and oligarchies; organizations of the anti-democratic Left get it from the Russians or Chinese; but organizations of the democratic Left have no obvious and reliable sources of support."[25]

Josselson had no knowledge of secret agencies in Washington, though he had shown eagerness to assist American intelligence officers in Germany long before his meeting with Lasky. "He is particularly useful because of his knowledge of Russian and his close liaison contacts with his allied opposite numbers," noted the head of the Berlin intelligence base a year earlier. "He has given us a number of valuable intelligence leads."[26] Josselson knew enough about European intellectuals to recognize that if they were to be funded, the support would have to be secret. In January 1950 he sent to Washington a proposal, bold for a junior cultural attaché, just as Lasky and his colleagues were rounding up participants for their offensive against the Cominform. Though he was ready to pounce on all sorts of bizarre operations that might become a meaningful counterforce to communism, Wisner sat on this proposal, by the unknown Josselson, for three months. When he finally granted the Congress for Cultural Freedom a budget of $50,000, it was on condition that "goats and monkeys" like Lasky be kept out of it.

The Congress convened on June 26, 1950, in the Titania Palace in occupied Berlin, a city newly buoyant with the triumph of the western cargo airlift that broke a communist blockade. Preparations were too far along to keep Lasky out of the American delegation, but he was surrounded by "safer" luminaries such as Schlesinger, the playwright Tennessee Williams, actor Robert Montgomery and even David Lilienthal, chairman of the government's Atomic Energy Commission. Coinciding with the communist invasion of South Korea, the Congress generated an unanticipated popular enthusiasm among European anti-Stalinists. "Friends, freedom has seized the offensive!" declared Koestler. Once a communist organizer for the Popular Front, he waved rhetorical banners, unwittingly, under the auspices of American intelligence.

In the aftermath Wisner was "very disturbed" that his strictures against Lasky and others had been ignored; persons like these threatened to be as inconvenient for OPC purposes as old Professor Melgunov in the Russian émigré front. But his annoyance was dulled as praise for the Berlin operation poured in, even from his nemesis, Defense Secretary Johnson, who commended the OPC effort to Truman personally. The president, Wisner advised his staff, was "very well pleased." Wisner's cautious strictures faded away.

Josselson resigned from his job with the military occupation regime to become executive director of the continuing campaign of the Congress for Cultural Freedom, with headquarters on the Boulevard Haussmann in Paris. Quietly he signed on to the professional staff of OPC.

For the next sixteen years his would be the deft guiding hand of a covert operation that succeeded in mobilizing intellectuals of the West and, eventually, the Third World, against the appeals of Marxism-Leninism. At its peak Josselson's apparatus had offices in nearly thirty-five countries with 280 employees, assisting in the publication of two dozen magazines and subsidizing countless books and reports.

As Josselson's eventual CIA case officer, Thomas W. Braden, recalled, visits to Washington were too risky for an undercover operator of such visibility. "The French bureaucracy was loaded with communists and someone might see him at the airport. But I traveled a lot and I'd meet him in Paris, often at bicycle races. We'd go in separately, get adjoining seats, talk business, and leave with the crowd."[27] CIA officers would try never to set foot in the Congress's Boulevard Haussmann headquarters.

Josselson was the anonymous officer proudly cited by Braden in a controversial magazine article in 1967, when the then-retired CIA executive decided to go public in defending the Congress amid a hostile public clamor.

> We had placed one agent in a Europe-based organization of intellectuals called the Congress for Cultural Freedom. Another agent became an editor of Encounter [a respected literary/political journal]. The agents could not only propose anticommunist programs to the official leaders of the organizations but they could also suggest ways and means to solve the inevitable budgetary problems. Why not see if the needed money could be obtained from "American foundations"?[28]

For all the growing impact of the subsidies, for which neither Josselson nor anyone else could take credit at the time, Wisner continued to be irritated by his intellectuals. In 1952, when the Congress's American affiliate denounced the anticommunist rampages of McCarthyism, Wisner complained that the group had no right to take such an independent stand.

> I can understand how an American committee for cultural freedom, standing alone, and being in fact a group of American private citizens interested in cultural freedom, would feel that it would have to take a position on McCarthyism. However, that is not the nature of the American Committee for Cultural Freedom which, according to my recollection, was inspired if not put together by this Agency for the purpose of providing cover and backstopping for the European effort.[29]

In the 1960s, as dissent started leaking out from behind the Iron Curtain (much of it published in journals of the Congress for Cultural Freedom), the CIA's funding mechanisms became careless. A series of media disclosures in 1967 cast the operation in a sinister light. The Vietnam war was shattering the earlier Cold War consensus in American life; intellectuals who had unwittingly benefited from CIA subsidies vented outrage at being duped. *Encounter* ceased publication; the Congress for Cultural Freedom was discredited. It was in this atmosphere that Braden wrote his article, published in the *Saturday Evening Post*. His effort backfired for Josselson. The long-serving operative resigned from the Congress the month Braden's article was published, taking upon himself personal responsibility for deceiving the wide array of intellectuals around him.

Though Braden's defense seemed unpersuasive in 1967, post–Cold

War generations may be able to appreciate the subtlety of an undertaking of a particular historical era better than Wisner did at the time. "By 1953 we were operating or influencing international organizations in every field where communist fronts had previously seized ground, and in some where they had not even begun to operate," Braden wrote. For all the deception involved, never "moral" but sometimes a lesser evil, Braden insisted that the OPC, and later the CIA, played by strict rules: "Use legitimate, existing organizations; disguise the extent of American interest; protect the integrity of the organization by not requiring it to support every aspect of official American policy."

"The choice between innocence and power," he wrote, "involves the most difficult of decisions."[30]

Into Battle

JUNE 24–25, 1950, MARKED THE END of "innocence" for the command center of America's secret political warfare; "power" took over. On that day, when armed forces from North Korea invaded the pro-western South, the specter of communist expansionism was forced upon the world. The Rollback campaign turned bellicose and urgent.

Kennan was drawn to larger foreign policy problems than those of the refugees and émigré intellectuals who had captured his imagination two years before. Wisner, who was not known to the general public, was attracting favorable notice in the higher reaches of the national security establishment as "a man of intense application" in fashioning a counterforce against communism, just as Truman's National Security Council had ordered. For his part, the misplaced Admiral Hillenkoetter at CIA seized upon the outbreak of war to leave the ship of intelligence, taking instead a command at sea in the Pacific.

There was no shortage of candidates eager to direct the exciting new Central Intelligence Agency. Leading the list in his own estimation (though not in that of many others) was the restive William Donovan. A more suitable choice would have been Allen Dulles, who was strongly supported by Kennan and the State Department. Both men were anathema to Truman. He had fired Donovan once, back in 1945 when he abolished the OSS, and nothing that had happened since had elevated the buoyant general in his confidence. As for Dulles, Truman was already employing his older brother, John Foster, as a gesture of bipartisanship on diplomatic missions, and one Republican Dulles in or near his administration seemed enough.

Instead the president ordered General Walter Bedell Smith to active duty. Recently ambassador to the Soviet Union and properly contemptuous of communists, Smith knew the diplomatic scene even as he complained he knew nothing about intelligence — a somewhat disingenuous claim, since he had served as Eisenhower's chief of staff all during World War II and was thoroughly familiar with the assertions and foibles of intelligence as practiced by the military.

Facing Smith, an acerbic martinet of dyspeptic disposition whose managerial style consisted of bullying everyone around him, Wisner felt intimidated. "He likened an hour with General Smith to an hour on the squash court," said a colleague of Wisner's, "and he did not mean by that to suggest that he enjoyed it."[1] At times Wisner even recalled the free and easy Hillenkoetter days with nostalgia. From the start, the general cast a jaundiced eye upon the covert political operations that the admiral had tolerated; to Smith's mind, Wisner's ventures had nothing to do with the real business of intelligence. Nor was Smith the sort to tolerate any freewheeling hybrid agency anywhere near his watch. After fuming at the haphazard structure he had inherited, the new CIA director simply abolished the OPC, absorbing it as the clandestine service of the CIA itself.[2] This had long been the intent of Kennan and his colleagues, but Wisner, accustomed to Hillenkoetter's hands-off attitude, now found himself under tight rein.

Even Smith, however, could not thwart the will of the National Security Council, where Wisner had gained the esteem of the policymakers. But he seldom missed an occasion to make clear that he regarded missions of political warfare as a nuisance. "They are costly by comparison with other intelligence operations," he once told the NSC, "and they present in most cases a gambler's chance of obtaining really significant critical strategic information." Smith's snarls peppered his staff meetings; clandestine operations, he charged, were suffering "from the use of improperly trained or inferior personnel."[3] If Wisner found himself personally undone by Smith's surly manner, he could take heart in seeing that he was not alone, that the general's scorn was routinely spread across the board.

❋

For all of Smith's griping, a fair judgment of OPC/CIA personnel when the move was made from innocence to power finds headquarters and field officers of impressive quality. Except for the occasional misfit,

Wisner's rosters were a world apart from the deadbeats Kennan had encountered at the start. "There was no CIA type," reflected Michael
Burke, an early OPC case officer. "The CIA's staff contained a crosscut
of America, people who by some different quirk of chance could very
well have found themselves in the Department of Agriculture, the Aetna
Life Insurance Company, the University of Arizona, or the Cincinnati
Police Department."

But they had chosen careers hidden from public view with the con-
viction that this unusual kind of work would be important to America.
As Burke put it, the price of anonymity was offset

> by an air of romance and mystery that cloaked the profession, by an elixir of
> glamour that curled up from their secret papers, by danger vicariously
> shared with agents operating on hostile ground, by the possession of a se-
> cret — a host of secrets — that set them apart, placed them among an elite
> few. . . . In practice, they could not afford to romanticize their work; they
> must be as pragmatic as dentists. Above all — and perhaps the most diffi-
> cult intellectual discipline to sustain — they could not allow themselves to
> fall in love with the game for the game's sake.[4]

To direct the eclectic operations conjured up for the lands behind the
Iron Curtain, Wisner hired a thirty-three-year-old army and OSS veteran from California named Frank Lindsay. Intending to pursue a career in business, Lindsay went to work for United States Steel after graduating from Stanford in 1938. Then came the war and mobilization into
the OSS. He parachuted into the mountains of Yugoslavia and for more
than a year served behind the lines, blowing up bridges and mining the
passes. He attached himself to partisan forces under Tito's command
and even arranged for some covert arms shipments — five shiploads of
innocent-looking boxes dispatched from Philadelphia. Lindsay was kept
away from discussions between the partisans and their sponsors in Moscow, but he reported to Washington at the end of the war that Tito's basic policy was pro-Soviet even without "day-to-day directives from Moscow."[5] In 1945 the notion of a home-grown communist movement was
not familiar to Washington.

Lindsay postponed his ambitions in business and entered graduate
school at Harvard, where in 1947 he heard with enthusiasm Secretary of
State Marshall's call for an American aid program to rebuild Europe.
He went to Washington to join the staff of a congressional committee set

up to document Europe's economic needs (a junior member of the committee was Representative Richard M. Nixon of California, and a staff colleague was Allen Dulles). Consulting briefly for the State Department, Lindsay and Charles Thayer, who had been his OSS colleague in Yugoslavia, produced the plan that attracted Kennan's attention in September 1947: "to extract for U.S. advantage disaffected foreign nationals." Lindsay, after moving on to Harriman's Marshall Plan headquarters in Paris, was spotted in Wisner's talent search: he seemed to be a man of operational experience and intellectual motivation to do a job of complexity and danger only dimly perceived at the outset.

On his desk at the OPC, Lindsay placed a little sign: "Kindly restrain your enthusiasm." That was his office stance. In the after hours, as he and his wife, the former Margot Coffin, settled into their little Georgetown house, Lindsay's enthusiasm for the daring new mission of the United States was unrestrained. If he was too cool-headed ever to "fall in love with the game for the game's sake," Lindsay's brisk efficiency and Californian geniality attracted an action-oriented salon of veterans, Foreign Service officers bored with the tedium of conventional diplomacy, young executives dismayed by the corporate ladder, and recent college graduates who wondered about the wider world.

One such prospect for a career in action appeared within his own family — Margot's brother, William Sloan Coffin, an idealistic and adventurous youth from Oyster Bay and New York's Upper East Side. Coffin was a veteran of four years in the army military government of Germany, a specialist in Russian language and society. To his later dismay, he had assisted in the forced repatriations of Soviet citizens immediately after the war. During his long-delayed senior year at Yale, he stopped in at his sister's Georgetown house and found himself being interviewed by two fellow Ivy Leaguers from CIA looking for potential recruits who spoke Russian. They told him about American ideas to make good use of grass-roots disillusionment with communism behind the Iron Curtain, and Coffin found the idea intriguing: "Although they said nothing specifically about how the disaffection within the Soviet Union was to be organized and supported, I had met plenty of anti-Soviet Russians eager to try."[6]

Coffin turned down that first approach, choosing instead to enroll at Union Theological Seminary for a career in the ministry. But with the changed national mood at the outbreak of the Korean war, the twenty-six-year-old divinity student reconsidered and accepted the offer of OPC employment. Staying at the Lindsays', he was put through a month of extraordinary training at various "safe houses" around Washington in the care of mysterious instructors whose names he never knew and who never knew his. "I was taught how to 'tail' and to escape surveillance, how to use passwords, dead-letter drops and 'live drops.' . . . I picked up good pointers: a fine place, for instance, to hide a pistol is in a broom, as people never associate the two in their minds."

Coffin's assignment would be to ingratiate himself with the Russian émigré communities in the European DP camps or wherever they gathered, with an eye to identifying able-bodied guys who might be willing to return to the Soviet Union on undercover missions. One instructor, whom he knew only as "Dave," told him that these volunteers would be asked to observe and report on specified sites and might be assigned certain other undefined activities. "I asked Dave how the volunteers were going to get into the Soviet Union. He replied, 'probably by parachute.' And when I asked how, once there, they were going to communicate, he said, 'mostly by radio, but don't ask any more questions now.'"

The divinity student decided to refresh his Russian language proficiency. But when he returned to his room at the Lindsays' every night, his chosen reading was *Anna Karenina* rather than *Pravda*.

Lindsay and Coffin clearly did not fit the popular image of the secret agent. Somewhat closer to the profile of a "CIA type," even as he denied that any such existed, was Michael Burke, a cheerful adventurer born in Connecticut and brought up in Ireland. Burke played football for the University of Pennsylvania, graduating in 1939, then headed to a job on the New York waterfront as a cargo inspector. In 1942 he was commissioned an ensign in the navy and assigned to the OSS. He dropped by parachute into occupied France; behind the lines in Italy he scouted out scientists with special expertise that would be of interest to the Allies. His career in wartime espionage seemed made for Hollywood, and so it was. After the war Burke signed on with Warner Brothers to help with the screenplay of a movie about war exploits called, inevitably, *Cloak and Dagger* and starring the gaunt and stringy Gary Cooper as the gaunt and stringy Michael Burke. (The epic production expired on the cutting-room floor.)

Real life resumed after Hollywood with the thud of aimless boredom; Burke and his wife rented a railroad flat on West Ninth Street in Greenwich Village and hoped for something to turn up. When two bland young men from some government office invited him to lunch at the Algonquin Hotel, Burke suspected that his fortunes were about to turn. He was not impressed when the men from Washington enjoyed their second martinis a little too obviously, then worked through two bottles of a fine Sancerre over lunch. But reassurance came when he heard a name well known to him from his OSS years; his commanding officer, in their vaguely defined proposition, would be Frank Lindsay.

With few alternative prospects, Burke packed up and headed for Rome to get established under an innocuous commercial cover; he presented himself as an aspiring entrepreneur on the prowl for good business opportunities. There he and his wife waited for the contact, which he had been assured would soon come, from the headquarters of America's secret political warfare.

Planning within a government proceeds on many levels, usually starting among imaginative idea men far below the heights where policy is made. Secrecy at this level is hard to maintain, for the idea folks are eager to be heard and appreciated. If senior bureaucrats are too pressed to listen, as they generally are at this stage, the idea men are perfectly ready to discuss their schemes with others who will listen — including even sympathetic reporters and commentators.

On December 14, 1949, *Life* magazine published a thoughtful article called "It Takes a Russian to Beat a Russian," written by Wallace Carroll, a scholarly journalist who consulted on psychological warfare for the Defense and State departments.* Spread out over six pages, the article was unusually heavy fare for the popular weekly of photographs and spectacles then at the peak of its popularity in Henry R. Luce's Time-Life empire.

"The Editors of *Life*, while not necessarily sharing all [Carroll's] conclusions, believe they provide a perceptive and fresh standpoint from

---

* Carroll later became Washington editor of the *New York Times* and then publisher of the Winston-Salem *Journal and Sentinel*.

which to re-examine U.S. strategic planning" read the disclaimer to the provocative passages that followed. Carroll gave the American public its first authoritative glimpse of the so-called Vlassov movement, made up of Soviet prisoners of war who switched sides to fight the Red Army alongside the Nazis. (Vlassov veterans were among the key targets of Kennan's and Wisner's émigré recruitment efforts.)

Carroll argued that wartime intelligence records of Hitler's march to the east exposed "menacing . . . disruptive forces within the Soviet Union, . . . millions of Soviet citizens who were willing to help a foreign power against the Soviet regime." As an outside consultant, Carroll probably was only vaguely aware of the closely held discussions relevant to this argument that were engaging the National Security Council and Kennan's State Department offices. But he might well have picked up on the strenuous recruitment efforts by an unidentified agency to build a counterforce against Soviet power.

An independent writer could float ideas that would be dangerous coming from a government official. Carroll was writing at a time when the atomic bomb was considered America's best line of defense, and he, like many other liberals, found the doctrine repugnant. "In the tragic event of a third world war, the U.S. has the power to drop the atomic bomb on Soviet territory and kill or maim millions of Russians. But can we hope to do something much more difficult?" he asked, can we "arouse those millions and propel them at the decisive moment against Stalin's regime?"

Instead of preparing to drop atomic bombs, Carroll argued, the United States should dispatch aircraft to

> plaster the Soviet Union with leaflets bearing the pledges and promises of the American government and people . . . [to drop] anti-Soviet agents and guerrilla leaders to any Soviet hamlet . . . [and] release the forces within the country which could destroy or cripple the regime. . . . We must prepare to support guerrilla warfare on such a scale as the world has never seen before. We must develop weapons such as guerrillas have never used before. We must train men to think guerrilla warfare and to plan guerrilla warfare.

A guerrilla war against the Soviet Union was not a prospect that most Americans would have endorsed in 1949 — hence the *Life* editors' disclaimers — nor was it precisely what the National Security Council had intended with NSC 10/2. But the nugget was there in the initial planning papers for the OPC. Wisner called it "preventive direct action, such as support of guerrillas, sabotage and related subversive practices"; Kennan's political warfare had included steps to "maintain contact with, sustain and influence underground movements." The call to battle, suitably sanitized and presented mainly to restive émigrés (and voters), became a crowd-pleaser for right-wing ideologues in the 1950s.

On careful reading, however, Carroll was arguing something a little different. He held no brief from the old Washington conservatives, nor was he sympathetic to right-wing journalists like Isaac Don Levine. ("Don't attack communism as such," Carroll advised, with the subtlety of a professional in psychological warfare; "better to raise questions about relations between the leaders and society, generate doubts about the wisdom of their leaders.")[7]

Carroll argued for guerrilla warfare only as an alternative to all-out nuclear war. No slouch in the nuances of public persuasion, he sought to make his point palatable to *Life* readers across the political spectrum. "Just as Hitler's reliance on physical force led him to scorn the help of the Soviet people," he concluded, "reliance on the atomic bomb could lead us into comparable folly."

Over the next decade, aggressive guerrilla operations against godless communism became the right wing's program to outclass the Truman (Kennan) doctrine of containment, and ban-the-bomb movements took over the left. Carroll's 1949 article represents a last ingenious bid to bridge the ideological divide: a strategy to roll back the Iron Curtain without dropping the bomb.

Most public talk of using the talents of refugees from eastern Europe centered on the intellectuals and politicians, professors, journalists, lawyers, and even former cabinet ministers ousted as the communist regimes took hold. But Wisner, Lindsay, Coffin, and Burke were attracted by refugees of a different class and inclination: manual workers from the Nazis' forced labor brigades, former soldiers for fascist or other armies, routine drifters, and downright mercenaries. These were men (even a few women) who had no surviving families or homes in postwar Europe; they were seeking to establish new identities fighting for a cause that would restore some sense of meaning to their lives and, in the process, cleanse whatever sins they may have committed during the Hitler years.

As the DP camps emptied out, many of these aimless souls sought to reconnect with life in the French Foreign Legion, with its long tradition of taking on men who did not fit into civilian society. Wisner and Lindsay were not about to let this element go to the French by default. A clear mission took shape for their new undercover man in Rome, Michael Burke. "Given the black-and-white definition of the Cold War there was no shilly-shallying about morality," Burke said as American covert action began. "Who is not with me is against me." Warming to the adventure, the new OPC recruit said his mission was straightforward: "Recruit a limited number of refugees, train them as agents, and place them clandestinely on their native soil. There they would seek out any incipient resistance elements that might exist."[8]

Wisner and Lindsay had reluctantly accepted the conclusions of the analysts that by 1947 the postwar resistance movements had been suppressed by Soviet power. The Forest Brothers of the Baltic, the manipulative politicians of Romania and Hungary, the partisans of Ukraine had been crushed, in spite of the efforts of émigré publicists abroad to keep the banners of anticommunist resistance flying. "The chances of finding resistance groups that had escaped annihilation were slim," Burke acknowledged. "We would be attempting to create an underground movement supported covertly from the outside. No one underestimated the difficulty."

You start with what you have. Two of the new communist regimes were dominated by former guerrilla forces with whom British and American intelligence services had enjoyed a tenuous wartime liaison, when those same partisans were active against the Nazis. The lands of Yugoslavia and Albania were known to some in London and Washington, and casual — though unofficial — contacts had been maintained with old comrades-in-arms even after the Iron Curtain descended.

Initial feints at reconnecting old ties were clumsy. An opportunistic and ill-conceived covert operation into Yugoslavia was sprung during the undisciplined formative months of the OPC late in 1948. Known to history only through informed spy fiction and the dismayed reports of third-country diplomats, this episode holds dubious distinction as the first of the Rollback missions.[9]

Lindsay knew Tito's partisans from the last years of World War II, but other OSS officers had been engaged on the other side of the Yugoslav civil war, with the so-called Chetniks, anticommunist monarchists who had collaborated with the Nazis in common cause against Tito. Lindsay understood that the Chetniks were discredited as a political force once Tito's communists took power. But he was new to his job in Washington, and others at the working level of intelligence had a less sure sense of Balkan realities. (A young CIA officer stumbled upon the registry of biographical data collected by the floundering successors to the OSS, and among the drawers of three-by-five index cards he came across the entry "TITO." The collective wisdom of American intelligence reported on the tattered card was: "FIRST NAME: unknown. LAST NAME: unknown.")*

One of the freewheeling American intelligence networks (records identifying the responsible officers have not survived) issued U.S. Air Force uniforms to a small cadre of Chetnik refugees and arranged for them to be dropped by parachute into Yugoslavia early in January 1949. Their mission was to contact old comrades from the struggle with Tito to see if the anticommunist spirit could be revived. Never mind that the United States government, the National Security Council, and President Truman himself were supporting Tito in his new defiance of Stalinism; old hands at espionage set out to dent the Iron Curtain by their own means.

The hapless agents (surviving records do not reveal whether there were two or three) jumped successfully into enemy territory, and Yugoslav security forces promptly arrested them. American uniforms might have offered some protection in the anti-Nazi alliance during the war, but no longer. On their way to prison camp, under escort, they passed through the central railway station of Belgrade, where an old-time Chetnik comrade happened to recognize them. Word of the episode got to the French military attaché, and his ambassador promptly queried his American counterpart as to what was going on.[10]

The United States ambassador to Yugoslavia, one Cavendish Can-

---

* To be fair, Tito was a *nom de guerre* adopted by the Yugoslav partisan leader during his guerrilla years. His real name, Josip Broz, was scarcely known to the outside world as the American file clerks were amassing their intelligence data.

non, was a Foreign Service veteran of difficult, if not illustrious, posts. No one had warned him about some gumshoe operation of the American military, but he invoked his ambassadorial prerogative to lambaste the State Department for undermining the subtle policy of encouraging Tito in his apostasy within communism. Jaded by long experience of failing to prick Washington's attention to judgments from the field, Cannon sought the support of the British ambassador, Sir Charles Peake, who cabled his own superiors in Whitehall. There, desk officers penciled in comments about "this idiotic American behavior," and Foreign Secretary Bevin weighed in with a cable to Washington. Bevin, it became apparent, yielded to no one in his enthusiasm for dirty tricks against commies, but this was too much. He advised that whatever the United States was trying to do in Yugoslavia, it should cease and desist forthwith.[11]

At the same time a more substantial Anglo-American collaboration in covert action began unfolding. The target was Albania, and the British planners conceiving the operation explained it to their American counterparts as "a clinical experiment to see whether larger Rollback operations would be feasible elsewhere."[12]

Clinging to the rugged Adriatic coast only fifty miles from Italy, the 11,000 square miles of Albania seemed nonetheless as remote as any corner of Europe. A poor population of three million survived in primitive conditions, the remnant of an ancient Illyrian civilization. After weathering the Greek and Roman empires and resisting the Visigoths, Huns, and Slavs, the Alblanians succumbed to the Turks in the fourteenth century. Never recognized as a nation by the international community, the Albanian outback of mountains, scrub, and bush would have been partitioned among the neighboring countries had President Wilson not insisted upon the independence of small peoples.

During World War II, as the OSS operated with competing factions of neighboring Yugoslavia, the British Special Operations Executive (SOE, the model for Wisner's enterprise) nurtured tenuous contacts with Albania. King Zog I, a feudal chieftain named Ahmed Bey Zogu before anointing himself with royal oils, had settled in bucolic exile at Henley-on-Thames in 1940 as Mussolini's fascists overran his land.

Through the war his British hosts casually encouraged his various partisans back home. Unfortunately, the wrong resistance factions, the communists, seized power in 1944 as the Italian and German armies withdrew, and with Moscow's support they embarked on the daunting task of turning a backward society into Stalin's satellite.

The United States had attempted to maintain a modest military mission in the Albanian capital of Tirana after the war, assigning Carmel Offie to the post. The communist authorities denied him a visa in 1946, branding him an "intelligence executive" — as Offie soon became, but at least at this early stage he was spared personal engagement in what became a covert-action disaster for both Britain and the United States.

When Bevin complained about an American operation behind the Iron Curtain in Yugoslavia, his ire was aroused by the amateurishness of the mission, not the principle. In 1946, long before the notion of either containment or political warfare had taken hold in Washington, Britain's Labour government had established a select "Russia Committee" of worldly cabinet undersecretaries to consider special means for confronting communism in Europe. They spotted, among other clandestine assets, the émigrés around King Zog at Henley and, upon investigation, discovered that Albania, his old domain, commanded a two hundred-mile coastline on the Adriatic accessible to landing craft of the Royal Navy. Though the empire's resources were crumbling, here was a prospect for projecting something of the old British verve.

In November 1948, the Russia Committee proposed testing the efficacy of paramilitary operations in one small target area. "Would it not be possible to start a civil war behind the Iron Curtain and, by careful assistance, to produce a state of affairs in Albania similar to the state of affairs that the Russians had produced in Greece?" asked Bevin's representative.[13] Well before American political warfare took shape, responsible British authorities decided on their own "that our aim should certainly be to liberate the countries within the Soviet orbit short of war." Informed of high-level interest in Albania, British intelligence operatives commissioned Greek shipbuilders to construct a forty-three-ton landing vessel; within a month she was launched in the Mediterranean as the *Stormie Seas.*

The Russia Committee determined that it could not proceed further without the assistance of the United States. If the germ of offensive action against communism sprouted in Whitehall, the power to make it flourish had passed to the other side of the Atlantic. British intelligence had the human assets and expertise to run agents, in the Balkans as well as the Baltics, but in the austerity of postwar Britain only the Americans had the money.

Enter Wisner. As Whitehall's Russia Committee devised the concepts, the OPC cranked up the funding and logistical support apparatus. Wisner was scouting out targets of opportunity to show his backers on Truman's National Security Council what his new agency could do; Offie was at his side, chafing at being excluded from Tirana as a diplomat and eager to activate his own Balkan networks. Desk officers in the State Department, unaccustomed to attention from high policymakers, produced workmanlike assessments of Albanian politics without the slightest awareness that anything more interesting — and unsettling to diplomatic practice — might be contemplated. Even Lindsay seemed dubious about Albania; recalling his experience in Yugoslavia, he cheerfully admitted to a British colleague that the very first Albanian he ever saw was hanging upside down from parallel bars.

Military intelligence officers concluded that despite its small size and political obscurity, Albania gave Stalin crucial access to international sea lanes or, as the strategists came to call it, "influence projection." The Pentagon learned that the Russian navy was developing a major submarine base at Valona Bay, just across from the Italian port of Otranto, with 1,500 "advisers" and 4,000 "technicians" training the Albanian military. In February 1949, Bevin approved a plan for a sea landing of saboteurs. The OPC signed on in March. A month later Kennan's Policy Planning Staff concluded that Albania might be worth serious attention.[14]

Thus were two governments and two secret services officially engaged in clandestine design upon a sovereign (albeit communist) state. The chairman of the Russia Committee, Gladwyn Jebb of the Foreign Office, journeyed to Washington to meet Wisner and learn about his mysterious new agency; he was accompanied by William Hayter, a fellow diplomat who knew a good deal about intelligence operations. Always eager to play the protocol, Wisner returned the visit a few weeks later, lunching at Buck's Club with the British experts involved with the myriad Albanian émigré factions, whose active participation would be crucial to the plan. King Zog, for one, judged that he had nothing to lose if the British and Americans chose to exert themselves in his behalf. But when he realized that his own factions would not be the only beneficiaries of largesse, he threw the Anglo-American emissaries out of the vacation villa in Alexandria where he was taking his ease as an exiled crowned head of Europe.

The Anglo-American agreement reached during these gentlemanly visits in the spring of 1949 committed the United States to underwrite the British mobilization of manpower among the Albanian resistance. But, overcoming his fulsome regard for British experience in covert operations, Wisner insisted that his own men must play the leading role in training Albanian penetration agents.

Enter Burke. His mission would be to energize the refugees who would return to their land from the *Stormie Seas* (or whatever other craft were provided); they were to be the harbingers of the anticommunist rebellion that experts in London and Washington (and Henley) were sure would erupt.* As he explained it:

> We met for the first time in a small spare apartment in a block of flats deep in a working-class district [he was not allowed to name the city], each of us coming alone by different routes to avoid notice by counterespionage agents or anyone else hostile. As each man arrived he introduced himself in broken French or English or Italian. In their own country they had been political activists — agrarians, socialists, royalists. In exile, like all refugees, they were a threadbare lot, drawn loosely together in common cause against a communist dictatorship and by a longing to go home.

Delivering the marching orders, Burke avoided political platforms and personal aspirations, saying nothing to "discourage the expedient pretext that they were a kind of government-in-exile." As was the case with the Russian émigrés lured to conferences at Bavarian inns, only "a modest but regular allotment of U.S. dollars was the glue" holding the Albanian resistance together.

> Each member committed himself to find among his political followers in the refugee camps and elsewhere suitable men who would volunteer to be pathfinders, who would parachute into their country in pairs, establish initial contacts and form the first resistance cadres. If the results were positive,

---

* A decade later, as paramilitary planners shifted their attentions from eastern Europe to the Third World, this same forlorn hope drove the strategists of the CIA's invasion at the Cuban Bay of Pigs. Some of the lessons of Rollback were never learned.

a larger body of men would be recruited for paramilitary training and would be infiltrated in commando-like units at some propitious time. . . . There would be casualties; this was not a parlor game.[15]

To front for the paramilitary force, the Anglo-American covert operation required political cover. By this time Wisner and Offie were having problems with the Soviet émigrés, but the Albanian front came about more easily — not because there were fewer differences among the factions but because these men had fewer resources and audiences to take them seriously. At a press conference that spring in Paris, the Committee for a Free Albania was proclaimed. Three émigré politicians claiming mass support among their people in Albania flew to New York for a public relations blitz. Offie and James McCargar, who became the OPC case officer for the operation, never personally met the supposed leaders of the Albanian resistance. The emissaries were received in the State Department by a (then) minor deputy assistant secretary, Llewellyn Thompson, who escorted them from his office saying only that they should keep in touch with the (private) Committee for a Free Europe in New York.

After weeks of sparsely attended press conferences, receptions, "exclusive" interviews with any newsmen who would seek them out, the Albanian visitors succumbed to a summer of boredom and aimless New York night life. Early in the morning of October 3, 1949, one of their number, the key agent in the Anglo-American front, Midhat Frasheri, a former diplomat and the owner of the largest bookstore in Tirana, was found dead in his room at the Hotel Lexington. It never became clear whether his death resulted from natural heart failure or something more deliberate (both were credible), but the OPC had to extend itself to hush up the uncomfortable incident. Such is the fate of officials engaged in undercover operations: Robert Low, the same American case officer who had clashed with King Zog in Alexandria, had to take on an adversarial role with the New York Police Department.

The very day of Frasheri's demise, the *Stormie Seas* offloaded nine of Burke's Albanian saboteurs and resistance agents onto the Karaburun peninsula of their homeland, springing the test case of Rollback. For eight days no one heard from them. When word finally came through over the clandestine radio frequencies, case officers in Washington learned that the men had tried to recruit villagers they encountered in the wilds, had skirmished with communist security units who just happened to be on the scene, and had eventually turned back to their escape routes. Four of the infiltration agents were killed; a fifth was missing.

At a small office deep inside the Pentagon, the Anglo-American head-quarters team held a postmortem on their doomed operation. McCargar held the watch for Wisner; his initial British counterpart had been an accomplished intelligence professional with experience in Greece and the Balkans who was known in Washington as George Jellicoe. (In England he was the second Earl Jellicoe, son of the British admiral in the World War I battle of Jutland.) Reviewing the disaster and Burke's re-ports from the field, Robert Low told his frustrated comrades that obvi-ously "there was a leak somewhere. . . . The communists just knew too much about these people we were sending in."

Sitting at the table that dismal day with McCargar and Low was Jellicoe's successor at the British Embassy, a likable thirty-eight-year-old expert on clandestine operations who had just taken over Whitehall's end of the Albanian planning. His name was H. A. R. (Kim) Philby.

Kim Philby seemed the exemplar of the old-boy network of responsible British civil servants, a Cambridge man, son of a distinguished scholar of Arabia. He had succeeded to Jellicoe's position as the first secretary of embassy but this merely covered his "real" role as liaison officer between the intelligence services of Britain and the United States. Only after a di-sastrous decade of Rollback missions gone sour was he exposed in his *real* "real" role as the highest-placed agent of Soviet espionage in the British and American security establishments.

When Philby first reported for Washington duty in October 1949, OPC executives and case officers were relieved to discover that the new man was already well briefed on Anglo-American plans for covert action behind the Iron Curtain. Over the months and years to come, this charming and well-recommended professional used his skills to pene-trate the most sensitive counterespionage secrets of the two govern-ments. Philby was more fully briefed than most American officials, for instance, on Arlington Hall's progress in breaking Soviet intelligence codes, for British expertise played a crucial role in the effort. The military codebreakers were not about to share the fruits of their labors with untested civilian agencies like OPC or CIA. The ludicrous situation thus developed that Philby, the Soviet mole, had to keep his silence in speaking with one branch of American intelligence about what he had learned from another branch of American intelligence — keeping Moscow fully informed all the while. Across the epic of the Cold War, the saga of Kim Philby stands as a record of elegant treachery.

Michael Burke, on the front line of the doomed Albanian operation, met Philby only five months later, when they both happened to be in London at the same time. Burke retained a poignant memory of their evening together.

> I was aware that he was legitimately privy to my assignment. What surprised me was his easy familiarity with operational matters. Frankly, too, I was pleasantly surprised and flattered that a man of his rank would invite me to dine with him privately. . . .
>
> After dinner we strolled along to pay our respects to Kim's father, St. John Philby. . . . The bearded, scholarly looking Philby Senior was dining at his club surrounded by a collection of Contemporaries, chairs pushed back from the dinner table, sipping their port, an archetypal nineteenth-century scene. The two Philbys embraced, Kim respectfully, his father benignly. . . . We went on to some late-hour club Kim knew. He was a heavy, indiscriminate drinker, but his protective mechanisms were so deeply rooted that no amount of drink betrayed him. . . . His considerable charm was disarming, his slight stutter sympathetic. . . . His social class and his education at Westminster School and Cambridge University presumed loyalty and commended him to the Establishment.
>
> It was unthinkable to suspect that those traditional credentials would conceal a Soviet agent, and the degree of self-control, of self-discipline demanded of Philby to sustain his enormous deception over so long a period of time is immeasurable.[16]

For all their determination to get on with the job, Wisner and Lindsay grew skeptical as further sea landings on the rugged Albanian coast met with further disaster. Each time the Anglo-American coordinating team in Washington struggled to absorb the lessons of failure, Philby was in attendance, paying dutiful and sympathetic attention. Burke, meanwhile, pursued his training mission with his Albanian protégés from the refugee camps of Germany. Starting with forty-nine Albanian toughs at a military barracks at Karlsfeld, a few miles out of Munich, the program rapidly grew to be called Company 4000, dispersed at various military bases and abandoned castles commandeered by the American occupation forces.

In their eagerness to get things moving, OPC officers took over any physical installations they could find. One of the training sites, an old barracks that had fallen into disuse, was established in the little village of Dachau near Munich. The fact that these facilities had recently been used as a concentration camp by the Nazis seemed irrelevant to the Americans arriving in 1949. But to local residents the sense of continuity with the Nazi past was inevitable. Too late did it dawn on the organizers of Rollback that the juxtaposition marred the moral position of the West against communism, as Soviet propaganda hammered the theme that the American imperialists were simply taking up where Hitler had been forced to halt.

By 1950 the test case of Rollback, of provoking rebellion behind the Iron Curtain, was not going well, just as the war in Korea gave urgency to the anticommunist effort. The British scheme for landing Albanian provocateurs by sea was clearly not working. All the restive partisans that King Zog had promised turned out to live miles inland from any coastline accessible to agents from the *Stormie Seas*. (The king himself, brought to the United States in 1951 for a public relations tour, seemed more preoccupied with the American real estate holdings in his investment portfolio than with the real estate of his homeland.)

Wisner and his OPC bypassed the provisions of the Anglo-American accord by switching to the tactic of dropping agents by air to pinpointed locations inland. Starting in November 1950 and continuing for two years, Burke's men were parachuted into Albania in two-man teams, sometimes even four in one drop, followed quickly by two more as backup. The missions were marred by mishaps on the ground even before they took off, as the men were secretly transported from German bases to equally secret takeoffs from neglected corners of Greek airfields. (American diplomats in Greece and Germany were not pleased to have their embassies embarrassed by unseemly operations of which they had no knowledge.)

Again and again the teams would land and go nowhere. Their pathetic attempts at radio contact were seldom heard. Those agents who survived for a few days were arrested and brought to show trials in Tirana, which were extensively covered by *Pravda* and other communist media to further blacken the image of the imperialists. Needless to say, no Albanian liberation movement rose up. Though the Americans did not yet realize it, the training camps at the former Nazi military bases had been infiltrated by Soviet agents, just as had happened among the refugees from the Baltic states, and Moscow had access to details of the operations in real time. "Seldom has an intelligence operation proceeded so resolutely from one disaster to another," wrote Yale professor Robin Winks, a latter-day scholar of intelligence.

Malcolm Muggeridge, a weathered survivor of the Russia Committee's action arm, representing British intelligence in its prime, was doleful as he recalled Wisner's Americans entering the Old World:

> From those Elysian days I remember so well in London when the first arrivals came among us, straight from their innocent nests in Princeton or Yale or Harvard, in Wall Street or Madison Avenue or Washington, DC. How short a time the honeymoon period lasted! How soon our British setup was overtaken in personnel, zest and scale of operations, above all in expendable cash! . . . The OSS-CIA network, with ramifications all over the world, came to outclass our once legendary Secret Service as a sleek Cadillac does an ancient hansom cab.[17]

Landing *agents provocateurs* by sea was the best Britain could offer in the declining years of its empire, against Albania in the Adriatic or, at the other end of the Iron Curtain, Estonia and its neighbors on the Baltic. The Americans pressed for the more expensive alternative of air drops. Unmarked C-47 aircraft manned by Czech defectors, pilots who had flown for the Royal Air Force during the war, began taking off from the U.S. Air Force base in Wiesbaden. Crossing into hostile airspace only 200 feet above the ground to elude air defense radar, the pilots would climb at the last moment to an altitude that allowed their human cargo to parachute to a safe landing. But most of the agents dropped into the Baltic states and Albania met the same dismal fate: suspicion among the local populace, arrest by security forces, and execution, with or without trials.

In later years, retired intelligence officers in London and Washington blamed the treachery of Kim Philby for their repeated failures in Rollback. This explanation is convenient, even perversely reassuring for the professionalism of their tradecraft: had it not been for this one epic mishap, they argued, the concept of rolling back the Iron Curtain might have worked.

In the Albanian test case, the unsealed records confirm Philby's mischievous role. But for the Baltics, and for countless other Rollback operations yet to be told, the excuse is less persuasive. As Wisner's OPC was amassing on-the-job expertise, even amateurs in clandestine operations understood the necessity of compartmentalizing information. Working knowledge of one set of operations was not shared with other case officers, the "need to know" principle was deeply ingrained from the start. Philby was intimately informed about operations to subvert communist power in Albania but far less so about the working details of operations toward similar ends in the Baltic states. He admitted as much in the last year of his life.

In November 1987, as Soviet domination over its satellites was dissipating (though still in place), Philby visited the Latvian capital of Riga for the first time. By then seventy-five and visibly ailing, he was permitted a mellow meeting organized by Latvian state television with a similarly retired Soviet intelligence officer, Major Janis Lukasevic, case officer for the Kremlin's campaign to suppress the Forest Brothers. Old spies reminisced. Philby relished his own exploits to preserve Stalin's communism against the designs of British and American imperialists. But when pressed by Lukasevic, he conceded that he could claim no credit for the failure of western efforts to revive the Forest Brothers. Of those British and American operations, he said, he had been operationally unwitting.[18]

Philby died in Moscow less than a year later, operationally unwitting of the final failure of his communism.

9

Combat High and Low

ROLLBACK'S FORAY into Albania, the first test of greater things to come, was faltering before the American people even knew it was under way. Public reference to other OPC operations — never identified as such, of course — sustained the tone of high purpose in which Wisner, and Kennan before him, had cast their mission of political warfare. An editorial in the *New York Times* in July 1950 urged Americans to send contributions to Radio Free Europe, "both to express their faith in a world of human liberty and to support the vigorous private effort now being made to bring a message of truth and encouragement to the millions of people held under Communist rule." The *Times* did not know that this "private effort" was in fact a million-dollar operation of a secret intelligence agency.

Candidates running for office across the country issued passionate appeals to "liberate the captive peoples" behind the Iron Curtain — at least when their constituents included significant numbers of first- or second-generation immigrants from eastern Europe, which Democrats as well as Republicans considered a potent voting bloc. Though the most extravagant rhetoric of Rollback came from Republicans, the Truman Democrats were not about to let this appeal drift toward the opposition party. The president himself assured a delegation of Romanian émigrés in May 1952 that "if I can continue our program which I have inaugurated, you are going to be a free country again, before you pass on to the next world."[1]

"Our program"? Details were not forthcoming, nor did a trusting populace, immigrant or native-born, consider it seemly to inquire. But in Whitehall the Foreign Office was dismayed at Truman's candor and or-

164

dered the BBC to ignore the statement in its news reports. "We can only hope that this unfortunate utterance of Mr. Truman's will not receive too much publicity," penciled one British official. "It provides a rather typical example of the difficulty of . . . absolute cooperation with the Americans in the application of a general policy."[2]

When astute journalists in Europe picked up on some strange agitations within the émigré communities, their published reports seemed opaque, lacking any meaningful context. The *News Chronicle* of London headlined at one crucial juncture "The Albanian Volcano Is Ready to Explode," leading a casual reader to expect a crisis of seismology rather than politics. A series of incisive columns in March 1950 by C. L. Sulzberger, foreign affairs columnist of the *New York Times*, revealed too much about the Albanian operation for the OPC's comfort, but his unique disclosures provoked no public interest or follow-up.

Truman had special reasons for his interest in OPC operations in Romania, for there foreign policy became most tangled with domestic politics. An ever-present danger in intelligence is the phenomenon called "blowback," when an action overseas provokes an unintended and often undesirable impact on the home front. After Albania, communist Romania was the target of the early OPC's most extensive subversion effort, and in the process a side effect of Rollback threatened to blow back on American politics at the height of the 1952 election campaign.

Wisner knew the territory and the players of his old stamping ground; Kennan, as it happened, had also targeted Romania for proactive American efforts at the end of World War II.[3] Once in command of political warfare in Washington, however, Kennan turned contemptuous of the old OSS networks: military adventurers like Ira Hamilton and Thomas Hall, and Robert Bishop, with his unsubtle political dispatches. (Thus came Kennan's early insistence that Wisner's OPC be held strictly accountable to the State Department — that is, to him.) Then, by chance, another of the old boys of wartime Bucharest appeared in a position of responsibility as Washington began its Cold War: General Courtlandt Van Rensselaer Schuyler was named assistant chief of staff of the army in June 1948. To Schuyler fell supervision of the Pentagon's support role in pursuing Kennan's and Wisner's concepts for guerrilla training among eastern European refugees.

As early as May 1948, with political warfare, NSC 10/2, and the OPC only in the planning stages, Romania's last noncommunist prime minister, General Nicolae Rădescu, who had departed for the West in 1946, approached the State Department with a proposal just a few months premature in its import. Some twenty thousand Romanians of military age were scattered across the occupation zones of Germany and Austria or were seeking new lives in France and Italy, Rădescu wrote. They were by and large impoverished, working at occasional odd jobs, often lacking food, clothing, and shelter. "Enlistment of these men in a military organization would save these men not only physically, but morally." He proposed that they be gathered in American refugee camps and trained for underground guerrilla action.[4]

To his credit, Rădescu was candid up front about one fact that would emerge to mar his cause as it later played out to the American electorate. Many of these potential fighters were Romanians of ethnic German background, he said, with strong fascist sympathies. They had volunteered to fight in the Nazi armies during the war; if not actual war criminals individually, most were partisans of the Iron Guard, the militant force that amassed a record of atrocities momentous even among fascists. Later attempts to obscure this issue could not conceal the reality that Wisner and his officers knew exactly the sort of men they were recruiting for their guerrilla warfare. James McCargar, fresh from his ventures to rescue anticommunist politicians of Hungary, surveyed the Romanian émigrés and reported that "the Iron Guardists, whatever their faction, because of the high percentage of youth among them and because of their militancy, are a fertile field for recruitment by Western intelligence services." Indeed, touching upon that early fear of Wisner's and Lindsay's that the French Foreign Legion might sign up the best fighters, McCargar noted that "the French take a very favorable view of the potentialities of the Iron Guardists for the furtherance of Western objectives in Romania."[5]

In screening for foot soldiers to fight the campaigns of Rollback, the OPC chose to overlook the record of Iron Guard atrocities. But the Washington strategists went even further in their judgment that a fascist past need not preclude a useful role in the combat with communism. Under a special dispensation for intelligence assets, the United States granted an immigrant's visa to one Valerian Trifa, graduate of a Romanian Orthodox seminary, whose record in organizing Iron Guard youth during the war included inflaming anti-Semitic violence in Bucharest in January 1941. Trifa, a person of undoubted political acumen, became archbishop of the Romanian Orthodox Episcopate of Cleveland in 1952, and for the next three decades he led the émigré communities of the American heartland in hatred of communism. He contributed regular commentaries to Radio Free Europe. The Republican-controlled Congress in 1955 invited Trifa to lead the Senate in daily prayer. Only in 1984 was he finally deported from the United States for his fascist past.

As communist authority tightened over Romania, resistance partisans held their ground longer than their Baltic counterparts, the Forest Brothers. Reliable intelligence flowed into Washington during the spring of 1949 that nationalistic partisan units in Transylvania, armed with enough hand weapons and ammunition for defensive tactics, were surviving the security forces' repeated liquidation sweeps. "The partisans have the support of the peasantry," concluded a report from the British Foreign Office, "without which, of course, they could not last long."[6] The CIA dispatched an able career officer named Gordon Mason to develop an intelligence collection station at the American legation in Bucharest; unlike Wisner's field officers under deeper cover, such as Burke, a "diplomat" like Mason was not initially allowed to contact antigovernment factions. But over the following year his post reported evidence of no less than eleven organized resistance groups, numbering overall perhaps thirty thousand men, in the central Carpathians, the Danube and Prut River lowlands, Bukovina, and northern Moldavia.

During Mason's tour in Bucharest, the purposes of the OPC and CIA merged, and CIA station chiefs (the equivalent of ambassadors in the intelligence services) became uninhibited by the old proprieties. Mason was empowered to send local agents out to make clandestine contact with resistance groups, pass around money to keep them going, and provide radio gear for keeping in touch. If the resistance movements grew large enough, Mason reasoned, they might be able to ignite a widespread insurrection; toward this end, case officers encouraged them into dramatic acts of sabotage. The CIA's interests went beyond the political warfare of Rollback, however. The same agents were asked for field intelligence on Soviet or Romanian troop movements that might indicate preparations for an attack on Yugoslavia or western Europe. Finally, Mason's networks positioned resistance fighters to harass Soviet troops in the event of a world war.[7]

The OPC set up training camps for potential guerrillas in France, Germany, Italy, and Greece, thanks to the mounting Marshall Plan counterpart funds. The mission of recruiting candidates for air drops into Romania fell to one of Wisner's less worthy lieutenants, none other than Robert Bishop, troubleshooter (and troublemaker) of the OSS mission in Bucharest, who had spent much of the three years since the war under threat of court-martial, in psychological therapy, suffering bouts of alcoholism. By 1948 he had reestablished himself as a freelance operator in Rome, assembling his own networks of anticommunist activists and taking on OPC assignments after the more disciplined Michael Burke had moved his Albanian operations to Germany.

For all his personal frailties, Bishop was effective in scouting out locations in the back streets of Rome for guerrilla training and filling them with a steady stream of destitute men. An unused room in a church basement, for example, became a classroom for lessons in operating clandestine radio transmitters, while normal religious instruction proceeded down the hall. Promising students would be transferred from Bishop's care to military bases near Athens, to be instructed in the mechanics of opening and concealing parachutes and surviving in the wild. Chosen infiltration agents would be handed false identification papers and small hand arms, then dropped into remote regions on the Soviet periphery with instructions to make mischief and seek out intelligence. Occasionally a desperate man would succeed in making radio contact for a few days; more typically they were arrested, and some were executed on the spot.

Through it all, the cynical doctrine of "plausible deniability" held firm; the United States government would disclaim any responsibility for the incidents, and the agents would be abandoned to their hopeless fates. This was the working pattern of Rollback from 1950 to 1953, against Romania and the other communist satellites, and even against the Soviet Union itself.

*

Romania held another distinction among the "captive nations," arising from the nature of its exile communities in the West. Not only were these émigrés blessed with fortuitous old friends in sensitive Washington agencies (a fact not at all lost upon their disparate leaders) but, setting them pleasantly apart from other émigré nationalists dependent on the

OPC's dole, they had access to considerable amounts of money. Their exiled King Michael, still popular both outside and inside his land, lived comfortably in Switzerland with a royal entourage. Leaders of the National Peasant Party had secreted some six million dollars in Swiss bank accounts before the war, funding their own émigrés, if not the rival factions, until the account was frozen in 1949. Finally, a handful of Romanian financiers had managed to diversify their assets around the world before their country fell to communism; they were only too ready to use their liquid wealth to gain political influence. This was the special circumstance that almost brought grief to the CIA and the Republican Party in the 1952 election.

Outstanding for his manipulative zeal, even among normally manipulative Romanians, was a corporate magnate named Nicolae Malaxa, head of his country's iron and steel industry before and during World War II. He bankrolled the Iron Guard in the 1930s, made common cause with Nazi industrialists until the war was lost, then turned around to collaborate with Romania's first pro-communist government. Visiting America in 1946 to line up partners among major industrialists for joint manufacturing enterprises, Malaxa sought to relocate himself and the command of his international holdings in the United States.[8]

His applications for a permanent entry permit were repeatedly turned down by the Immigration and Naturalization Service. Testifying against him were old Romanian hands in the American government, including Frank Wisner while he was still in the State Department. Wisner found collaboration with fascism objectionable (in Malaxa's case at least), and even worse was his subsequent collaboration with the communist government of Romania. When Wisner moved over to the OPC, he feared that Malaxa would contrive to buy control of the Romanian émigré community to serve his own agenda rather than the American government's.

This animus had a history. Among Wisner's favorite social companions during his glory days in wartime Bucharest was one of Malaxa's rivals, an industrialist named Max Ausnit, who also sought an American base for his corporate empire. To represent his interests after the war, Ausnit retained none other than Allen Dulles, then still in private law practice, who knew his way around émigré politics as well as secret operations. Fearing himself outclassed, Malaxa retained his own establishment counsel, Roosevelt's former aide Adolf Berle, a Democrat. As General Rădescu was gaining a hearing in Washington for anticommunist activities, Malaxa offered Rădescu's favored émigré organization a million dollars should he receive permanent residence papers.

Early in 1951 Malaxa tried another tack. He publicized plans to build a massive seamless steel tubing plant in the small California town of Whittier. As his local representative he retained the former law partner of the newly elected Republican senator from the town, Richard M. Nixon. A colleague of Nixon's in Congress introduced special legislation to grant Malaxa a resident's visa, but the measure stalled. It emerged that Romanians loyal to the steel magnate's rivals (Wisner's friends) had approached the CIA with evidence that Malaxa had surreptitiously passed Nixon the sum of $200,000. The informant, an enterprising Romanian immigrant working up the promotion ladder of a California bank, asked a mere $5,000 to produce the evidence: photocopies of two canceled checks, for $100,000 each, signed by Malaxa, written to the accounts of Richard Nixon and his brother Ed.

By this time Nixon was Eisenhower's running mate in the 1952 election. The CIA's Romanian desk sent the suddenly explosive evidence upstairs to Wisner, who promptly sent it to the CIA director, Walter Bedell Smith. Smith ordered the full Malaxa file brought to his desk and proceeded to discuss it at the White House. Press reports were mounting of a Nixon "slush fund," reportedly provided by business friends in Whittier (no disclosure of their nationalities), and the beseiged vice-presidential candidate went before the nation on television to defend his finances in the famous speech that invoked his wife's cloth coat and his dog, Checkers.

Even in the ugliness of election combat, the Truman White House withheld its evidence against Nixon and the apparent attempts at influence peddling by dubious east European interests. The Malaxa file, it was feared, could eventually implicate the Democrats through Berle as well as the Republicans. And it might open for untoward inspection the OPC's program of employing European émigrés in the Rollback campaign.*

---

* Some in the CIA wondered if Bedell Smith had himself suppressed the Malaxa evidence so as not to endanger Eisenhower's presidential election campaign. This has to be regarded as unlikely. Smith had no taste for partisan politics. His friendship with his old World War II commander clearly endured, but it became known long after all the principals were dead that Smith also had an overarching reason for loyalty to Truman:

In the Eisenhower-Nixon administration of the 1950s, Malaxa finally received his green card, though never American citizenship. He never got around to building the seamless steel tubing plant in Whittier; he died at his home on New York's Fifth Avenue in 1972. Decades later Wisner's daughter, Elizabeth W. Hazard, argued that in Rollback, foreign interests "like Nicolae Malaxa, General Rădescu and Valerian Trifa had found a way to manipulate the electoral process and insinuate themselves into the political dynamics of the United States."⁹

✳

If ethnic community leaders courted by candidates running for office, from Truman and Nixon on down, were not, and did not ask to be, briefed on the workings of Rollback, Soviet intelligence learned soon enough that the inscrutable "Organization X" meant business.

Two unmarked C-47s dropped groups of two or three Ukrainian scouts near major Soviet airfields in September 1949, with orders to radio back messages on conditions observed. The men disappeared, but just eighteen days later the Soviet Defense Ministry issued a printed alert to all hands: "Guard Military Secrets!" Imperialists, the military command warned, were training agents at the Bavarian village of Oberammergau to spy on the Soviet Union.¹⁰ (As usual, the information was a little wrong: agents were indeed being trained in the American occupation zone, but "Detachment R" in placid Oberammergau, site of the famous Passion Play, was no Organization X; it was an academic Russian-language school for promising American army officers.)¹¹

Attempts at infiltration were then mounted all along the length of the Iron Curtain, and they continued for three years. "British and Americans exchanged precise information about the timing and geographical coordinates of their operations," explained Kim Philby, who received the crucial data on behalf of his British seniors and passed it on to his Soviet seniors. "I do not know what happened to the parties concerned," he wrote in one of his most cynical asides, "but I can make an informed guess."¹²

Actually, Soviet intelligence had a well-established record about pro-

as president, Truman had quietly granted Smith a blanket pardon, undated, for any legally questionable decisions he might make as director of central intelligence, a professional comfort that, as far as is known, none of his successors at CIA could enjoy. (See Grose, *Gentleman Spy*, p. 327.)

tecting networks and sources, including Philby. "We were careful not to use his information to conduct a systematic dismantling of the networks concerned," wrote his case officer in Moscow, Yuri Modin, long afterward. A candid (and thus highly classified) American retrospective assessment of counterespionage, even before Philby's treachery became known, noted that "usually the Russians avoided direct action until they had learned almost all the details. . . . Sometimes we were even able to follow their progress through attempts at kidnapping. . . . We have since learned something of the cost to the agents themselves: sentences of five to twenty years in Siberia, misery and even destitution among the families left behind."[13]

This was not a massive military effort. Top-level CIA and Pentagon officers were ever concerned to avoid creating any perception of an "invasion," however puny, and, above all, to sustain the National Security Council's requirement of plausible deniability whenever an operation was exposed. Individual missions were discreet and sporadic, pinpointed to precise locations and purposes — and the available manpower. No overall account of the quality and quantity of Rollback infiltrations has escaped from the secret intelligence and military archives; they probably numbered in the many dozens rather than the many hundreds. Each was conceived and ordered from Washington and London well in advance, though the officers on the ground generally learned only a day or two before the launch the exact location of the target zone and the mission to be carried out.[14]

In March 1951 Philby alerted Moscow that three teams, of six men each, would soon be parachuted into Ukraine; the drop came in May, from British aircraft taking off from Cyprus.[15] The eighteen infiltrators were survivors of the old SS Galizien division who had been among those POWs settling into an ostensibly working-class existence in England. Their landing zone was the remote backwater between Lvov and Ternopol in Galicia and near Kolomyva in the Carpathians at the headwaters of the Prut River. A few months later, communist security forces in Bulgaria picked up several purposeful stragglers slipping in under the averted eyes of Turkish border police. Kennan's "counterforce," after all, was to be applied "at a series of constantly shifting geographical and political points."

Two men, A. I. Osmanov and I. K. Sarantsev (according to their identity papers) were dropped by parachute into Soviet Moldavia one night in August. They carried, according to the Russians after their capture, "false documents, weapons, vials of poison, tools for diversionist and terroristic activities and large sums of money." Open parachutes were found nearby as they were arrested. They were said to have admitted "their entire guilt" and were executed.[16]

In October Vilhelm Spinder and Constantin Saplacan were dropped into the mixed Hungarian-Romanian district of Fagaras. Both were alumni of Bishop's church-basement training academy; communist authorities said they were arrested on the ground carrying four radio receiving and transmitting sets, ten grenades each, seven automatic weapons and handguns, money in gold and local currency, and vials of poison. They told interrogators that their mission was to set up clusters of resistance among the local population and to report back field intelligence on Romanian army deployments and armaments, "about airdromes, military plants, railroad bridges, petroleum reservoirs, etc." Romania filed a diplomatic protest two months later, charges that the United States rejected as "conjured up . . . ridiculous . . . fantastic." A formal note from the American legation in Bucharest declared: "The Government of the United States is unwilling to dignify them with further comment."[17]

In the far north two rootless survivors of wartime displacement, Vladimir K. Galai and Yury A. Khramtsov, were apprehended in Murmansk province and put on show trial. They told of their intelligence training in a small German town and their flight in an American plane from Wiesbaden to Oslo, where a single-engine Norwegian seaplane ferried them to the Soviet border. Galai and Khramtsov were among the few agents whom Soviet authorities allowed to survive, sentencing them to twenty-five years in the gulag.

Sporadic accounts filtered out to the West of communist police actions in Poland, Ukraine, and elsewhere to break up resistance groups receiving clandestine funds from the OPC. West German border police along the porous Czech frontier were ordered to look the other way when certain wandering drifters — "bandits" in the communist terminology — came by, and stragglers entering Germany from Czechoslovakia were not to be searched or disarmed. Such sources brought word late in 1951 that Czech dissidents were ready to mount an internal uprising whenever the United States wanted — an offer Washington rejected as too ambitious even for the gathering march of Rollback. Later testifying in closed session as the new deputy director of the CIA, Allen Dulles admitted to the House Foreign Affairs Committee, "There are times when I feel we have almost stirred up Czechoslovakia too much, without the military ability to do something."[18]

One incident that November forced unwelcome publicity. An American military transport plane was tracked flying over Romania and Hungary. When it was forced to land, the four members of the crew were confined in separate solitary cells. This was no unmarked spy plane piloted by crews of indeterminate nationality; it bore official United States insignia. The public reaction to the news in America was incredulity and contempt. A conservative commentator, William Henry Chamberlin, railed against "the forcing down of an American airplane over Hungary and the virtual holding for ransom of its crew members."[19]

The incident intruded upon the United Nations General Assembly. Speaking for the United States, Democratic senator Mike Mansfield of Montanta declared that the plane had wandered off course, its crew "hopelessly lost and appealing for help over its radio." The Soviet delegate, Andrey Y. Vyshinsky, retorted that examination of the downed aircraft revealed all its navigation equipment in "perfect operational order." American spokesmen then defended the flight as routine, its gear only standard. The Russian side disclosed that on board were found detailed maps of the Volga and Ukrainian terrain, portable radio communication equipment, more than the normal number of parachutes, and large amounts of cash in local currencies. "Were those the standard equipment of the aircraft?" a sarcastic Vyshinsky asked; if so, it was clear evidence that the plane "had been over that area on intelligence activities."[20] (Washington ultimately paid $120,000 to get the American fliers back, a courtesy not extended to the Czech and Polish defectors flying the regular Rollback missions. The embarrassed Senator Mansfield became a stern critic of the CIA.)

A few days before Christmas of 1951, Secretary of State Dean Acheson was personally challenged in public about Moscow's espionage charges; his seemingly offhand reply stands as a textbook exampler of plausible deniability in action, of smooth diplomatic technique to deceive without technically lying.

On December 19, the *New York Times* carried on its front page Moscow's announcement that Osmanov and Sarantsev, the two agents dropped a few months before into Moldavia, had been executed. The next day, at a scheduled State Department news conference, Acheson ridiculed the Soviets' story, according to a *Times* headline, calling it an "obvious fabrication . . . designed to worry their peoples about the aggressive character of the United States." Then, to tie it all up, the *Times* reported a memorable assertion by the secretary of state: "The United States had declared again and again that officials here had absolutely no knowledge of such spying efforts."[21]

This careful phrasing, as reported by a trusting press, was true: that is what the United States had indeed declared again and again. As for the real point at issue, the deception was more subtle, but the words uttered were equally true. Acheson himself, as a member of the National Security Council, knew a good deal about Kennan's political warfare tactics and Wisner's aggressive program, and as much as he wanted to know about individual operations. But "officials," in diplomatic custom, often means civil servants down the line, below the levels of cabinet officers. Given the restrictions and secrecy surrounding NSC decisions on political warfare, a cause of frustration for Kennan himself as he tried to recruit Foreign Service officers for the OPC, it was surely true, as Acheson blandly said, that "officials here had absolutely no knowledge" of clandestine paramilitary operations.

A new United States ambassador to Czechoslovakia presented his credentials to President Klement Gottwald on the last day of 1952. This diplomatic ritual, formal and elegant, is traditionally marked by professions of good will and promises of pleasant working relations between governments. George Wadsworth, a sixty-year-old veteran of proper diplomacy, was somewhat taken aback when the president turned on him, saying, "What about spies you are sending to this country? They are many; they come armed; some have murdered." The new ambassador muttered polite evasions: covert actions have been carried on throughout history but are certainly not the business of statesmen or embassies. As Wadsworth cabled to the secretary of state, Gottwald persisted, saying the Czech Foreign Ministry had a room "filled with arms and apparatus of obvious US origin seized with arrested agents and I could be shown room and some spies so might report to Washington." Wadsworth finally managed to divert the conversation to more agreeable topics. In closing his cabled report, he allowed a gentle sarcasm to intrude upon the parlance of diplomats: "Department may wish to instruct me telegraphically whether it would wish me accept invitation, if again extended, to visit collection arms and equipment allegedly seized with apprehended spies."[22]

✳

In the classified annals of Rollback, Poland occupied for British intelligence a position analogous to that of Romania for the Americans. The men of Whitehall knew the territory, and their instincts were sympathetic. Britain's SOE had developed covert-action capabilities in Poland even before World War II; SOE's fabled chief, Sir Colin Gubbins, had served in prewar Poland and maintained sentimental and practical ties to anticommunist Poles. Gubbins, known during his years of secret service only by the cryptic initials CD, allowed himself a rare public comment in 1944, after the Soviet army refused to come to the aid of the Warsaw uprising against Nazi rule: "Perfidy had reached its climax; we are left stunned by this appalling betrayal."[23]

During and after the war, "Poland" existed in London as well as in the Nazi- and Soviet-occupied homeland. Here there was a government in exile and an émigré community 150,000 strong, including an active Polish Boy Scouts Association claiming 22,000 members. Underground political factions had more or less tenuous links to the Home Army resistance in Warsaw. An army in exile was commanded by General Wladislaw Anders, who had earlier fought alongside the Red Army in resistance to Nazi rule, then had turned against the Soviets. Anders escaped with cadres intact and fought under General Eisenhower in the invasion of North Africa and Italy. (In 1951 the United States briefly considered assigning Anders's skeletal force to NATO command, but the idea was dropped.)

Should the Russians decide to advance toward western Europe, the route of march for the Red Army led through the Polish heartland. Thus the Pentagon's need for early-warning military intelligence and the interests of the OPC in political resistance were joined. From the swirl of émigré activity, British and American intelligence singled out one faction in London that held promise of serving effectively both to collect intelligence and to provoke anticommunist unrest.

It was called the Freedom and Independence movement, or in Polish Wolnosc I Niepodleglosc — whose initials, WIN, English speakers found reassuring.[24] Gubbins and his agents had encountered the WIN underground inside Poland in the last months of the war, but as the communists imposed their grip during 1946 and 1947, security forces decimated the WIN networks. Only the London outpost held on, claiming to represent some 500 active members remaining in Poland, another 20,000 partially active, and 100,000 men ready for mobilization in the event of war against the Soviet Union. WIN-Outside, as it was known, became the Anglo-American instrument for what Pentagon and OPC strategists called a retardation program. Years later the veteran CIA Soviet specialist Harry Rositzke felt free to describe WIN's mission: provide on-the-ground and real-time military intelligence, establish underground paramilitary units, and prepare measures to sabotage any Soviet march toward western Europe, an ever-present fear in those early years of the Cold War.

British intelligence started supplying modest subsidies to the WIN emissaries in London, who managed late in 1948 to send a courier into Poland to reestablish personal contact, after three years of separation, with whatever remnants of the underground could still be located. This courier found his way to an old resistance comrade named Sienko, who confided that he had settled into Polish life as a "sleeper," under the code name Wiktor, awaiting freer days when the old national cause could be reactivated. Sienko and a partner named Kowalski, described as the shadow commandant of WIN-Inside, started casual correspondence with "family" and "friends outside," and the case officers in London saw promise of a revived WIN network. In the guarded ways of émigré correspondence, the Polish operatives began complaining that the British subsidies were nowhere near enough to support the tasks of resistance to communism. Try hard, the letters from Poland pleaded, to get in touch with the Americans.

No one on the receiving end had to try very hard, for Britain's Russia Committee and the American OPC were already working together to penetrate the Iron Curtain. In February 1949, Wisner and Lindsay took over the financing of the nascent WIN network. As the OPC was learning in its other operations, dealings with émigré organizations were never straightforward; they involved touchy issues of ego and personal standing, to say nothing of the amounts, nature, and method of delivery of cash. Among the American cutouts in the negotiations with WIN was Arthur Bliss Lane, a former ambassador to Poland, still well connected in Polish church circles, and a stalwart of Wisner's front groups in the New York establishment.

Over the next three years, more than a million dollars of Rollback funds went to WIN. The "family" letters to London and, increasingly, the couriers who passed back and forth as tourists and commercial travelers would indicate exactly what — and how much — WIN-Inside needed. Replies from London and Washington asked for hard intelligence from the network: exact locations of Soviet troops, names of commanding officers, construction sites that might serve military purposes, technical equipment issued to Polish and Soviet forces, descriptions and coordinates of industrial facilities. By November 1951 the British and American case officers felt confident enough in their Polish contacts to reveal their full contingency plan to retard the feared Soviet advance. It was called Operation Vulcan. WIN-Inside was ordered to "select and point out . . . objects for bombing, mainly railway junctions and reloading areas, and also to destroy those objects."[25]

Even as the WIN interrogatories and responses flowed back and forth between Warsaw and London, a certain wariness developed among the top Rollback officers in Washington, burned by their accumulation of operational failures in Albania, the Baltic states, and almost everywhere else they had tried. John Bross, recruited by Wisner to serve as Lindsay's deputy for east European operations, reminisced in an interview decades later, when he could afford to be mellow about it all, that he first grew uneasy about WIN when they "asked for a high-ranking American military officer to be sent in, to show support and help morale." As Bross, an urbane and level-headed clandestine operator, put it: "The prospect of an American general dangling from a parachute, hooked on a tree in some Polish forest, gave me pause."[26]

In November 1952, the first crack appeared in this heated clandestine operation. Polish air defense reported an intrusion by an American plane over Polish territory — there had been many before — and the government prepared a diplomatic protest. Three days after Christmas, British and American case officers woke up to discover the worst: the communist press headlined the story of WIN, with ample corroborative detail. The "sleeper" Sienko and his comrade, reputed commandant of WIN-Inside, told of their three years of contacts with "family" and "friends outside," the hard currency they had received in cash, the requests put to them for intelligence and sabotage.

Washington pieced together the evidence of debacle. During the security sweeps of 1946 and 1947 against WIN, Sienko had been arrested. In the classic way of counterespionage, security police turned him to serve as yet another double agent. He was ordered to collect all the data he could about western intelligence requirements; under his carefully crafted credibility, information, suitably doctored by his new communist masters, would be returned for the edification of WIN-Outside and its sponsors in the British and American intelligence services.

In the battle of Rollback, the Polish WIN had been a fraud from the start.

＊

The strategy of rolling back the Iron Curtain and liberating the east European "captive nations" under Soviet domination seemed even to liberals and Democrats a worthy goal of American political warfare at the turn of the 1950s. But the real prize of Kennan's "counterforce," an offensive campaign proceeding under cover of defensive "containment," would be in weakening and, eventually, overthrowing communist power in the Soviet Union itself.

An ever-tempting target zone for clandestine infiltration by persons seeking access to forbidden territory was the remote and boggy district of Volhynia, near the border between Ukraine and Belo-Russia. Crushed between the rival Hapsburg, Polish, and Russian empires, the forests and grasslands of Volhynia were sparsely peopled by humble souls with no enduring national allegiance. "Sandy roads and narrow paths connect the scattered villages," as a Ukrainian geographer described the area. "The unbridgeable marshes preclude all but a rudimentary network of communications. . . . The inhabitants live isolated for months at a time, untouched by the civilization of the cities."[27] The Nazi occupiers of Ukraine had been no more effective in controlling Volhynia than the Soviets or the Poles. It was from this forsaken terrain that the Ukrainian Insurgent Army (UPA) had broken out for American-occupied Bavaria in 1947, and it was to this point that Ukrainian nationalists and their new sponsors in the British and American intelligence services sought reentry.

The UPA stragglers of 1947 might have fared better had they been able to reach the British zone of occupation in northwestern Germany, for British intelligence had a clearer idea of who they were. From before the war, Gubbins and his Polish networks knew well the Ukrainian revolutionary Stepan Bandera, and once Bandera took refuge among the DPs in Germany, Whitehall was far ahead of Washington in reestablishing contact. Watching the effort closely, of course, was Kim Philby. "The trouble was," Philby wrote in the memoirs his Soviet masters allowed him to publish in the 1960s, "that although Bandera was quite a noise in the emigration, his claim to a substantial following inside the Soviet Union was never seriously tested, except in the negative sense that nothing much ever came of them."[28] Perhaps not, but an important corrective to Philby's soothing account came three decades later from Soviet spymaster Sudoplatov. If "nothing much ever came" of the Ukrainian resistance, it was not for their lack of trying; its collapse came only after a massive and concerted security crackdown under Sudoplatov's command.

Terror and assassination were part of daily life in Ukraine at the turn of the 1950s, at the bloody hands of state security forces and partisans alike. A Soviet propagandist against the "bandits," one Yaroslav Galan, was butchered with an ax in his Lvov apartment in November 1949. Four months later Sudoplatov's men killed a partisan commander, Roman Shukheyevich, in a shootout, losing two of their own in the raid. Sudoplatov succeeded in planting one of his own agents among the Ukrainian stragglers crossing into Germany, just as American intelligence officers had feared. But British intelligence accepted the man in question and took him with other Ukrainian refugees to England for paramilitary training. The agent allegedly met Bandera in person and proceeded over the coming months to send a stream of coded postcards to a cover address in Germany, to be passed on to Moscow. "There was nothing we didn't know about Ukrainian emigrant organizations and the Bandera movement," Sudoplatov claimed.[29]

In the boredom and relative safety of exile, the Ukrainian nationalists fragmented into competing factions. Bandera's first emissary to the West, Mykola Lebid, broke with his partisan chief in 1948 and set up his own "legal foreign office" of the Ukrainian underground, gaining more interest and support from American intelligence — and from Ukrainian emigrants to the United States and Canada — than Bandera ever would. In his memoirs Philby describes the Anglo-American tensions over which Ukrainians to use in the cause of Rollback and how to use them. (This passage, at least, is not disputed by knowledgeable western intelligence officers.)

"CIA proffered three serious objections to Bandera as an ally," Philby wrote: his "extreme nationalism," which undermined the American attempts going on at the time to unite the Soviet nationalities in a common anticommunist front; his lack of appeal to "the new, 'more realistic' emigration . . . which the Americans were busy cultivating"; and finally, the old-time firebrand's anti-American views. Philby scoffed that the CIA brandished field intelligence from "couriers from the Ukraine in the winter of 1949–50, but the wretched quality of their information suggested rather that they were tramps who had wandered into the wrong country."[30]

Philby naturally savored the disputes between London and Washington over the best use to be made of the Ukrainian resistance, but perhaps even he was not aware of an equally angry conflict inside the American intelligence services themselves over Ukrainian nationalist movements. This came into public view only when selected American intelligence archives were declassified in 1994.

Through their formative years, the OPC and CIA had vied for resources, assets, and the attention of top policymakers for their differing tasks. Both intelligence branches engaged in espionage and covert operations, of course, but while the CIA sought to collect information about the communist enemy, the OPC's mission was to take action against the enemy. Wisner inevitably clashed on day-to-day operations with his opposite number on the intelligence-collection side, Richard Helms. One night in April 1950, as the OPC was still feeling its way toward fulfilling NSC Directive 10/2, Carmel Offie learned that the Voice of America had transmitted code messages to the Ukrainian resistance; on Wisner's behalf he complained to Helms. If, as it seemed, both branches were running separate and uncoordinated operations, they were bound sooner or later, as Allen Dulles had warned years before, to get their wires crossed. Even worse for the national interest, messages on the official broadcasting service could hardly be "plausibly deniable." Offie reported that "Helms expressed astonishment" at the slipup, but found that his explanations "constituted a complete admission that OSO [that is, the intelligence collection branch] has been and is pretty far gone in connection with the Ukrainian underground." Whether the OSO men had wandered into the wrong country or not, the OPC was frustrated in its effort to forge an action front.[31]

The tensions between the American services were officially resolved only in 1952, when the OPC lost its independent status and was folded into the CIA (though working rivalries between the two branches continued for years ahead). Anglo-American tensions lingered on. Wisner and his British counterparts tried to find a common strategy at a conference in London in April 1951. Again, Philby's brief account of the meeting stands unchallenged: "Rather to my surprise, the British stood firm, and flatly refused to jettison Bandera. The best that could be agreed, with unconcealed ill temper on the American side, was that the situation would be re-examined at the end of the 1951 parachute-dropping season."

In the event, Whitehall and Washington pursued separate infiltration missions into Volhynia and nearby areas over the next three years, and Philby was right: "nothing much came of them." Which is not to say that Soviet intelligence had lost interest: Bandera was assassinated in Munich in 1959 by an agent sent from Moscow. Sudoplatov, no longer inhibited, as Philby had been in his memoir, to hew to the party line, wrote of learning in passing that Khrushchev himself had ordered Bandera's liquidation.*

Troubled or, indeed, bored with the feudings of impossible Ukrainians, the OPC and its successor apparatus within the CIA turned to potential clients of more lofty ambition and, perhaps, capability. Separatist Ukrainians were a sideshow; Wisner and Lindsay now looked to exploit discontent within Stalin's Russia itself.

Lindsay had picked out the young Russian-speaking divinity student William Sloan Coffin to recruit and train volunteers for dangerous missions into Russia. After proper vetting, Coffin was sent to Munich,

---

* Here is a splendid example of Philby's ingenuity at "disinformation," which requires extreme caution in reading his Soviet-sponsored memoirs. Ignoring the public confession of the Soviet assassin (already known at the time he was writing), Philby writes in his cavalier style on p. 202: "Some eight years later, I read of the mysterious murder of Bandera in Munich, in the American zone of Germany. It may be that, despite the brave stand of the British in his defense, CIA had the last word." The CIA, of course, had nothing to do with it, as Sudoplatov acknowledges on p. 355 of his book.

where the OPC and the data-collection side of CIA shared an uneasily combined operation on the top two floors of a former German army barracks called the McGraw Kaserne. They served under cover as employees of the Department of the Army. "Everyone knew we were doing something different from regular Department of Army civilians, but no one in Munich those days would be crude enough to ask what," recalled Fenton Jameson, one of Coffin's fellow officers. "Our job was to recruit young toughs to go into Russia. We had to talk about 'liberation' and such, but we all knew this was not to be taken literally."[32]

Coffin had encountered anticommunist Russians during his army service right after World War II, but he was impressed to find that, whatever the American newcomers thought, "rolling back the iron curtain" had more than academic appeal to homeless individuals who had nothing much to lose and were ready to put their lives on the line. He first fell in with some refugees from the wartime Vlassov army, who were understandably reluctant to return home.

For all else that separates them, émigrés and bureaucrats find common comfort in organizational charts and labels; the Vlassov veterans (and their new American mentors) adopted the grand title "Union of the Struggle for the Liberation of the Peoples of Russia" or, in the Russian initials, SBONR. Coffin escorted a cohort of SBONR men to the CIA station in Berlin, where it was thought that they might be helpful in encouraging defections from the Red Army occupation units in East Germany. The visit went poorly; the SBONR men seemed clumsy and careless, showing none of the ingenuity and aptitude required for clandestine operations. "When pressed they conceded they had no volunteers to offer," Coffin said, "a fact which rather relieved me because I didn't trust any of them." Indeed, he began to feel that the three or four men he had found "were just about all there was to the organization."[33]

Setting out in a rented second-hand Volkswagen, Coffin toured the DP camps on his talent search. Gradually he became aware of a different émigré organization, secretive, suspicious of outsiders, but demonstrably active in the refugee communities.

The shadowy political party called the NTS was known all too well to Wisner and Offie in Washington. In the OPC's futile effort to unite the Russian emigration into a common anticommunist front, NTS representatives had stood out in their arrogance and their refusal to play the Americans' game. But unlike other émigré associations, whose aggres-

sive energies were displayed mostly in vigorous mimeographed press re-
leases, the NTS seemed to be actually doing something. Their Russian
nationalist ideology dated from before World War II, and their furtive organizational cohesion was far-flung. While their rivals were stewing and
agitating in German refugee camps, NTS operatives were organizing in
Russian émigré communities the world over. Supporters of their cause
had penetrated the Georgetown University Russian language faculty in
Washington, center of Father Walsh's prewar anticommunist networks,
where young Americans, military and civilian, learned about the Soviet
enemy. The NTS built a major presence in the hospitable air of Morocco, establishing schools, conversation circles, and mutual-support societies to preserve the culture of noncommunist Russia among the refugees. By 1950 NTS activists had begun trickling back to Germany to
work closer to the front line of the battle against communism.

British and American intelligence representatives agreed that, for all
the problems it created, the NTS was worth notice. While Coffin interviewed potential foot soldiers for infiltration into Russia, CIA executives
met in a private room at the Frankfurter Hof and, over a lavish lun-
cheon, agreed to turn the NTS loose for operations from Berlin. NTS
officers found German intermediaries to make friendly contact with
men of the Soviet occupation forces, seeking potential defectors or other
malcontents. They spread anticommunist pamphlets in Red Army barracks and even launched short-range balloons to drop propaganda leaflets by the millions into the Soviet zones of Germany and Austria, where
a few might strike receptive readers among the lonely Russian troops.

Traditional intelligence officers looked somewhat askance at this sort
of activity. "In classical counterespionage terms NTS was a poor operational risk for CIA," wrote one of the Berlin base chiefs, David Murphy.
"The nature of their work in emigration continually exposed them to
KGB agents. Further, some NTS leaders welcomed direct confrontation with their Soviet opponents. . . . NTS agents did not despair
when one of their number fell into Soviet hands; rather, they chose to
believe that one more Russian patriot had penetrated the enemy's de-
fenses."[34]

But as they worked up to their mission, NTS operatives became more
subtle in their approach and avoided inciting unrealistic acts of rebellion or sabotage. The group's purpose at this stage was simply to let ordi-

nary Russians know that an alternative to communism existed, that there were countrymen at work who cared. As the NTS managed to insert agents behind Russian lines, a favored device was simple graffiti, the furtive scrawling of a trident on buildings and walls and at bus stops, to rattle the KGB security forces and to reveal the presence of anticommunists in the Russian midst.

Understanding full well that the NTS, like the Soviet emigration as a whole, had been deeply penetrated by Soviet agents in the guise of homeless refugees, Coffin and his fellow officers established their own private and secure training camps across Germany, just as Burke had done with his Albanians.

*

The American zone of Germany had evolved from one of occupation into the front line of political warfare against the lands behind the Iron Curtain. While the cities were rebuilding Germany's sovereignty and industrial might, village life survived in the routine of ages past. Michael Burke visited an NTS training base at Bad Homburg and found it "a quaint town that looks like a charming photograph found in your grandmother's attic." Hoping for better security than the NTS could offer, Coffin and Jameson trained their recruits deep in the woods and lake country of southern Bavaria, in Kaufbeuren, an old Free City of the fifteenth and sixteenth centuries, where Kaiser Maximilian I had often taken pleasure in the Gasthaus.

Now, in the twentieth century, strangers from America came to town, bringing motley cohorts of Russians and Ukrainians. The new residents could hardly move about unnoticed, but they tried to fade into the village landscape as they mounted incongruous secret missions. Jameson settled his wife and small son in the elegant villa of a former Nazi general; Coffin, a bachelor, lived in a safe house at the edge of town with the men he was training. They studied radio repair, and pored over recent Soviet magazines to acquaint themselves with the local scenes they would soon encounter. They made test parachute jumps from a tower built in the abandoned hangar of a former Luftwaffe base and went for four-mile runs every morning, cloth caps pulled low over their foreheads to foil any attempts by curious outsiders to photograph or recognize them. None of the men knew each other's real names, as they constructed elaborate cover identities for themselves. Burke, with his ready eye for the ironic, summed up the life of a Bavarian village in the early 1950s: "Innocent and sinister people inhabited the same turf, passed through the same revolving doors, traded at the same fish market."[35]

When mission orders came from Washington, the NTS recruits had to do much more than scrawl tridents on walls. Each man, Coffin explained, would be told the coordinates of the place where he was to land, "the railroad station, miles away, where he was to catch a train, the city where he was to live, the factory where he was to look for work. For the first 48 hours he was to travel at night, . . . avoid the nearest railroad station . . . It was sure to be covered if anyone reported his landing." Each man, once radio or courier communication was established, "knew what signals to give should he be captured and 'turned,' and what other signals he was to tell the Soviets he had been given." That was the theory. Long afterward, in bitter reflection upon his failed operation, Coffin summoned up the memory of one young recruit he called Serge, with whom he endured, and grew to relish, the four-mile runs. "We heard from Serge only once, a quick all's well message transmitted on the same night in which he jumped. Thereafter his silence was total."[36]

For a brief spell shortly after the death of Stalin in March 1953, the internal politics of the Kremlin gave the Kaufbeuren operation an unexpected assist. Lavrenty P. Beria, contending for power in the Kremlin succession, released from the gulag thousands of Stalin's political prisoners. Soviet towns and villages were suddenly overrun with rootless men seeking jobs and homes and the NTS men could readily mingle.

Jameson heard of two Kaufbeuren "alumni" who actually worked their way to Moscow, where they made the fatal mistake of contacting an NTS activist from before the war, now long retired — and long under surveillance by the KGB. Another mission may actually have succeeded in its limited, strategically important purpose. Two men from Kaufbeuren were ordered to make their way into the Ural Mountains to an obscure town called Kyshtym to collect a vial of river water downstream from what appeared to be a strange, newly constructed industrial plant. If they could then make their way south, to a pickup point just across the Turkish border, chemical analysis of the water might reveal the nature of the work being done there. (Eventually Kyshtym was revealed to be the Soviet Union's major nuclear processing plant.)[37]

For the most part, the infiltration missions were "stalked by tragedy," as Coffin acknowledged. On April 26, 1953, a team of four recruits from the NTS, twice as many as usual, dropped into the Ukraine by parachute from an unmarked four-engine plane. For all the careful preparations at Kaufbeuren, they were immediately arrested. A month later Moscow Radio announced that Alexander V. Lakhno, Alexander N. Makov, Sergei I. Borgunov, and Dmitri N. Remig had been executed. There was no way to know their birthplaces, their families, their wartime experiences, even their real names.

For close to four decades, authentic records of the Rollback operations were suppressed, denied, or ridiculed. The Soviet side did not want to admit any outcroppings of discontent within its new empire; the American and British sides did not want to admit their failures.

A few veterans made the argument that it had not all been futile. Granted, the Iron Curtain was not rolled back, but snippets of hard intelligence were garnered, from halting radio signals and, more important, from defectors systematically interviewed by western intelligence analysts. Whether or not that vial of water from Kyshtym actually reached western laboratories, American intelligence was soon able to pinpoint and monitor the site of Soviet plutonium production, no small prize in the nuclear arms race as it unfolded. John Paton Davies, one of Kennan's first idea men on his Policy Planning Staff in 1948, concluded long afterward that the operations were indeed ill conceived; "they were unnecessarily dangerous and provocative," he said in a 1994 interview, and they "never seriously undermined the regimes in power."[38] In the last months of the Truman administration, even members of the National Security Council, source of the early pressure for Rollback, began expressing concern that the Soviet Union might be provoked into a drastic response.

Wisner's star in the Washington bureaucracy was fading. Walter Bedell Smith, the CIA director, completed his reining in of OPC by naming a new deputy for political warfare operations to whom Wisner would have to report. This was none other than Allen Dulles, the OSS master of clandestine operations. Once Dulles had been Wisner's mentor; now he became his restraining rival. Even Frank Lindsay's early enthusiasm was turning to skepticism.

In October 1952, even before the public debacle of WIN and the secret failures of the paramilitary air drops, Lindsay composed a secret nine-page memorandum to Dulles and Wisner, arguing point by point why Kennan's notion of a counterforce was not working. In intellectual (if not yet political) terms, this memo quashed the campaign of political warfare conceived in May 1948, activated by NSC directive 10/2 and the mysterious "Organization X."

Lindsay concluded:

> The instruments currently advocated to reduce Soviet power are both inadequate and ineffective against the Soviet political system. The consolidated Communist state . . . has made virtually impossible the existence of organized clandestine resistance capable within the foreseeable future of appreciably weakening the power of the state. . . . Guerrilla action in interior areas of the Soviet Union is impossible because of the impossibility of establishing a base relatively secure from Soviet police control. Areas bordering the Soviet sphere are without exception controlled by minor or secondary states, and the fear of provoking Soviet aggression effectively deters these states from supporting guerrilla operations across their borders.[39]

The language was bureaucratically proper, but the message carried blunt import. What later became a commonplace in Washington was shocking to the true believers of 1952. Allen Dulles summoned the apostate Lindsay to his Georgetown home one Saturday morning early in October, and the two men argued over virtually every phrase of the memo. "Frank, you can't say that," argued Dulles again and again. "You can't say things like that."[40]

Allen Dulles had a personal and political reason for his discomfort that Saturday morning, leaving aside the expression of internal dissent from a respected deputy. The presidential election of 1952 was just a month away, and the Eisenhower-Nixon ticket had a good chance of sweeping the Democrats from power. The spokesman for the Republicans' future foreign policy was Dulles's older brother. Among the vote-catching appeals most favored by John Foster Dulles (less so, as it turned out, by Eisenhower himself) was the call to roll back the Iron Curtain and liberate the captive nations of eastern Europe. This was precisely the campaign that the Truman administration had been secretly pursuing for four years (under cover of containment), which the senior responsible officer within the CIA was now declaring a failure.

Dulles and Lindsay worked over some softening language of compromise, but the base was laid for what Wisner eventually — and diplomatically — termed "a thoroughgoing re-examination of means and methods." Policies that the Dulles brothers considered politically desirable now stood in stark contrast to operations the CIA professionals considered futile. The week after the election, with anticipation of change in the air, Wisner wrote an old comrade in political warfare: "Many persons who will certainly hold key positions in the new Administration have a keen and demanding interest in this field and will want to be satisfied that everything possible is being done."[41]

PART V
Aftermath

10

Anticommunism on the Hustings

"ROLLBACK," USED AS A BATTLE CRY, is most often associated with the rhetoric of John Foster Dulles, a bland international lawyer for most of his career, who ultimately became the indispensable statesman for the Republicans as they took charge of the Cold War. Expecting to become secretary of state under "President Thomas E. Dewey" with the election of 1948, his ambition was deferred for four years until his party finally gained the White House under Dwight D. Eisenhower. After the holding pattern of those years, as he turned sixty, Dulles gained public stature as a symbol of bipartisanship, the spokesman for the loyal opposition to Truman's foreign policy.

In the decades before World War II and the Cold War, Foster Dulles had been too busy in his corporate law practice to dwell upon the politics of the Washington anticommunists. To be sure, he and his younger brother, Allen, had been reared in the tradition of their uncle, Robert Lansing, Woodrow Wilson's secretary of state, who had first set the diplomatic service off on its anti-Bolshevik mania. But early on Foster had decided to leave matters of diplomacy and public policy to Allen, then aspiring to a career in the State Department, while he worked his own agenda of enriching the industrial world (and himself) through the sale of risky foreign debentures to an unwary American public. (This was before the Depression.)

When his friend Governor Dewey first ran for president in 1944, Foster Dulles discovered the temptations of partisan politics. He began to wonder if his Republican Party had made enough of the old suspicions of communist influence within the New Deal. Presuming to rough out a political speech, he wrote Dewey: "The important facts are, first, that Mr. Roosevelt has so weakened and corrupted the so-called Democratic Party that it is readily subject to capture, and secondly, that the forces of communism are, in fact, attempting that capture." Dewey was properly unimpressed, for nothing known to him or the electorate at that time justified such hyperbole, and Dulles himself seemed hesitant to go public on the matter. Once the partisan bug had bitten, however, Dulles was not immune. A few years later, he professed outrage at Moscow's restrictions on American newsmen: "The more I think of it," he wrote Republican senator Arthur Vandenberg, then eyeing the presidency, "the more I think I can make a pretty good issue."[1] Again, politicians experienced at winning votes were not impressed.

After World War II, with the Soviet-American partnership collapsed and Roosevelt replaced by the untested Truman, Dulles's suspicions of communist inroads in Washington became more pragmatic, a "pretty good issue" for the Republicans and, indeed, for Americans of the heartland in general. "Rolling back" the tide of communism or radicalism or un-Americanism (or, indeed, nudism) — whatever the currently resonant name of evil — was becoming as vivid a political image to Americans as Churchill's descending Iron Curtain.

To Dulles and the Republican Party after its disastrous losses in 1948, what Washington officials were calling psychological warfare simply would not do. The Truman Doctrine against communist expansion in Europe, the Marshall Plan, and containment might have been "good so far as they go. But they do not go far enough," he wrote in 1950. Allen, who knew much more than Foster about what the Truman administration was actually doing, must have dropped hints during the fierce chess games the brothers enjoyed in their nearby Manhattan townhouses during those years when they were out of government. But along with most other Americans, Foster could reasonably claim no knowledge of the secret operations launched by the Truman administration, "Mr. X," or Wisner's OPC. So he could blandly declare, "It is time to think in terms of taking the offensive in the world struggle for freedom and of rolling back the engulfing tide of despotism."[2]

*

Evidence was accumulating in the most secret counterintelligence offices of the Truman administration that Republican charges of communist infiltration were not so far-fetched after all. The codebreaking efforts at Arlington Hall started bearing fruit late in 1946, and army specialists finally began to read secret messages sent to Moscow from Soviet agents in the United States. Added to this source were fragmentary clues from communist defectors that seemed to link respected names of the New Deal with Soviet espionage.[3] Since none of this counterintelligence data could be shared beyond the most sensitive confines of government (and, indeed, was not authoritatively disclosed to the public for fifty years), Truman could go on denouncing the Republican charges as partisan politics — even as, within his own councils, the suspicions were mounting.

Quietly, officials who had seemed overly sympathetic to the Soviet Union during the war were encouraged to leave government service. Alger Hiss accepted a prestigious post in the private sector in 1946; sponsored by a then-unsuspecting John Foster Dulles, Hiss became president of the Carnegie Endowment for International Peace. State Department archivists began reviewing old memorandums of troublesome conversations that had seemed irrelevant at the time, including the Russian defector Krivitsky's meetings with Loy Henderson in January 1939, and the disheveled Whittaker Chambers's conversation with Adolf Berle at Woodley later that year.[4]

This was the context, still known only to Truman and his closest aides, in which the president announced a loyalty program to vet civil servants for their patriotism, Executive Order 9835 of March 22, 1947. New Deal stalwarts promptly denounced Roosevelt's successor for pandering to the Republicans, just because they were making noise and had won control of Congress in the 1946 elections.

One government insider saw the goal posts shifting. After years of keeping silent about American communists firing up the social activism of the New Deal, then rushing in with his half-baked advisories to make up for lost time, J. Edgar Hoover and his FBI were ready to make a break with the White House. The loyalty program gave him his opening; his breathless alarums would no longer go unheeded. And, like most Americans of the day, Hoover assumed that Truman was a lame-duck president, poised for defeat in 1948.

Always before, Hoover had refused to testify before Congress on substantive matters, for fear, he said, of disclosing counterintelligence techniques and sources (and, not so incidentally, of offending his chief executive). Truman was "very strongly anti-FBI," according to presidential aide George Elsey, but "J. Edgar will in all probability get this backward-looking Congress to give him all he wants. It's dangerous." As the loyalty program was announced, the durable FBI director offered to appear immediately at a congressional hearing. On March 26, Hoover testified before an overawed House Select Committee on Un-American Activities. "This is a big day for me," he wrote a friend.[5]

Hoover's testimony that big day was a virtuoso display of rhetoric that would grip the public mind of America for decades to come. The anguish of Lansing in the earliest Bolshevik years, of Georgetown's Fathers Walsh and Cronin, Sidney Hook and the New York intellectuals, and the Washington anticommunists ignored in the late 1930s — it all came suddenly to life on Capitol Hill, marked by a dazzling array of historical nonsequiturs and enduring buzzwords.

"In 1917, when the communists overthrew the Russian government," Hoover declared, "there was one communist for every 2,277 persons in Russia. In the United States today, there is one communist for every 1,814 persons in the country."

> I do fear . . . for the liberal and progressive who has been hoodwinked and duped into joining hands with the communists, . . . for the school boards and parents [who] tolerate conditions whereby communists and fellow travelers under the guise of academic freedom can teach our youth a way of life that will eventually destroy the sanctity of the home, that undermines faith in God, that causes them to scorn respect for constituted authority and sabotage our revered constitution. . . .
>
> Communism, in reality, is not a political party. It is a way of life — an evil and malignant way of life. It reveals a condition akin to disease that spreads like an epidemic and, like an epidemic, a quarantine is necessary to keep it from infecting the Nation.[6]

For decades to come, Hoover's theme would itself become a "way of life" in the Cold War. Half a century later, when the "epidemic" of communism seemed eradicated, right-wing preachers merely transferred the image of "disease" to other disliked tendencies of society — abortions by choice, homosexuality, poverty, and crime — and went on fanning the fears of their faithful.

Substantive charges of communist influence in New Deal Washington became public in July 1948, when the Un-American Activities Committee presented a star witness, Elizabeth Bentley, the former courier of communist espionage who had told her story to the FBI three years before. She was followed by Whittaker Chambers, finally emerging in public as the accuser of Alger Hiss. (Interestingly, in this first appearance Chambers charged Hiss only with being a comrade in the American Communist Party in the 1930s; charges of Soviet espionage came later.)[7]

A month later, far from the klieg lights (as they were then called) of congressional hearings, the code rooms of Arlington Hall were unlocked for a collaboration between military intelligence and its longstanding and distrusted rival, the FBI. Hoover sent a single special agent, Robert Lamphere, on the case of the decoded cables. Decades later, Lamphere wrote of his awe at being assigned to a sanctum of the protective military: "I stood in the vestibule of the enemy's house, having entered by stealth."[8] Arlington Hall had pinpointed the British embassy in Washington as the locus of a crucial leak to Soviet intelligence; it took the codebreakers three more years to identify the source more precisely. Only in 1951 could the code name in the Soviet traffic, HOMER, be assigned to Donald Maclean, the trusted diplomat whose sudden defection to the Soviet Union rang the alarm bells.

Truman's loyalty program, Hoover's new readiness to cooperate with the House Un-American Activities Committee, and the hitherto spurned voices of anticommunist researchers in the Washington think tanks opened the way for the national obsession known in American history as McCarthyism, after Joseph R. McCarthy, the previously obscure junior senator from Wisconsin. McCarthy can be credited with no original research of his own, but he grabbed the headlines in the early 1950s with his indiscriminate accusations of communists in government.

Modest and often unremarkable Americans, many of them civil servants of the New Deal, turned their lives around in fear of what old records might show about their reformist or even communist zeal of the 1930s. Noel Field, a Foreign Service officer with a distinguished intellectual heritage, disappeared upon the first accusations against his friend Alger Hiss; he spent the rest of his life as a defector behind the Iron Curtain. Laurence Duggan, a Latin American specialist in the State Department and a stalwart of left-wing discussion circles in Washington (he likely was the man who introduced Hiss to Field) fell to his death December 20, 1948, an apparent suicide; twelve days before, his name had been cited in a closed session of the Un-American Activities Committee. Harry Dexter White, a brilliant and irascible economist who, with John Maynard Keynes, had conceived the postwar economic order at Bretton Woods, was named by Elizabeth Bentley, his courier to Soviet intelligence; he died of a heart attack as the investigations bore down upon him.

McCarthy and Hoover found cells of eager informants in the old anticommunist networks of Washington and New York, including frustrated activists like Isaac Don Levine, who had never managed to attract the attention he thought he deserved during his Krivitsky campaign. It was Levine who informed the Un-American Activities Committee about Duggan, citing information he had received from Chambers. (This was well before Wisner and Offie recruited Levine to help forge the OPC's anticommunist front of Soviet émigrés.)

Hiss, seeking to regain his respectability with the establishment after the charges of betrayal leveled against him, long placed that dreadful man Levine high on the list of his accusers. Levine had allegedly employed forged typewritten documents in an early journalistic coup, branding Stalin as a member of the tsar's secret police before the Bolshevik revolution. Since incriminating typewritten documents figured prominently in the Hiss case, Hiss charged Levine with using the same old trick again.[9] More serious evidence against Hiss was turning up elsewhere. Without the knowledge of the principals in the case, the Arlington Hall codebreakers were on the verge of finding a smoking gun: an intelligence cable intercept that identified Hiss as the source of secret information received by the Soviets.[10] Unfortunately for the right-wing partisans who made Hiss their prime villain, this crucial evidence was finally deciphered and triangulated only in June 1950, after Hiss had been convicted for perjury, and not until 1996 was it made known to a public that still doubted that Hiss had been a Soviet informant.

The late 1940s were ugly years for American politics, for the communist lands behind the Iron Curtain, and for the promise of a new world understanding. Communists won the civil war in China late in 1949. In September the Soviet Union tested an atomic bomb, fundamentally altering the post-war power equation. Anticommunism was finally, as John Foster Dulles had foreseen, a "pretty good issue."

Kennan, Wisner, and the National Security Council had found their foot soldiers in the rootless émigrés of Europe. Anticommunist zealots running for public office found theirs in the east European ethnic communities of the American Middle West.

❋

The official census tabulated 25 percent of the American population in 1948 as being of "foreign origin": 35 million "white" people (that was the category in those days). Electoral strategists, Democrat and Republican, noted that a formidable 11 million of these Americans were eligible to vote.[11] Though hardly a monolithic bloc — American ethnic communities were as politically and socially fragmented as the émigré communities in Europe — the foreign-born had been a major source of electoral strength for the New Deal. With the end of World War II and the change in attitudes toward the Soviet Union in the nation and in the Truman White House, this solidarity began to fracture.

The left wing had long found popular support among the foreign-born; indeed, during the war Stalin had considered it a promising target for Comintern infiltration. By 1946 one influential group, the American Slav Congress, was judged to have been effectively infiltrated by communists; it came out for Truman's left-wing challenger, Henry Wallace, in 1948.[12] A more significant shift occurred in the right wing amid widespread disillusionment at the Yalta accords, which seemed to many immigrants a sellout of Roosevelt's principles and a token of the surrender of eastern Europe to the Soviet Union. The powerful Polish-American Congress promptly denounced Yalta; its president, Charles Rozmarek, took the dramatic step of breaking with the Democrats and declaring himself a Republican.

Republican speakers started receiving unexpected invitations to address Polish audiences; in the 1946 congressional elections, Democratic candidates were defeated in their old stronghold of Milwaukee. In Chicago's mayoralty election the next year, the conservative *Chicago Tribune* wrote that a vote for the Democrats would only be "an encouragement to continue the policies of loot, starvation, and exile that have brought despair to the peoples of Poland, Hungary, Czechoslovakia, Yugoslavia and the Baltic states."[13]

Polish Americans constituted the largest of the eastern European immigrant communities, though the claim of 6 million members was a stretch that would have to include third- and fourth-generation Poles. Even with 3 million of the first and second generations, however, Democratic strategists were ever-mindful of the Polish vote — as Roosevelt and Hopkins had regularly reminded Stalin, who was not impressed. Facing his last election in 1944, Roosevelt had even asked Churchill for a two-week delay in announcing discussions with Moscow about the future of Poland; "you will understand," was all the president had to say to the politically savvy prime minister.

The ethnic vote was important in the industrial states of New York, Illinois, Ohio, Pennsylvania, Indiana, New Jersey, Connecticut, Michigan, and Wisconsin; in the first four the Polish vote alone could tip the balance between the national parties. Ukrainian Americans, supporting twenty-nine local radio stations and no less than forty-seven newspapers and periodicals, were concentrated around the Great Lakes, in Michigan, Wisconsin, Illinois, Indiana, and Ohio. The two hundred thousand or so Romanian Americans were not numerically powerful, but they were politically active and well connected, and, unlike most of the other groups, they commanded ample cash resources.

Even with the crossover of the Polish-American Congress and other Republican inroads into immigrant communities, Truman and the Democrats overwhelmingly won the votes of Americans of foreign descent in 1948. Polish voters in Buffalo, for instance, accounted for 25 percent of the city's Democratic victory; Truman carried Chicago.

Both Republicans and Democrats faced a delicate challenge in addressing this ethnic vote: the various nationality groups felt a certain ambivalence toward their old countries. Making good in America had been the overpowering goal for decades, and party politics seemed to welcome those seeking public stature. Ties of culture and heritage to the homeland endured, even among the American-born, but these were complicated after World War II when refugees from the Iron Curtain lands began to swell the numbers of the longer-established communities in the United States. Immigrants of the late 1940s had to be regarded as suspect for their perhaps necessary but unsavory collaboration with either the Nazi invaders of their homelands or the subsequent Soviet occupiers. "Nothing destroys conversation with new immigrants more than questions like 'What did you do in the war?'" said one American scholar of the immigrant experience. For those insecure in their new roots, redemption and mutual support came in the form of an old American ideology now rising to new prominence: anticommunism. The anticommunist networks pressed their case upon the Republicans. At lunch one day in Albany, Senator Styles Bridges of New Hampshire; William Loeb, publisher of the Manchester (New Hampshire) *Union Leader* and an influential voice of conservatives; and the ever-active Don Levine urged Dewey to keep hammering away at the theme of a communist threat in government.[14]

At the turn of the 1950s, Kennan's containment doctrine (increasingly associated with the Democrats and with indifference to eastern Europe) was being challenged by the alternative doctrine of "liberation," billed as the dynamic Republican alternative to a foreign policy corrupted by old New Deal and outright communistic influences in Washington.[15] Even after the 1948 election, which confirmed the Democrats' hold on the White House and Congress, and after Hoover's publicized tirades to the Un-American Activities Committee, the testimonies of Bentley and Chambers and, in response, Hiss, only 3 percent of Americans declared themselves concerned about an internal communist danger.[16]

Both before and after the 1948 election, Dewey relied on John Foster Dulles for visionary foreign policy guidance, a role that suited Dulles happily. His accomplished younger brother had thrown himself into mobilizing émigrés for the Republican Party in previous election years and seemed to have a good feel for what worked in partisan terms. Furthermore, Allen had developed a head of enthusiasm for the role that refugees, both those still holding on in Europe and those settling into the United States, might play in efforts to roll back the Iron Curtain.

Recoiling from Dewey's astonishing defeat in 1948, Allen Dulles vented to James Forrestal his chagrin that his Republicans had not challenged the Democratic administration more vigorously about the future of Soviet-American relations and of communism against the free world, and specifically about Roosevelt's deals with Stalin at Yalta. Dulles accepted a share of the blame, for he had been one of Dewey's campaign advisers and had argued that "injecting these issues into the campaign would have been destructive of the effort toward bipartisan foreign policy." Bipartisanship might be a noble idea, Allen Dulles felt, but it had cost the election; it was the Republicans' "greatest mistake," he said.[17]

Determined not to repeat that error as anticommunism and the Cold War grew into an American obsession, the Republican opposition launched its own political warfare on the American home front.

＊

The spring before the 1948 election, Senator Henry Cabot Lodge of Massachusetts introduced a bill to recruit up to fifty thousand single European men from the DP camps into the U.S. Army and to train them in paramilitary and espionage skills for future deployment behind the Iron Curtain. The well-meaning senator, a moderate Republican, could not have known the delicacy of his initiative, for he was not privy to the deliberations of the executive branch; in fact, his public proposal closely paralleled what Truman's NSC, Kennan, and Wisner were already contemplating in secret. Once the Lodge bill was passed in 1950, the right wing of his party warmed to the idea, both as a vote-getter in the ethnic precincts and as a tangible alternative to passive containment. Senator Robert A. Taft of Ohio, leader of the conservative Republicans and a presidential aspirant for 1952, advocated "an underground war of infiltration in Iron Curtain countries." Alexander Wiley of Wisconsin, in line to be chairman of the Foreign Relations Committee in a Republican-controlled Senate, urged a "commando-type program of psychological and revolutionary penetration, including the use of 'silver bullets' — money."[18]

Such talk put Wisner and the OPC in a bind. Not only were public statements about secret doings imprudent, but the calls from the Republican opposition came as the Democratic administration was already mounting paramilitary operations, disbursing its "silver bullets" wherever suitable recipients could be located. A CIA study dismissed Lodge's so-called Volunteer Freedom Corps as having no serious military significance but warned of its propaganda value to Moscow, which could lambaste a cynical device to recruit European "cannon fodder" to fight for American imperialism.[19]

None of the intelligence insiders' doubts could muffle the "foreign origin" voters' applause for a strategy of liberation going into the 1952 elections. In an otherwise unremarkable congressman from Wisconsin the hyphenated Americans found their most outspoken champion. A Milwaukee lawyer named Charles J. Kersten had won his first election to the House of Representatives in 1946, part of the unexpected Republican sweep in a former Democratic stronghold. He was defeated for re-election in 1948 but returned to the House in 1950 and served for two more terms. Conservatives found his critical scrutiny of the tax code appealing, and his constituents loved the down-home stories of his musical family and his abandon in playing the marimba. But it was in denunciations of a "bankrupt" Democratic foreign policy that he made his public stand.[20]

"In the past our policy has been that of containment — to prevent the Kremlin influence from expanding, but to do nothing to undermine its influence where it is already established," he claimed, unaware of what was being done. In an angry public letter to Secretary of State Dean Acheson, a particular target of conservative ire, Kersten charged the administration with blocking congressional initiatives that run "counter to the negative policy of containment you have sponsored" and demanded a change of "our foreign policy to one that looks toward the liberation of the peoples of the captive nations."[21]

"The historic friendship of the American people with the Polish people" was a natural theme in Kersten's rhetoric, given his large Polish-American constituency. He moved on to Hungarians, even Albanians, taking no notice of the secret OPC/CIA operations already attempted to foment an Albanian uprising. No nationality of eastern Europe was too obscure or tainted by history; Kirsten defended the memory of the Slovak wartime leader Joseph Tiso in the pages of the *Congressional Record*, apparently assuming that his audience at the Slovak League of America would not care that Tiso had been a Nazi puppet. He heralded the "Czechoslovakian" people, as if this artificial "nationality" had its own ancient heritage. Kersten's rhetoric finally became tiresome when he invoked "the historic friendship of the American people with the Bulgarian people."[22]

Building up to the 1952 election, Kersten pressed the Republican National Committee to include a pledge in the party platform: "to assist in bringing about . . . liberation from communist slavery, we shall offer positive aid and moral support to active fighters now struggling." The committee's Ethnic Origins Division produced a fiery pamphlet called "Betrayal! Over 100,000,000 Eastern Europeans by the Democratic Administration." Liberation, by contrast, was a "Republican policy in the making," and delegates to the Republican National Convention were reminded that the idea was "especially well received by American citizens of Polish, Hungarian, Czech, Slovak, Lithuanian, Latvian, Estonian, Bulgarian, Romanian, Ukrainian, Belorussian and Russian descent." Looking at the 1950 census, that roster totaled close to eight million potential voters, conveniently concentrated in states of high electoral votes.[23]

In 1950, John Foster Dulles had warned against campaign statements "making novel and unseasoned proposals, designed primarily to win votes. . . . The end of that campaign would leave our foreign relations in a shambles." In 1952, determined to become secretary of state in a Republican administration, Dulles changed his tack: the United States, he declared, should make "it publicly known that it wants and expects liberation to occur."[24]

From Wisner's point of view, all this public talk was destructive to the actions already being taken. Kersten's mischief reached its peak in the summer of 1951 with the congressman's proposal to allocate $100 million of American military aid "for any selected persons who are residing in or escapees" from the lands behind the Iron Curtain. "We have the opportunity of taking the offensive in the Cold War," Kersten declared. "Let us make some trouble for Joe Stalin in his own back yard."[25] The so-called Kersten amendment passed on October 10.

The irony was not only that Congress thus gave official sanction to a program dubious under international law but that as a practical matter the OPC did not need the money; the Marshall Plan's counterpart funds were more than ample. (Kersten's later complaints that "his" monies had not been spent would have required too complicated and sensitive an answer for a wary State Department or CIA to discuss in public.) At the Foreign Office in London, officials could only cluck at American naïveté; the British chargé d'affaires in Bucharest cabled Whitehall that as far as he could see, the only effect of the Kersten amendment was a modest increase in the number of Romanians calling at the American legation seeking "a cut of a hundred million dollars."[26]

Six weeks after the Kersten amendment became law, the Soviet Union charged the United Nations General Assembly to consider the "aggressive acts of the United States of America and its interference in domestic affairs of other countries, as instanced by the appropriation of

$100 million to pay for the recruitment of persons and the organization of armed groups." The activities Moscow had known were going on through "Organization X" suddenly became a target of opportunity for formal diplomacy. The General Assembly in that era was still regarded as a hallowed body of statesmanship, and United States delegates struggled to explain not only the repeated incursions of American aircraft and their parachuted human cargo but also a solemn act of Congress.

The Republican convention of 1952 turned against its conservative wing, headed by Taft, and chose as the candidate the surer winner, Eisenhower, whose views on liberation, as well as any number of other issues, were not clear. Foster Dulles tried to press liberation upon the candidate, even arranging for Eisenhower to meet Kersten at the start of the campaign. The two men held a joint press conference, with Eisenhower proffering a bland statement of his hope to obtain "by peaceful means, freedom for the people now behind the Iron Curtain." This was not enough for Kersten, who launched into his tirade about the "captive nations" and the need for an American policy to support resistance to "Stalin's hold." At the end of the news conference, Eisenhower's press secretary made a point of explaining that the presidential candidate was "in no way" endorsing Kersten's position.[27]

Eisenhower and Dulles both delivered statements concerning eastern Europe late in August, and the presidential candidate was furious that his senior foreign policy adviser had "carelessly" omitted the phrase "by peaceful means" in speaking of rolling back the Iron Curtain. Indeed, Eisenhower's men could not figure out exactly where Dulles stood on the matter of "liberation." Emmet John Hughes, the candidate's speech writer, said "we would chase this proposition around and around and around, but it never acquired substance beyond [Dulles] affirming the desirability of it."[28]

The Ethnic Origins Division of the Republican National Committee naturally claimed credit when Eisenhower won in November 1952 with a plurality of over 6.6 million votes. Independent polls did not bear out the claim of a major swing in the ethnic vote. To be sure, Polish-American voters, traditionally 70 percent Democratic, now seemed evenly split between the national parties. Moving beyond the Polish community and down into precinct-by-precinct returns, however, analysts had a harder task demonstrating that the Republican appeal of liberation had significantly weakened the traditional Democratic allegiances of the immigrant communities.[29]

*

Wherever the votes came from, and for whatever policies, John Foster Dulles finally achieved his ascent to power as secretary of state in the incoming Eisenhower administration. His more pragmatic but equally ambitious younger brother, however, was conflicted in the aftermath of the election. Allen Dulles assumed (though could not be sure) that he too would rise in his chosen profession to become director of CIA. But as deputy director in the last Truman years he had seen ample evidence, and had been specifically warned by Lindsay and his other covert-action professionals, that the political warfare he and Kennan had championed since 1948 was futile. The conflict could not be finessed: the drive to roll back the Iron Curtain was central to the new Republican foreign policy; the methods for doing the job were not working.

Reined in by Eisenhower, Foster Dulles had avoided the more extravagant declarations of liberation bandied by the likes of Kersten in the heat of the campaign. One modest line of evidence suggests that in their off-hours together Allen had made his brother at least vaguely aware of the Truman administration's secret operations, even of the peculiar Washington agency established to conduct clandestine political warfare. Thus, in one statement, the elder Dulles conceded what he had not admitted before, that "some highly competent work is being done at one place or another to promote liberation," an admission that did not sit well against Republican complaints of the Democrats' passive policy of containment and was not repeated.[30]

Once sworn in and, as Wisner had expected, determined to see "that everything possible is being done," Dulles could learn as much as he wanted about all the Rollback operations gone sour and the few that were proceeding well, such as Radio Free Europe and Josselson's Congress for Cultural Freedom, for which, of course, he and his party could take no credit. But Secretary Dulles also heard candid assessments from within both CIA and his State Department to confirm the futility of the political warfare envisaged with such gusto in the secret councils of 1948. Eisenhower had temporized on the stump; if the gloom of Lindsay and others in the OPC trenches was evident in their classified discussions, no one at the policy level knew how to admit it all to the public and the restive Republicans in Congress.

It fell to the starchy and unruffled Bedell Smith to make these insiders' assessments more (if vaguely) public, shortly after the death of Stalin in March 1953. The former CIA director had been named undersecretary of state in the Eisenhower administration. Smith told the Senate Foreign Relations Committee that "it would be a mistake on our part to do anything" that would prevent "disruptive influences" in the Soviet Union from playing out. "You know how the Russian is, he resents even the thought of interference in the affairs of Mother Russia." Volunteering his doubts about the kinds of covert operations that had long troubled him, Smith said that, for instance, "we should be very cautious in our dealings with the Ukraine problem." A judicious Democrat, Guy Gillette of Iowa, found himself moving the interrogation, in increasingly guarded language, into the long-forbidden topic of clandestine operations. Smith knew he could not discuss these matters, but his capacity for circumspection failed him.

> SENATOR GILLETTE: Does Central Intelligence, or any of the intelligence agencies, have any information which might justify the hope that within any of these satellites, or groups, there are centers of nucleii from which this might give an opportunity for revolutionary expression?
>
> MR. SMITH: Senator, I am afraid I cannot very well answer that question.
>
> SENATOR GILLETTE: You mean through lack of information, or that you don't . . .
>
> MR. SMITH: Partly through lack of information, and partly, . . . that is one that I don't think I should discuss. But . . . among the larger ones, . . . I am afraid not at this time.[31]

Smith went on to mutter something about various American-sponsored operations in eastern Europe, but the Senate committee's stenographic report deleted the passage. The new undersecretary of state then turned the discussion off with the statement that "the policy for the United States is to say we hope for freedom for all of the countries behind the Iron Curtain and for self-determination, and that is about as far as we can go."

Fair enough as a measured statement from the responsible diplomats of the executive branch, but not nearly far enough for the Republicans in control of Congress. Smith's caution flew straight in the face of all that the anticommunist networks of Washington had been preaching. The doctrine of the right wing found astute expression in James Burnham's philosophical study *Containment or Liberation*, published as the Eisenhower administration took office, but Burnham defined the choice too starkly for policymakers — Democrats or Republicans — accustomed to nuance and complexity. Kersten and his Capitol Hill colleagues demanded creation of a new policy board to sit alongside the National Security Council for a single purpose: to "break the grip of the Red rulers." (Don Levine, just back from his stormy OPC operation to unite the Soviet émigrés, proposed himself as a member.)

Republicans in executive responsibility quickly began to see things differently from their partisans on the campaign trail and in Congress. John Foster Dulles, as secretary of state, and Allen, as director of central intelligence, could not ignore the classified evidence from within their own departments. As they quickly discovered, the president they served had no intention of risking anything for captive nations. Then, in the sixth week of the Eisenhower presidency, the dictator Stalin died, and the premises that had spurred political warfare came up for fundamental reconsideration.

*

Before all that, Secretary Dulles had to confront an awkward personnel problem: George Kennan. After his journeyman days in Moscow, the author of the Long Telegram and the pseudonymous "X" article had acquired public stature as one of the country's most respected career diplomats. By 1952, however, his name had become inextricably entwined with containment, the doctrine despised on the Republican campaign trail. Those who condemned the doctrine had no way of knowing, of course, that its author was also engaged in secret planning for active political war against communism.

Early in 1952, as the political convention season loomed, Truman named Kennan ambassador to the Soviet Union. On his background, no one was more qualified for this difficult assignment; surely more than incidental, however, was the convenient side effect that the appointment would move an inevitable target of partisan controversy out of town. The ploy failed, both in culminating a diplomat's career and in serving the political interests of the Democrats under challenge. For reasons not fully clear but easily conjectured, Stalin took offense at this too-knowledgeable American diplomat, and when Kennan blurted out some casual statements critical of life in Moscow, the Kremlin seized on the pretext to declare him *persona non grata*. After twenty years' preparation as the diplomatic service's most thoughtful expert on communist power, Kennan lasted as United States ambassador to the Soviet Union a mere five months.

His expulsion came early in October. The last thing Truman and Acheson wanted, just one month before the election, was the return home of the author of containment, a high-profile diplomat who would attract press attention and dramatize Republican criticism. Acheson ordered Kennan to take a compassionate rest leave in Germany for a few weeks, providing for his comfort a government guest house at Bad Godesberg. Only in mid-November, a few days after the election, was Kennan invited to return to the United States. At home he went on "resting" in limbo through the transition of administrations. He made only one public statement, a typically thoughtful speech on the future of Soviet-American relations to the Pennsylvania Bar Association on January 16. Neither Kennan nor the State Department officers who cleared his text in advance considered this a high-profile event. It came just four days before the presidential inauguration.

Kennan spoke his complex mind and spoke it eloquently, without regard for the mood and setting in which he would be heard. His tone was cautious and wary about political realities on the global scene; gone was all his patriotic enthusiasm for the "counterforce" against communism he had espoused five years before. He even criticized unnamed champions of aggressive policies for capitalizing on "what they believe to be the unhappiness of the various peoples under Soviet rule."

A few people attending his speech noted the contrast between Kennan's measured assessments and the battle cries of the incoming Republican administration. The *Washington Post,* mincing no words, headlined its news story: "Dulles Policy 'Dangerous,' Kennan Says." Never mind that he had not used the word "dangerous" in the crucial passages and had never mentioned Dulles's name. Kennan's prospects for a responsible assignment in the Eisenhower administration were ended.

John Foster Dulles fired Kennan from the Foreign Service. Allen Dulles moved in quickly to offer his old colleague in political warfare a responsible position within CIA, but Kennan refused to be "pawned off." Secure with a retired ambassador's pension, Kennan set out on a new midlife career as a scholar at Princeton University.

From afar he "shuddered and winced" at the redbaiting of the McCarthy era, in which the diplomatic service was a particular target. To his dismay, Foster Dulles did nothing to defend career diplomats against the venom of their accusers (Allen did better, ruling his CIA out of bounds even to the McCarthyites). From his academic security, Kennan mounted a defense himself; he testified repeatedly before loyalty boards and in public statements on behalf of professionals whose judgments on the job over the years looked suspect to the rampant right wing coming along so much later.

Kennan had never imagined that his strategy of clandestine political warfare would mutate into the conservative battle cry of Rollback; for that matter, he never conceived of his containment doctrine as a "Democratic policy." He took satisfaction in the fact that the logic of Mr. X survived the political squalls of 1952 — even if its author did not — to become the fundamental and successful policy of successive administrations, Republican and Democratic, for the duration of the Cold War.

But the secret side of Kennan's vision also left its heritage in American politics. Long after its efficacy had been found wanting, the aggressive rhetoric of anticommunism flourished, and Kennan's concept of a counterforce against Soviet power brought legitimacy to an old jeremiad. Here, in the jargon of intelligence tradecraft, was "blowback" with a vengeance. For decades into the future, Kennan wrote in concluding the second volume of his memoirs, "there would not be a president who would not stand in a certain terror of the anticommunist right wing of the political spectrum, and would not temper his actions with a view to placating it and averting its possible hostility."[32]

11

Legacy

PRESIDENT EISENHOWER GRASPED more quickly than many who had elected him that the death of Stalin on March 5, 1953, changed everything. A window upon the Soviet Union was opening after the decades of rigid hostility defined by suspicious souls like Krivitsky, Chambers, and the anticommunist brigades. Truman's impulse to land "the old one-two punch on Uncle Joe" no longer served, as Eisenhower saw it; he began looking to signal that in Washington, at least, there was readiness to make a new beginning. "Look, I am tired — and I think everyone is tired — of just plain indictments of the Soviet regime," he told an aide. "It would be wrong — in fact, asinine — for me to get up before the world now to make another one of those indictments."[1]

Such sentiments, understandably, did not sit comfortably with the political warriors who saw the passing of the communist dictator as the moment to exploit uncertainties and foment trouble in the satellite countries. John Foster Dulles, for one, saw no reason to abandon the rhetoric and thought habits of his rise to power.

Frustrated by skepticism among his diplomats, Eisenhower set his own staff to work, with a few invited scholars and specialists outside the government, on a presidential address he called "The Chance for Peace." Delivered on April 16, the president's statement held out a guarded olive branch to the untested post-Stalin leadership. The dour White House chief of staff, Sherman Adams, called it "the most effective speech of Eisenhower's public career." In barely a week the CIA showed Congress a list some twenty single-spaced pages long of "peaceful or friendly gestures by the Soviet Union since Stalin died."[2] Most were trivial courtesies among diplomats proffered where before none had been forthcoming. Even Dulles, who took a dim view of outsiders to his preserve presuming to articulate foreign policy, embraced the signal that the post-Stalin Soviet Union was to be treated as a political adversary, not a holy enemy. A good lawyer sees where his client wants to go; Dulles was a good lawyer, and Eisenhower was his new client.

✳

Under Eisenhower, political warfare against Soviet communism was reined in by the rigors of bureaucratic procedure, leaving no room for freewheeling agencies, operations, and case officers. On the agenda for one of his early NSC meetings, on February 19, 1953, was Senator Lodge's old proposal, beefed up by Congressman Kersten, to mobilize east European refugees into a Volunteer Freedom Corps to serve under American military command. The Joint Chiefs of Staff aired their reluctance to divert jealously hoarded resources to support undisciplined elements from the DP camps. But a staff study won respect on at least one point: "The estimated per capita cost of raising a U.S. combat soldier stood at $5,560," the NSC was told, "compared to a cost of $3,500 for a Volunteer Freedom Corps member."[3] Though creation of such a corps was authorized in May, the Republican administration found repeated pretexts to delay its implementation.

Similarly with Kersten's call for a high policy board to manage Rollback: in 1951 the Truman administration had created an advisory group called the Psychological Strategy Board that had no operational facilities and no authority. The Eisenhower administration tried to mollify the Republican right by reconstituting this passive board and putting an old personal friend of the president's, C. D. Jackson, in charge. Jackson, an executive of the Time-Life empire, yielded to no one in his militancy for liberation, and the board (Don Levine was not appointed to it) proceeded to generate reams of reports and proposals over the years. Eisenhower, however, showed no more readiness than Truman to bestow upon these militants any functional clout.[4]

These layers of decision-making and the heavy hand of orderly procedures did not sit well with Wisner's political warfare brigades. More to the point, disillusionment and defection were spreading among his energetic and highly motivated officers as they confronted the repeated failures of their idealistic paramilitary missions. Frank Lindsay was among the first to leave government, after his final contretemps with Allen Dulles just before the election. Court jester Carmel Offie stayed in the business of undercover operations, but in the private sector. As a "fixer" for the American Federation of Labor International Section, he clashed endlessly with the more rigid operational disciplines of the CIA clandestine services.[5]

Severe burnout hit William Sloan Coffin as his lovingly nurtured Russian agents flew off into the night with their parachutes and code-books, disappearing behind the Iron Curtain, never to reappear in person or deed. Coffin left the CIA in 1953, returning to the seminary and then a distinguished career in the ministry. (He became a national figure in the 1960s as the outspoken chaplain of Yale, a champion of civil disobedience in the civil rights and anti–Vietnam war campaigns.) Michael Burke's zest for the game vanished; he was hired away from the CIA by John Ringling North, another OSS veteran, to manage the Ringling Brothers Barnum & Bailey Circus. In 1956 Burke stepped onto the executive ladder at the Columbia Broadcasting System, eventually becoming president of the CBS-owned New York Yankees, then chief executive of New York's Madison Square Garden until his retirement in 1981.

Even Allen Dulles, at the top of his chosen profession of intelligence, had to admit to doubts about the efficacy of the paramilitary part of the political warfare program he and Kennan had championed four years earlier. He had warned a congressional committee, in closed session, that outside efforts to stir up resistance movements behind the Iron Curtain would need outside military support, which the U.S. government was not ready or able to provide. Within the classified councils of the executive branch, Dulles was proud of the anticommunist impact of the Congress for Cultural Freedom and of Radio Free Europe and Radio Liberty. But when it came to inserting agents anywhere from Stettin to Trieste, from Poland to Albania, he had to concur in Frank Lindsay's sorry conclusions. With only sporadic exceptions of rare opportunity, the air drops of infiltrators ended in 1953.

As head of the CIA, Allen Dulles turned his enthusiasm to targets outside of Europe. In the summer of 1953, with great authority but little guidance from headquarters, an old Middle Eastern hand named

Kermit Roosevelt managed an operation in Teheran to depose the radical prime minister of Iran, Mohammad Mossadegh, whom American policymakers thought was becoming pro-Soviet. A year later Washington believed that an earnest Guatemalan leader, Jacobo Arbenz, was poised to become a communist tool in Latin America; case officers no longer needed in Germany joined old Latin American operators to mount a military operation that deposed him. The policymakers of 1954, Democrats almost as much as Republicans, still envisaged an "international communist conspiracy" with strings pulled by the Kremlin to nurture revolutionary movements wherever it saw fertile ground.

Cuba became the most daunting target of all for CIA. The charismatic revolutionary Fidel Castro, who had led his militia in the mountains down into Havana to overthrow the corrupt Batista regime, loomed as a puppet of the Kremlin just off the coast of Florida. Veterans from the OPC set up training camps in nearby lands to prepare for an invasion and imported east European paramilitary instructors from the German refugee camps. "They were a strange bunch of people," said Robert Amory, an iconoclastic case officer of the new generation that had replaced the CIA's founders, "pretty goddamned good at blowing up barns and power stations, . . . absolutely no sense or feel about the political sensitivities."[6] Speaking no Spanish, émigré drill sergeants shouted obscenities in Hungarian and Russian at boys from Cuba in the mountains of Guatemala.

Into the 1960s and 1970s, from Castro's Cuba to Ho Chi Minh's Vietnam, a lingering spirit of political warfare held on in Washington, operating over and over on the convictions that peoples suppressed by authoritarian regimes, given just the slightest encouragement, would rise up in armed rebellion.

Such rebellions did happen at a few momentous junctures. On the night of June 16–17, 1953, Rollback was put to a dramatic test, though without the planning or encouragement of America's political warriors. East German construction workers had been complaining for weeks about their communist leaders' demands for higher productivity without higher pay. An unprecedented protest rally in East Berlin — a couple of hundred workers at the most — called for a general strike the next day.

The military occupation regimes of both East and West were startled at this outburst of local anger.

Ultimately, communist authorities reached a sober judgment on what had happened. From the comfort of retirement decades later, Yevgeny Pitovranov, Soviet intelligence commander of Berlin at the time, admitted that the 1953 East German uprising had been "the reaction of people to the blunders of the country's leadership, an abscess that in those circumstances could not help but break open."[7] Wallace Carroll, that intuitive American architect of psychological warfare, had years before advised that, contrary to the ideological intuitions of the political warriors, the winning technique was not to attack "communism" as such but rather to highlight the incompetence and injustice of the imposed regimes.

On duty that June night at CIA headquarters in Washington was Lindsay's deputy and successor, John Bross. A message came in from Berlin reporting on the growing intensity of the workers' protest, including warnings that the demonstrations, and the communist authorities' efforts to suppress them, could turn violent. Bross retained a vivid memory of the question posed to him that night: could the CIA surreptitiously supply small arms and grenades to strengthen the workers' position? On his own authority, he drafted a quick response to the Berlin base authorizing CIA operatives to provide "sympathy and asylum, but no arms."[8]

In the immediate aftermath, C. D. Jackson and his Psychological Strategy Board countered that the East German protest was "the greatest opportunity for initiating effective policies to help roll back Soviet power that has yet come to light."[9] The Eisenhower administration responded to the crisis with a huge, and hugely publicized, campaign to supply food packages to East Germans facing shortages and dislocations, a gesture that brought more popular credit to the United States and shame to the communist regime than any measure since the Marshall Plan.

Early that autumn, American ambassadors and senior diplomats from eastern and western Europe gathered for a regular policy review. Not surprisingly, the diplomatic establishment was united in condemning unorthodox measures to undermine governments in place, however hateful and authoritarian those regimes may be. An envoy in eastern Europe stated the case against the militancy of Rollback: "The pressure of events and the shortcomings of the communist system will contribute more inexorably than we can through psychological warfare activities which are essentially uncontrollable and whose results may too often prove the opposite to those intended." An ambassador from a western European capital weighed in from another perspective: "psychological operations at times serve to increase fears on the part of our allies that we were prepared to break in the windows; to bring the pot to a boiling over condition, the grave consequences of which we have perhaps not weighed and carefully considered."[10] Driving yet another nail into the coffin of the strategy favored on the Republican right, the diplomats advised Secretary Dulles: "We should never consider that eastern Europe can be liberated by political warfare devices no matter how well planned and energetic they may be."[11]

For three years after Stalin's death, his successors in the Kremlin were consumed in internal power struggles. By the beginning of 1956 one of their number, Nikita S. Khrushchev, was poised to complete his ascendancy; to secure his power base against a Stalinist old guard, he spoke out openly (more or less) to denounce crimes and betrayals in the Stalin era. Over two days in February, he delivered a rambling but explosive indictment to a closed meeting of world communist parties. Delegates took notes; fragments of a secret text slowly made their furtive way to outsiders, including those in Washington whose business was collecting intelligence.

Wisner and his powerful counterespionage chief, James J. Angleton, had not given up on the effort to stir unrest in the satellite countries. They advocated using the charges by Khrushchev, as they were authenticated, for maximum political advantage: they wanted to dribble the changes out in a carefully orchestrated campaign to encourage resistance forces, which, according to the doctrine of Rollback, were only waiting for their moment to rise up.

Thus came another juncture in the undermining of Rollback's militancy, comparable to Bross's restraint toward the East German workers three years before. This time it came from the top: as the fragments of text came together on his desk, Allen Dulles considered Khrushchev's secret speech to be a historic document, not a device for political warfare; he wanted the whole text out in public, in full, without connivance. Musing with one of his analysts of Soviet affairs, he suddenly blurted out, "By golly, I am going to make a policy decision." Sweeping aside his deputies' schemes, he picked up the secure telephone to his brother, the secretary of state, to say that an important text would shortly arrive at the State Department by messenger.[12] Secretary Dulles and the department's press office did their parts; on June 5, some three months after its delivery, Khrushchev's secret speech was printed in full, over four dense pages, by the *New York Times*. (The *Times* said it received the confirmed text "through diplomatic sources.")

That October, popular discontent erupted against the ruling communists in Hungary, and the scale and scope of rebellion grew to dwarf the earlier East German workers' protest. To blame (or credit) the CIA with instigating the Hungarian revolution of 1956 is to assume a far greater competence than the American intelligence agency possessed, but in both East and West, Radio Free Europe was accused of broadcasting extravagant newscasts to fan a spontaneous combustion. After it was all over, the station was able to refute the charges, though officials had to concede lapses in policy control on the fringe of the radio's operation. It emerged that small freelance transmitters were in service around the communist periphery, manned by émigré announcers who had earlier served American intelligence (Wisner's pioneering undercover agent in Romania, Teodore Manacatide, was one such, broadcasting from Athens), and their anticommunist zeal could indeed have sounded like incitements to violence and even promises of American support.[13]

The Soviet response to the Hungarian uprising was firm and massive, and as the Red Army tanks rolled into Budapest, refugees by the tens of thousands began flowing into neighboring Austria. By long-standing and unrelated plan, Wisner was off on one of his periodic world tours to inspect CIA stations. He arrived in Germany just as the Soviet repression reached its tragic climax; on November 7 he made a quick side trip to Vienna, the last outpost before the Hungarian frontier. There he stood helplessly watching the flow of refugees, even as Dulles advised him that the CIA was determined "not to incite to action." "He saw it so close, he was right there, it was happening under his nose," said Richard Bissell, the new CIA deputy for clandestine services. "He felt this was the first big break of the Cold War. . . . Frank believed that the agency was created to take advantage of this situation."[14]

By all accounts, then and later, Wisner cracked. As his inspection tour came toward its end, the founding political warrior "was rambling and raving all through dinner, totally out of control."[15] He took to drinking too much in Rome, and in Athens he wolfed down a heaping plate of clams. The alcohol brought him relief temporarily; from the bad clams he contracted hepatitis, which endured. Reluctantly, as Wisner's long-evident mania gave way to depression, his old mentor Allen Dulles removed him as head of CIA's clandestine services, arranging a sinecure post for him at the CIA station in London. There sympathetic intelligence colleagues grasped the problem. In the early postwar years, Wisner had been there when the British needed his zeal for action — and the funds at his disposal. Over luncheons at Buck's and elaborate Anglo-American strategy meetings, he had embodied the promise and the naïveté of the Yanks. After three years of enforced retirement and under psychiatric care, on October 29, 1965, Frank Wisner killed himself.

*

Independent of actual crises, the Eisenhower administration ordered yet another study of the CIA and of the clandestine operations against communism that few in power — and none away from power — fully comprehended. Named to conduct a presidential inquiry were two seasoned veterans of high-level political combat, former ambassador David Bruce and former undersecretary of state Robert Lovett. Expecting to spend a few weeks looking over CIA political operations, they found themselves embroiled in investigations for nearly three months. As Lovett told a subsequent board of inquiry, "The idea of these young, enthusiastic fellows possessed of great funds being sent out in some country, getting themselves involved in local politics, and then backing some local man and from that starting an operation, scared the hell out of us."[16]

The Bruce-Lovett report, completed in the fall of 1956, remains one of the most pungent — and embarrassing — policy documents of America's Cold War. It has never been declassified; CIA historians forty years later reported they could not find a copy anywhere in the agency files. But the classified text can be fairly reconstructed from detailed notes taken of a copy found in the personal files of Robert F. Kennedy when he was attorney general. The report discloses no operational secrets. Rather, it conveys the mature opinions of two formidable elders of the establishment, judgments that undercut the entire concept of political warfare as it was played out within the OPC and CIA.[17]

The supporters of the 1948 decision to launch this government on a positive [psychological and political warfare] program could not possibly have foreseen the ramifications of the operations which have resulted from it. No one, other than those in the CIA immediately concerned with their day-to-day operation, has any detailed knowledge of what is going on. . . .

The CIA, busy, monied and privileged, likes its "kingmaking" responsibility. The intrigue is fascinating — considerable self-satisfaction, sometimes with applause, derives from "successes" — no charge is made for "failures."

The two authors built up to their devastating conclusion.

Should not someone, somewhere in an authoritative position in our government, on a continuing basis, be counting the immediate costs of disappointments, . . . calculating the impacts on our international position, and keeping in mind the long range wisdom of activities which have entailed our virtual abandonment of the international "golden rule," and which, if successful to the degree claimed for them, are responsible in a great measure for stirring up the turmoil and raising the doubts about us that exist in many countries of the world today? What of the effects on our present alliances? What will happen tomorrow?

For three decades after the Hungarian uprising of 1956, Rollback lingered on as a hollow slogan, to soothe the ethnic communities of America and the ideologists of the right wing, while the Soviet-American confrontation proceeded in earnest at a higher level of intensity and danger. Each year Congress would pass a meaningless resolution to honor the "captive nations"; low-ranking diplomats would attend national-day receptions for the three Baltic republics at their (precommunist) "embassies" in Washington. Records and memories of the old political warfare efforts were judiciously concealed in the West — no one enjoys reliving failures — and in the East as well, where it remained awkward to acknowledge that there had ever been resistance to the arrival of communism.

By the mid-1980s a new generation had come of age behind the Iron Curtain, accustomed to the disciplines of communist regimes but also chafing at the restrictions on their thoughts and movements. The Hungarian revolution of 1956, simmering unrest in Poland, and the Prague Spring of 1968 were well remembered, if not often discussed. Lost to collective memory were the audacities of the resistance movements of the

1940s, nurtured by western intelligence agencies, crushed so definitively by Soviet internal security in the early 1950s.

Occasional incidents of "blowback" provided inconvenient reminders of operations gone wrong. Across western Europe, from Italy to Belgium, angry politicians reported the discovery of secret arms caches, dating from the 1950s, that were intended initially to support an anticommunist resistance in the event of a Soviet invasion — the old "stay-behinds" — but that had allegedly become the arsenals of right-wing terrorism. Confronted by the charges, the CIA asserted that it had long ago wound up the stay-behind operations, but perhaps they had missed some of the hidden arsenals.

An unprecedented mood of discourse and inquiry was becoming acceptable within the Soviet bloc. It was called *glasnost*. Early in the 1980s in Estonia, Mart Laar, a graduate student in history at the University of Tartu, began taking advantage of this new openness to explore episodes long since relegated to obscurity. He sought out survivors of the Forest Brothers to assemble their oral histories and locate whatever archives could be unearthed in the records of the Soviet Baltic republics. Because of his research, the Forest Brothers are the best documented of the early anticommunist resistance movements, both in their indigenous origins and their subsequent support by western intelligence. Laar was elected prime minister of independent, postcommunist Estonia on October 19, 1992.

Of all the original shock troops of Rollback, it was the strange and shadowy Russian NTS that survived. Deprived of facilities for clandestine air drops, the émigré zealots turned to legal means to dispatch tourists, academics, and businessmen into Russia through the 1960s to scrawl the tridents when no one was looking, to slip their pamphlets into hands that might be friendly. The energy expended in the 1960s and 1970s by Soviet security forces to discredit the NTS is perhaps a better measure of its disruptive potential than the patronizing tolerance shown by jaded intelligence case officers in Washington and London.

Then, under *glasnost*, the mood changed. NTS spokesmen were actually allowed to appear on Soviet television; though criticized and mocked for their pretensions, they were out in public, a status long sought and long denied. Old men living quietly in towns across Russia were invited by newly adventurous Soviet journalists to speak of their years in Stalin's hard-labor camps, their previous indoctrinations by

Nazi and western intelligence, their parachute drops into the Soviet Union in the bad old days of the Cold War. The names by which they were identified in the Soviet media do not seem to match up with any names known to the OPC in the West German training camps — which is not really surprising, since names, backgrounds, and identities had been contrived from the start. But *glasnost* may well have resurrected some of the obscure tough guys whom American covert operators like Michael Burke and William Sloan Coffin had assumed were gone forever.

Once the Soviet Union collapsed, political agitation long suppressed by the monolithic Communist Party burst into the open. No longer content merely to appear on state television, the NTS declared itself from Moscow to be "the only opposition organization in our country that has existed for decades."[18] The faction took its chances amid some seventy other political parties in regional and national elections in the 1990s; the NTS appeared on the nationalist, right-wing side of the Russian political spectrum, but fully supportive of President Boris Yeltsin, free-enterprise reform in the Russian economy, and, above all, assertion of Russian supremacy over the other nationalities of the former Soviet Union.[19] Not too much had changed, it would seem, from the fractious days of disputations among the delegates to the American Committee's conferences in Bavarian country inns fifty years earlier.

In 1993 Yeltsin himself paid personal tribute to the American Committee's ultimate achievement, Radio Free Europe and Radio Liberty: "It would be difficult to overestimate the importance of your contribution to the destruction of the totalitarian [Soviet] regime." And Vaclav Havel, the anticommunist dissident of Czechoslovakia who became his country's first postcommunist president, spoke in personal terms.

> For many years, I myself was one of those who could address their fellow countrymen mainly or even solely through the medium of this radio station. I am not sure that I would not have been in prison for another couple of years, were it not for a certain amount of publicity which I had because of these radio stations. . . .
>
> During the period of the Cold War, these stations spread objective information about the world, spread the ideas of freedom, democracy, human rights and the rule of law.[20]

As the Soviet Union was imploding at the beginning of the 1990s, Frank Lindsay was one old political warrior roused into action. By then turning eighty, comfortably retired as chief executive officer of a large defense company (specializing in classified hardware for satellites and remote sensing devices), Lindsay left his Cambridge home overlooking Harvard's John F. Kennedy School of Government and took a flat in Kiev to stimulate entrepreneurs and enterprises in the newly independent and sovereign Ukraine. Seeking to help build the postcommunist society, therefore, was the pioneer OPC/CIA executive who half a century before had tried to subvert Soviet rule in Ukraine through covert action.

The founding father never returned to Moscow after the fall of the Soviet Union. George Kennan celebrated his ninety-fifth birthday at home in Princeton, New Jersey, on February 16, 1999.

Notes on Sources

Author's Note

Index

Notes on Sources

A huge cache of Secret and Top Secret documents about American intelligence was gradually declassified during the 1990s, sometimes attracting public attention, other times scarcely noticed. The most important of these archives, cited throughout *Operation Rollback*, as abbreviated in the notes, are:

FRUS Intelligence: C. Thomas Thorne, Jr. and David S. Patterson, eds., *Emergence of the Intelligence Establishment* (Washington: Government Printing Office, 1996). Supplementing this important publication in the *Foreign Relations of the United States* series, the State Department history office provided a large file of additional related documents available for consultation at the Truman Library in Independence, Missouri, and at National Archives II in College Park, Maryland.

CIA-Truman: Michael Warner, ed., *The CIA Under Harry Truman* (Washington: Center for the Study of Intelligence, Central Intelligence Agency, 1994). This large softcover volume reproduces photocopies of actual documents.

CIA-OPC: "Office of Policy Coordination, 1948–1952," CIA Historical Study. Dated February 1973, this fifty-seven-page typescript was declassified only in March 1997, after my appeal under the Freedom of Information Act.

CIA-Berlin: Donald P. Steury, ed., *On the Front Lines of Cold War: Documents on the Intelligence War in Berlin, 1946–1961* (Washington: Center for the Study of Intelligence, Central Intelligence Agency, 1999).

VENONA: Robert Louis Benson and Michael Warner, eds., *VENONA, Soviet Espionage and the American Response, 1939–1957* (Washington: National Security Agency and Central Intelligence Agency, 1996). Additional documents and somewhat fuller commentaries were found on the National Security Agency Web site: www.nsa.gov:8080/.

CIA, HS-1: Arthur B. Darling, *The Central Intelligence Agency: An Instrument of Government* (University Park, Pa.: Pennsylvania State University Press, 1990). This was the first of the CIA Historical Studies, drawing on documents that are still classified.

CIA, DCI-1: Ludwell Lee Montague, *General Walter Bedell Smith as Director of Central Intelligence* (University Park, Pa.: Pennsylvania State University Press, 1992).

Additionally, anyone doing serious research on developments in eastern Europe will do well to have close at hand the excellent *Historical Atlas of East Central Europe* by Paul Robert Magocsi (Seattle: University of Washington Press, 1995).

Overture

No one has told the story of Kennan's Long Telegram better than its author, in George F. Kennan, *Memoirs 1925–1950* (Boston: Little, Brown, 1967), cited below as Kennan, *Memoirs I*. He carried developments further, though more guardedly, in his *Memoirs 1950–1963* (New York: Pantheon, 1972), cited below as Kennan, *Memoirs II*. The Long Telegram itself is cited and discussed more fully in Chapter 5. For more comments and color about that time, see Walter Isaacson and Evan Thomas, *The Wise Men* (New York: Simon and Schuster, 1986).

1. Kennan, *Memoirs I*, p. 293.
2. *Foreign Affairs* reprinted "The Sources of Soviet Conduct," the "X article," intact fifty years later, in July 1997, along with excerpts from Walter Lippmann's contemporary criticism and useful retrospective reflections, including some by Kennan himself.
3. Burnham's various comments are found in his *The Coming Defeat of Communism* (New York: John Day, 1949), pp. 43, 24; and his *Containment or Liberation?* (New York: John Day, 1952), pp. 31, 61.
4. *Congressional Record*, Jan. 2, 1951, pp. 96, A7975–77, "Penetration Program Against Communism."
5. *Foreign Relations of the United States 1945*, vol. 5, pp. 884–86. This series is cited hereafter as *FRUS* with year and volume number.
6. Principal author of the memo was John Paton Davies, a career diplomat who proceeded to make the refugee programs his pet project. In one of the minor ironies of the era, Davies later fell afoul of the McCarthy brigades as insufficiently anticommunist. See Wilson D. Miscamble, *George F. Kennan and the Making of American Foreign Policy, 1947–1950* (Princeton: Princeton University Press, 1992), pp. 182, 210; also Kennan, *Memoirs II*, pp. 202–7.
7. This decision, known as NSC 10/2, is discussed in Chapter 5.
8. Kennan, *Memoirs I*, p. 356; see also Kennan, *Memoirs II*, pp. 202–3.

1. Nazis and Communists

1. The progression of the image, from *Das Reich* on February 25, 1945, to Fulton, Missouri, on March 5, 1946, is conveniently assembled in Alfred M. de Zayas, *Nemesis*

at Potsdam (London: Routledge & Kegan Paul, 1979), p. 220. In addition, see Churchill to Truman, May 12, 1945, quoted in Martin Gilbert, *Churchill: A Life* (London: Heinemann, 1991), pp. 843–44.

2. John Charmley, *Chamberlain and the Lost Peace* (London, Hodder & Stoughton, 1989), pp. 134–35.

3. Robert I. Gannon, *The Cardinal Spellman Story* (Garden City, N.Y.: Doubleday, 1962), pp. 222–23; see also Bennett Kovrig, *The Myth of Liberation* (Baltimore: Johns Hopkins University Press, 1973), p. 7.

4. Quoted in Robert L. Messer, *The End of an Alliance: James F. Byrnes, Roosevelt, Truman and the Origins of the Cold War* (Chapel Hill: University of North Carolina Press, 1982), p. 168. See Ronald Steel, *Walter Lippmann and the American Century* (Boston: Little, Brown, 1980), for a discussion of Lippmann's skeptical attitudes toward American responsibilities in Eastern Europe, particularly pp. 425–29.

5. William J. Casey, *The Secret War Against Hitler* (Washington: Regnery Gateway, 1988), pp. 205–6.

6. Alan Bullock, *Ernest Bevin, Foreign Secretary* (New York: Norton, 1983), p. 486.

7. See Louise Atherton, *SOE in Eastern Europe* (London: Public Record Office, 1995), p. 32.

8. Alexander Dallin, *German Rule in Russia 1941–1945* (Boulder, Col.: Westview Press, 1981), p. 657.

9. Quoted in Nikolai Tolstoy, *Victims of Yalta* (London: Corgi, 1979), p. 123.

10. Louise Atherton, *SOE Operations in Scandinavia.* (London: Public Record Office, 1994), p. 21.

11. National City Bank report of Feb. 1920, pp. 7–9; I am grateful to James M. Hester for calling this source, from his own research file, to my attention.

12. A recent study is Mary Ellen Reese, *General Reinhard Gehlen: The CIA Connection* (Fairfax, Va.: George Mason University Press, 1990).

13. Chamberlin is quoted in Linda Hunt, *Secret Agenda* (New York: St. Martin's Press, 1991), pp. 38–39; John Gunther, *Behind the Curtain* (New York: Harper, 1949), p. 18.

14. FRUS Intelligence, pp. 243–45.

15. Memorandum, Jan. 15, 1946, "Assets of SSU for Peacetime Intelligence Procurement," reproduced in CIA-Truman, pp. 21–27.

16. Arnold M. Silver, "Questions, Questions, Questions: Memories of Oberursel," *Intelligence and National Security* 8, no. 2 (April 1993): 199–213.

17. James V. Milano and Patrick Brogan, *Soldiers, Spies and the Rat Line* (Washington: Brassey's, 1995), pp. 43–44.

18. Milano and Brogan, *Soldiers, Spies*, pp. 46–52.

19. Allan A. Ryan, Jr., *Klaus Barbie and the United States Government* (Washington: Department of Justice, 1983), pp. 135–41.

20. This memorandum of Apr. 10, 1950, is reprinted in Milano and Brogan, *Soldiers, Spies*, pp. 224–27.

2. Resistance

1. Silver, "Questions," p. 211; see also Frantisek Moravec, *Master of Spies* (London: Bodley Head, 1975), one of the most intriguing espionage memoirs of the period. As in

all memoirs, particularly those of shadowy intelligence figures, what the author does not include is often as revealing as what he writes. Moravec gives little hint that he had a close working relation with Soviet intelligence as well as with the British.

2. A thorough account of the Forest Brothers is Mart Laar, *War in the Woods* (Washington: Compass, 1992). This is one of the most important of the post–Cold War historical studies to come out of the former communist bloc. See also V. Stanley Vardys and Judith B. Sedaitis, *Lithuania: The Rebel Nation* (Boulder, Col.: Westview Press, 1997).

3. Laar, *War in the Woods*, p. 107.

4. The double agents are described ibid., pp. 208–10; see also Tom Bower, *The Red Web* (London: Mandarin, 1993), pp. 122–23, 127–28.

5. Elizabeth W. Hazard, *Cold War Crucible* (Boulder, Col.: East European Monographs, 1996), pp. 44, 46, 158–60. Hazard's extensive archival research and personal interviews provide all future scholars with a commendable point of entry for considering Romanian politics in the late war and early postwar years. Amusing as a period piece is Robert Bishop, *Russia Astride the Balkans* (New York: McBride, 1948).

6. For recent explorations of Bishop's controversial role, see Hazard, *Crucible*; Ryan, *Klaus Barbie*; and Eduard Mark, "The OSS in Romania, 1944–45: An Intelligence Operation of the Early Cold War," *Intelligence and National Security* (April 1994): 320–44. See also Anthony Cave Brown, *The Last Hero: Wild Bill Donovan* (New York: Times Books, 1982), pp. 679–81.

7. Hazard, *Crucible*, pp. 99, 119.

8. Ibid., p. 164.

9. McCargar is the real name of the pseudonymous "Christopher Felix," author of one of the finest books on Cold War intelligence: *A Short Course in the Secret War* (Lanham, Md.: Madison Books, 1992). This went through three editions between 1963 and 1992, each one successively more candid. The most definitive edition, obviously, is the third, particularly pp. 163–70.

10. See *UPA in Western Europe* (New York: Ukrainian Press Service, 1948), pp. 66–69; also Yuriy Tys-Krokhmaliuk, *UPA Warfare in Ukraine* (New York, privately published, 1972), pp. 390–91. These and other Ukrainian records are found in the Stanislav A. Ausky Collection, Boxes 1 and 4, Hoover Institution, Stanford University. Also useful is "The Nature and Extent of Disaffection and Anti-Soviet Activity in the Ukraine," State Department Intelligence Research Report OCL 4228, Jan. 16, 1947, and a series of articles by Sydney Gruson, *New York Times*, beginning June 13, 1946; see also Orest Subtelny, *Ukraine: A History* (Toronto: University of Toronto Press, 1994).

11. *UPA in Western Europe*, pp. 69–70.

12. State Department, "Nature and Extent"; Will Cates typescript (see note 18 in Chapter 7 below); Ian Sayer and Douglas Botting, *America's Secret Army* (New York: Franklin Watts, 1989), pp. 351–52.

13. Pavel Sudoplatov and Anatoli Sudoplatov, *Special Tasks* (Boston: Little, Brown, 1994), p. 235.

14. Ibid., p. 249.

15. "NTS, the Russian Solidarist Movement," Department of State External Research Paper (series 3, no. 76), 1951; Dallin, *German Rule*, pp. 525–26; Cates typescript. For the Soviet view on the NTS, see Konstantin Cherezov, *NTS: A Spy Ring Un-*

masked (Moscow: Soviet Committee for Cultural Relations with Russians Abroad, undated, probably mid-1960s).

16. Interview with Rahr, 1988.

17. SSU Intelligence Reports 1945–46, RG 226, National Archives (microfilm) E153a, A66407, Feb. 8, 1946, and A66619, Jan. 28, 1946.

18. Quoted in Kovrig, *Myth of Liberation*, p. 71.

3. Liberals and Conservatives

1. American reactions to Bolshevism are discussed in David S. Fogelsong, *America's Secret War Against Bolshevism* (Chapel Hill: University of North Carolina Press, 1995); see also Lawrence E. Gelfand, *The Inquiry* (New Haven: Yale University Press, 1963); and Peter Grose, *Gentleman Spy* (Boston: Houghton Mifflin, 1994). For Wilson's attitudes, see George F. Kennan, *Russia and the West Under Lenin and Stalin* (Boston: Little, Brown, 1961), p. 123.

2. Richard Gid Powers, *Not Without Honor: The History of American Anticommunism* (New York: Free Press, 1995), pp. 52–53, 109, 123–24; Seth P. Tillman, *Georgetown's School of Foreign Service* (Washington: Georgetown University, 1994), pp. 6, 31. See also John E. Haynes, *Red Scare or Red Menace?* (Chicago: Ivan R. Dee, 1996), pp. 89, 92.

3. Richard Gid Powers, *Secrecy and Power* (New York: Free Press, 1987), p. 281.

4. Kennan, *Memoirs II*, p. 191.

5. Flora Lewis, "Who Killed Krivitsky?" *Washington Post*, Feb. 13, 1966; VENONA, p. xii. Krivitsky's own story (ghost-written by Isaac Don Levine) was published in 1939, then reissued with an important introduction by William J. Hood: Walter G. Krivitsky, *In Stalin's Secret Service* (Frederick, Md.: University Publications of America, 1985).

6. William Henry Chamberlin, *Beyond Containment* (Chicago: Henry Regnery, 1953), p. 12.

7. See Harvey Klehr, John Earl Haynes, and Fridrikh Igorevich Firsov, *The Secret World of American Communism* (New Haven: Yale University Press, 1995).

8. Isaac Don Levine, *Eyewitness to History* (New York: Hawthorn, 1973).

9. VENONA, pp. 5–10.

10. House of Representatives, Special Committee to Investigate Un-American Activities, Hearing, Oct. 11, 1939, pp. 5719–42.

11. Hood, introduction to Krivitsky, *In Stalin's Secret Service*.

12. Hearing, House Un-American Activities, Committee, p. 5737.

13. Sidney Hook, *Out of Step* (New York: Harper & Row, 1987), p. 263.

14. Verne W. Newton, *The Cambridge Spies* (Lanham, Md.: Madison Books, 1991), pp. 26–27.

15. Sudoplatov and Sudoplatov, *Special Tasks*, p. 49.

16. A recent and comprehensive discussion of the vast Chambers literature is Sam Tanenhaus, *Whittaker Chambers* (New York: Random House, 1997). Still important is Chambers's own story, originally published in 1952 and reissued with new comments: Whittaker Chambers, *Witness* (Washington: Regnery Gateway, 1980).

17. Levine, *Eyewitness*; Jordan A. Schwarz, *Liberal: Adolf A. Berle and the Vision of*

an American Era (New York: Free Press, 1987), pp. 298–99; Tanenhaus, *Chambers*, pp. 159–63.

18. Spruille Braden oral history, Butler Library, Columbia University, pp. 1866–67.

19. *VENONA*, pp. 121–28. The following sequence is drawn from this internal FBI memorandum of Dec. 29, 1948, made public in 1996.

20. *VENONA*, p. 123.

21. Ibid., p. 128.

22. This anonymous letter was unknown to the public until July 1996, when it was released by the CIA in the context of World War II Soviet espionage. One can speculate with amusement about the motives of the CIA in publishing a document that puts its rival, the FBI, in a bad light. *VENONA*, pp. 51–52, xvii–xviii.

23. *VENONA*, p. xii and following.

24. Harvey Klehr and Ronald Radosh, *The Amerasia Spy Case* (Chapel Hill: University of North Carolina Press, 1996).

4. "Did I Do Right?"

1. William Taubman, *Stalin's American Policy* (New York: Norton, 1982), pp. 96–98; W. Averell Harriman and Elie Abel, *Special Envoy to Churchill and Stalin* (New York: Random House, 1975), pp. 440–43.

2. KGB Archives, Moscow, quoted in Allen Weinstein and Alexander Vassiliev, *The Haunted Wood* (New York: Random House, 1999), pp. 167–68.

3. Taubman, *Stalin's American Policy*, p. 259.

4. Vladislav Zubok and Constantine Pleshakov, *Inside the Kremlin's Cold War* (Cambridge: Harvard University Press, 1996), p. 95.

5. Taubman, p. 102; *Stalin's American Policy*, see also Harriman and Abel, *Special Envoy*, pp. 448–54.

6. Charles E. Bohlen, *Witness to History* (New York: Norton, 1973), pp. 212–13.

7. Zubok and Pleshakov, *Kremlin's Cold War*, p. 304.

8. Quoted in Messer, *End of an Alliance*, p. 76.

9. Eduard Mark, "Venona's Source 19 and the 'Trident' Conference of May 1943: Diplomacy or Espionage?" *Intelligence and National Security* (Summer 1998): 1–31.

10. Harriman and Abel, *Special Envoy*, p. 268.

11. Sudoplatov and Sudoplatov, *Special Tasks*, p. 227.

12. Records of the exchanges leading up to the Hopkins mission and the conversations themselves are in *FRUS* 1945, vol. 7, pp. 21–62; see also Robert E. Sherwood, *Roosevelt and Hopkins* (New York: Harper, 1948).

13. Taubman, *Stalin's American Policy*, p. 104.

14. Quoted in Messer, *End of an Alliance*, p. 82.

15. Bohlen, *Witness to History*, p. 219.

16. Sherwood, *Roosevelt and Hopkins*, p. 905.

17. *FRUS* 1945, vol. 7, p. 61.

18. The story of Colonel Neff was found in VENONA release no. 2 on the NSA web site: www.usa.gov:8080/.

19. Messer, *End of an Alliance*, p. 82.

20. Powers, *Secrecy and Power*, p. 282.
21. Quoted in Powers, *Not Without Honor*, p. 196.

5. Kennan's Design

1. CIA-Truman, pp. 81–83.
2. *VENONA*, pp. xxi–xxii. An interesting account of this process as Moscow learned about it, largely from Philby, is found in Yuri Modin, *My Five Cambridge Friends* (New York: Farrar, Straus & Giroux, 1994), pp. 194–96.
3. FO 371, 51626, London: Public Record Office, cited by John Lewis Gaddis, "Intelligence, Espionage and Cold War Origins," *Diplomatic History* 13, no. 2 (Spring 1989): 198.
4. Quoted in Robert Garson, "The Role of Eastern Europe in America's Containment Policy, 1945–1948," *Journal of American Studies* 13, no. 1 (April 1979): 76.
5. *FRUS* 1946, vol. 6, pp. 696–709.
6. Reproduced in Kenneth M. Jensen, ed., *Origins of the Cold War* (Washington: United States Institute of Peace, 1991), pp. 5–6, 69.
7. Quoted in Clark Clifford and Richard Holbrooke, *Counsel to the President* (New York: Random House, 1991), pp. 110–11, 123–25.
8. CIA-OPC, p. 2.
9. Clifford and Holbrooke, *Counsel*, pp. 123–24. In this memoir, Clifford quotes from a penultimate working draft he found in his personal files.
10. FRUS Intelligence, p. 669.
11. Robert Murphy, *Diplomat Among Warriors* (New York: Doubleday, 1964), p. 343.
12. *VENONA*, pp. xxi–xxiv.
13. CIA-Truman, pp. 99–104.
14. JCS document 862/3, P&O 350.2 TS, RG 319, National Archives. This memorandum, dated Aug. 2, 1948, reviews the various discussions of proposals to deploy émigré paramilitary units.
15. The Finnish offer was relayed to the State Department by the former OSS director, William J. Donovan. Details of guerrilla activity against the communist regimes of Eastern Europe are routinely deleted from classified documents selectively released in the 1990s. This one, however, survives in an unclassified letter from one Alpo Marttinen to Donovan, which Kennan commended to the JCS chairman, Major General Alfred Gruenther. See also Hunt, *Secret Agenda*, pp. 134–35, with detailed citations to other JCS records on p. 296.
16. CIA-Berlin, p. 111.
17. CIA, HS-1, pp. 245–47, 266.
18. This fundamental memorandum, quoted extensively over the following pages, appears in heavily censored form in FRUS Intelligence, pp. 668–72; passages deleted from this official release were unearthed from a clear text of the penultimate draft of April 30, thanks to a Freedom of Information Act appeal by Douglas Selvage of Yale University.
19. This section is deleted in the memorandum as declassified for FRUS Intelligence; the passage quoted is from the penultimate draft.

20. Testimony to the Senate Select Committee on Intelligence chaired by Frank Church of Idaho, Oct. 28, 1975, pp. 8–10, quoted in the committee's final report, vol. 4, p. 31.
21. FRUS Intelligence, pp. 684–85; 690.

6. The Secret Game

1. CIA, HS-1, p. 247. Darling's history, written in 1952–53, so angered the leadership of CIA that it was suppressed even within the classified circles of the agency. It was finally declassified only in 1989.
2. CIA-OPC, p. 6.
3. FRUS Intelligence, pp. 622–23.
4. CIA, HS-1, p. 247.
5. FRUS Intelligence, pp. 702–4; also Kennan, Memoirs II, p. 203.
6. FRUS Intelligence, p. 684–85.
7. Ibid., pp. 681–83.
8. Ibid., pp. 684–85, 690.
9. Ibid., p. 691.
10. Ibid., p. 652.
11. Ibid., pp. 716, 723.
12. CIA, HS-1, pp. 277–79; FRUS Intelligence, pp. 719–22.
13. William Colby, Honorable Men (New York: Simon & Schuster, 1978), p. 73.
14. FRUS Intelligence, p. 729.
15. Morris interview with Ted Morgan, who was generous in sharing his notes with me. See also Ted Morgan, A Covert Life (New York: Random House, 1999), pp. 231–32.
16. Murphy Papers, box 59, Hoover Institution, Stanford University.
17. CIA-OPC, pp. 10–12.
18. Quoted in The Intelligence Community (New York: Bowker, 1977), p. 738.
19. CIA-Truman, pp. 441–43.
20. Revealing clues to the sensitivities of intelligence secrets appear when least expected: this phrase was one of those deleted in the official FRUS Intelligence release. It can be recreated only from the penultimate draft of April 30.
21. Records of the Exchange Stabilization Fund for the early years are understandably sparse. An authoritative, if highly sanitized, statement of its history was given to the House Budget Committee on Feb. 18, 1976, by Edwin H. Yeo III, undersecretary of the treasury for monetary affairs. The following account also draws upon the ESF Annual Report of June 30, 1974.
22. NSC 58/2, quoted in James D. Marcio, "Rhetoric and Reality: The Eisenhower Administration and Unrest in Eastern Europe, 1953–1959," dissertation, American University, 1990, p. 32.
23. FRUS Intelligence, pp. 732–33.
24. CIA-Truman, pp. 321–22.
25. Congressional Record, Apr. 9, 1956, p. S5292.
26. Quoted in Sallie Pisani, The CIA and the Marshall Plan (Lawrence: University Press of Kansas, 1991), p. 73.

7. Starting with Intellectuals

1. *Pravda*, Aug. 22, 1948.
2. George F. Kennan, Lecture of Dec. 18, 1947, in *Measures Short of War* (Washington: National Defense University Press, 1991), p. 314.
3. *U.S. News and World Report*, Apr. 9, 1948, pp. 26–27.
4. Speech to the American Society of Newspaper Editors, Apr. 17, 1948.
5. FRUS Intelligence, pp. 730–31. Again the CIA's sensitivities about financial matters are revealed, even fifty years later: the version of this memo from Wisner to Hillenkoetter, Oct. 29, 1948, reproduced in CIA-Truman (pp. 241–42) deletes the explanations of commodity and fiscal operations; the State Department editors of the Foreign Relations series knew no such inhibitions and released the clear text.
6. FRUS Intelligence, p. 734.
7. Sig Mickelson, *America's Other Voice* (New York: Praeger, 1983), pp. 56–57.
8. CIA, DCI-1, p. 214. Tantalizingly, four lines following Smith's sardonic remark were deleted by the CIA when this official history was declassified; here is one instance where simple prudence discourages a historian's attempt to rebuild the missing material.
9. FRUS Intelligence, pp. 737–40.
10. Ibid., p. 670.
11. Interview with Leich, 1988, and his unpublished memoir, "Great Expectations: the National Councils in Exile" (Dec. 1, 1988), p. 3.
12. Mickelson, *America's Other Voice*, p. 21.
13. Interview with Washburn, 1998.
14. Leich, "Great Expectations," p. 4.
15. Ibid., p. 6.
16. FRUS Intelligence, pp. 735–36.
17. X-2 Washington to X-2 Munich, Aug. 27, 1946; Timothy J. Naftali, then of the University of Hawaii, found this cable in the National Archives' SSU microfilms (RG 226) while researching American counterespionage (X-2) in Germany.
18. The following account of the American Committee's founding effort is drawn largely from an unpublished historical study by Will Cates, an early case officer. A senior official of Radio Free Europe pulled the tattered typescript of perhaps three hundred (unnumbered) pages from a bottom desk drawer and gave it to me in 1988.
19. Offie to Lovestone, May 24, 1951. Ted Morgan found this letter in the Jay Lovestone papers at Stanford's Hoover Institution and called it to my attention.
20. Jon Lodeesen, "Radio Liberty (Munich): Foundations for a History," *Historical Journal of Film, Radio and Television*, 6, no. 2 (1986): 197–210.
21. David E. Murphy, Sergei A. Kondrashev, and George Bailey, *Battleground Berlin: CIA vs. KGB in the Cold War* (New Haven: Yale University Press, 1997), pp. 447–48.
22. An authoritative new source for the following controversial episode is the CIA internal history of the Congress for Cultural Freedom, declassified in 1995 and edited by Michael Warner of the CIA History Staff. It was posted on the Internet (www.odci.gov/csi/) as an article from the CIA's in-house journal, *Studies in Intelligence*; quotations

not otherwise cited are drawn from this source. A serious academic study of an intellectual movement is Peter Coleman, *The Liberal Conspiracy* (New York: Free Press, 1989). This still enlightening account was written, unfortunately, without benefit of documentation about CIA's essential role in the whole effort.

23. Quoted by Coleman at a conference in Berlin in October 1992. For calling this to my attention, I am grateful to the late A. Spenser Braham, himself a seasoned but discreet operative in the campaigns of the Congress for Cultural Freedom.

24. Quoted in Leonard Bushkoff's useful article "Counter-Intelligentsia," *Bostonia*, Jan./Feb. 1990, p. 44.

25. Schlesinger, in "Liberal Anti-Communism Revisited: A Symposium," *Commentary*, Sept. 1967, p. 70, quoted in the research paper of Abra Edwards, one of my undergraduate students at Yale in 1996.

26. CIA-Berlin, p. 69.

27. Bushkoff, "Counter-Intelligentsia," p. 44.

28. Tom Braden, "I'm Glad the CIA Is 'Immoral,'" *Saturday Evening Post*, May 20, 1967, pp. 10–14.

29. CIA-Truman, p. 455.

30. Braden, "I'm Glad," p. 14.

8. Into Battle

1. CIA, DCI-1, p. 92.

2. From Aug. 1, 1952, the OPC officially became the Directorate of Plans within the CIA, with Wisner as its director. Like their Soviet counterparts (Lenin's Cheka, the NKVD, and the KGB), the American clandestine services passed through a series of bewildering titles, both to obscure their functions and to meet the requirements of bureaucratic organizational charts. What had been OPC finally mutated into the CIA's Directorate of Operations (DO), where it seems to have come to rest. Where the KGB will settle down in the post–Cold War era is not yet certain.

3. CIA-Truman, pp. 457–62, 469–70.

4. Michael Burke, *Outrageous Good Fortune* (Boston: Little, Brown, 1984), p. 157.

5. Franklin Lindsay, *Beacons in the Night* (Stanford, Calif.: Stanford University Press, 1993), pp. 337, 332.

6. William Sloan Coffin, Jr., *Once to Every Man* (New York: Atheneum, 1977), pp. 86–94.

7. Carroll to William Harlan Hale, box 18, folder 26, Hale Papers, Yale University.

8. Burke, *Outrageous Good Fortune*, pp. 142–43.

9. Lawrence Durrell, a British intelligence officer in Belgrade at the time, recreated the mood of the venture in an early novel, *White Eagle over Serbia* (1957), which bears little resemblance to the actual operation. The factual, or at least archival, record was pieced together from guarded and opaque British, French, and American records by Beatrice Heuser of Oxford University, published as "Covert Action Within British and American Concepts of Containment, 1948–1951," in Richard J. Aldrich, ed., *British Intelligence, Strategy and the Cold War, 1945–1951* (London: Routledge, 1992).

10. Heuser cites the British Foreign Office records, PRO FO 371/7815, R 2160, and French military attaché to Ministry of Defense, Jan. 14, 1949.

11. Heuser, "Covert Action," pp. 72–73.

12. The published literature on the Albanian operation is more extensive than that of any other venture of Rollback. Most important are Michael W. Dravis, "Storming Fortress Albania: American Covert Operations in Microcosm, 1949–54," *Intelligence and National Security* 7, no. 4 (1992); Nicholas Bethell, *The Great Betrayal* (London: Hodder and Stoughton, 1984); Robin W. Winks, *Cloak and Gown* (New York: William Morrow, 1987); and Burke's own *Outrageous Good Fortune* (though his former superiors in CIA never allowed him, throughout the memoir, to name the country described). See also Anthony Verrier, *Through the Looking Glass: British Foreign Policy in an Age of Illusions* (London: J. Cape, 1983).

13. W. Scott Lucas and C. J. Morris, "A Very British Crusade: The Information Research Department and the Beginning of the Cold War," in Aldrich, *British Intelligence*, pp. 101–2.

14. *FRUS* 1949, vol. 5, pp. 12ff.

15. Burke, *Outrageous Good Fortune*, pp. 143–44.

16. Ibid., p. 145.

17. *Esquire*, Jan. 1973, p. 48.

18. This television encounter is described in Bower, *Red Web*, pp. 247–48.

9. Combat High and Low

1. Quoted in Kovrig, *Myth of Liberation*, p. 116.

2. FO 371/100749 XC 22978, Public Record Office, London, cited in Hazard, *Crucible*, p. 231.

3. *FRUS* 1944, vol. 4, p. 260.

4. Hazard, *Crucible*, p. 196.

5. Ibid., pp. 200–202.

6. Ibid., pp. 205–6.

7. Mason spoke of his long-secret missions only after the Cold War had ended, when interviewed by Wendy Hazard, the daughter of his former boss, Frank Wisner. See Hazard, *Crucible*, p. 207.

8. Hazard carefully researched the Malaxa episode, with Mason's help, and her work was further developed in Seymour M. Hersh, *The Dark Side of Camelot* (Boston: Little Brown, 1997), pp. 158–61.

9. Hazard, *Crucible*, p. 225.

10. *New York Times*, Sept. 23, 1949, as cited by Chris Costa of the School for Advanced International Studies, Johns Hopkins University in his unpublished thesis, "The CIA and the Ukrainian Resistance, 1949–1954" (1991), a diligent gathering of the evidence available at the time of his research.

11. Interview with Brewster Denny, a Detachment R alumnus, 1999.

12. Kim Philby, *My Secret War* (New York: Grove Press, 1968), pp. 201–2.

13. Modin, *Cambridge Friends*, pp. 126–27; CIA-Berlin, p. 23.

14. Historians embark on an exercise in futility in seeking to unearth the operational cable traffic. The culture of CIA, unlike that of the State and Defense departments, has always been nonaccountable and antihistorical; operational messages are routinely destroyed after only a few years, whether judged politically sensitive or not. Allen

Dulles did have a sense of history, and he established the agency's Historical Office, but researchers and authors were constantly plagued by the lacunae in even the classified files to which they had access. Details of individual Rollback missions emerge primarily from the memories of the case officers involved and the complaints of communist propagandists. Worth noting, however, is the plaint often expressed by American case officers that the stories in *Pravda*, *Tass*, and the like were generally too accurate for comfort.

15. Philby's courier for this tip was his fellow diplomat and spy, Guy Burgess, just then returning to London from Washington. Modin, *Cambridge Friends*, p. 189; and Philby, *My Secret*, p. 201.

16. Proceedings of the United Nations General Assembly, First Committee, Dec. 21, 1951, p. 118.

17. Department of State Bulletin, Dec. 24, 1951.

18. The transcript of this 1952 hearing was made public only in 1980. See Marcio, "Rhetoric and Reality," p. 43.

19. William Henry Chamberlin, *Beyond Containment* (Chicago: Henry Regnery, 1953), p. 86.

20. UNGA, First Committee, Dec. 21, 1951; *UN Bulletin*, Jan. 15, 1952, p. 60.

21. *New York Times*, Dec. 19 and 20, 1951.

22. *FRUS* 1952–54, vol. 8, pp. 33–34.

23. Quoted in M.R.D. Foot, *SOE* (London: Mandarin, 1990), p. 278.

24. The following account of the rise and fall of WIN is drawn from *Current Digest of the Soviet Press* 4, no. 52 (Dec. 29, 1952), p. 17; and Harry Rositzke, *The CIA's Secret Operations* (Readers Digest Press, 1977), pp. 170–71.

25. Current Digest, p. 17.

26. Interviews 1988–89 with Bross, who also supplemented the above sources with additional details.

27. Tys-Krokhmaliuk, *UPA Warfare*, pp. 1–2.

28. Philby, *My Secret War*, p. 199.

29. Sudoplatov and Sudoplatov, *Special Tasks*, pp. 253–58.

30. Philby, *My Secret War*, pp. 200–201.

31. CIA-Truman, pp. 325–26. Helms was director of central intelligence from 1966 to 1973.

32. Interviews with Jameson from 1967 to 1990. "Jamie," as he was known to a generation of CIA case officers, was one of the few early Wisner recruits who stayed on for a long career in clandestine operations. A fluent Russian speaker, he was tapped as the escort for Svetlana Alliluyeva, Stalin's difficult daughter, when she abruptly defected to the United States in 1967. One of Jamie's first moves in this unanticipated situation was to seek advice and solace, for himself and her, from the long-retired George Kennan.

33. Coffin, *Once to Every Man*, p. 95; see also Murphy, Kondrashev, and Bailey, *Battleground Berlin*, p. 111.

34. Murphy, Kondrastev, and Bailey, *Battleground Berlin*, p. 110.

35. Burke, *Outrageous Good Fortune*, p. 165.

36. Coffin, *Once to Every Man*, pp. 102–5, 111.

37. Interviews with Jameson, 1988–89.

38. Hazard, *Crucible*, p. 209.
39. "A Program for the Development of New Cold War Instruments," Oct. 1952. Lindsay lost his own copy of this memorandum, but years later found a version of it deep within the files of the Eisenhower Presidential Library; he gave me a copy during our frequent interviews.
40. Interviews with Lindsay, 1989.
41. Wisner to Gordon Gray, Nov. 11, 1952. Lindsay found this letter in the Eisenhower Presidential Library as he built his own files on the demise of his effort.

10. Anticommunism on the Hustings

1. Quoted in Ronald W. Pruessen, *John Foster Dulles: The Road to Power* (New York: Free Press, 1982), pp. 267, 276, 296.
2. John Foster Dulles, *War or Peace* (New York: Macmillan, 1950), pp. 174–75.
3. VENONA, pp. xx–xxi.
4. Ibid., pp. 87–92.
5. Powers, *Secrecy and Power*, pp. 286–87, 290.
6. *Congressional Record*, Mar. 28, 1947, pp. A1409–A1412; Powers, *Secrecy and Power*, pp. 288–89.
7. VENONA, pp. xxi, xxiv, xxvii; Powers, *Secrecy and Power*, p. 298.
8. VENONA, p. xxiii; see also Robert J. Lamphere and Tom Shachtman, *The FBI-KGB War* (New York: Random House, 1986), p. 89.
9. Alger Hiss, oral history, Butler Library, Columbia University. See also Allen Weinstein, *Perjury: The Hiss-Chambers Case* (New York: Vintage Books, 1979), pp. 581–82.
10. VENONA, pp. xxvi, 423.
11. Jack Redding, *Inside the Democratic Party* (Indianapolis: Bobbs-Merrill, 1958), p. 208. For a more thorough electoral analysis of the period, see Louis L. Gerson, *The Hyphenate in Recent American Politics and Diplomacy* (Lawrence: University of Kansas Press, 1964). A useful breakdown of national origins is in pp. 263–65.
12. Gerson, *Hyphenate*, pp. 173–76.
13. Athan G. Theoharis, *The Yalta Myths* (Columbia: University of Missouri Press, 1970), pp. 52–53.
14. Joseph Keeley, *The China Lobby Man* (New Rochelle, N.Y.: Arlington House, 1969), pp. 220–21.
15. Kovrig, *Myth of Liberation*, pp. 100–102.
16. Haynes, *Red Scare or Red Menace*, pp. 188–89.
17. Walter Millis, ed., *The Forrestal Diaries* (New York: Viking, 1951), p. 520.
18. *Congressional Record*, Jan. 2, 1951, p. A7975. See also Robert A. Divine, *Foreign Policy and U.S. Presidential Elections, 1952–1960* (New York: New Viewpoints, 1974), pp. 9–10.
19. Hazard, *Crucible*, p. 217.
20. *American Mercury*, Nov. 1953, pp. 93–95.
21. Quoted in Marcio, "Rhetoric and Reality," p. 45; see also *Congressional Record*, June 25, 1953, p. A3841.

22. *Congressional Record*, 82nd Congress, 2nd session, vol. 98, part 10, pp. A3763, A3744, A3748–49, A3503, A3754, A3757.

23. Gerson, *Hyphenate*, pp. 183, 263.

24. Ibid., pp. 183–84.

25. Kovrig, *Myth of Liberation*, p. 103.

26. Hazard, *Crucible*, p. 219.

27. Theoharis, *Yalta Myths*, p. 145.

28. Divine, *Foreign Policy*, p. 25.

29. Gerson, *Hyphenate*, p. 199; Theoharis, *Yalta Myths*, p. 149.

30. John Foster Dulles, "A Policy of Boldness," *Life*, May 19, 1952, cited in Marcio, "Rhetoric and Reality," p. 46.

31. This transcript from an executive session of the Senate Foreign Relations Committee is quoted in John Joseph Yurechko, "From Containment to Counteroffensive," dissertation, University of California at Berkeley, 1980, pp. 226–28.

32. Kennan, *Memoirs II*, p. 228.

11. Legacy

1. Emmet John Hughes, *The Ordeal of Power* (New York: Atheneum, 1963), p. 103.

2. Dwight D. Eisenhower, *Mandate for Change* (Garden City, N.Y.: Doubleday, 1963), pp. 145–47; Hughes, *Ordeal of Power*, pp. 113–14; House Committee on Foreign Affairs, *Hearings on U.S. Foreign Policy and the East-West Confrontation*, Executive Session, Apr. 24, 1953, pp. 470, 479.

3. NSC files quoted and cited in Marcio, "Rhetoric and Reality," pp. 139–42.

4. Marcio, "Rhetoric and Reality," pp. 38–41.

5. Morgan, *Covert Life* (New York: Random House, 1999), particularly pp. 210–14.

6. Robert Amory, Jr., oral history interview, John F. Kennedy Presidential Library, Boston, pp. 123–24.

7. Murphy, Kondrashev, and Bailey, *Battleground Berlin*, p. 163.

8. This exchange remains a point of controversy even now, decades later. David Murphy, a CIA officer in Berlin, reported in 1997 that he found no record of any such request put to Washington (See Murphy, Kondrashev, and Bailey, *Battleground Berlin*, pp. 163–70). This is not surprising, given the CIA's practice of promptly shredding operational traffic. But Bross, who rose to become one of the CIA clandestine service's most respected officers, clearly remembered his dilemma that night, and the corroborative details he gave me in several interviews make his story convincing. He said, for instance, that when Allen Dulles learned of the exchange the next day, he seemed disappointed at the ease with which a midlevel officer had made a decision fateful for the course of anticommunist political warfare.

9. Quoted in Christian F. Osterman, *The United States, the East German Uprising of 1953, and the Limits of Rollback* (Washington: Cold War International History Project, Woodrow Wilson International Center for Scholars, 1994), pp. 23–24.

10. Marcio, "Rhetoric and Reality," pp. 147–48.

11. *FRUS* 1952–54, vol. 8, p. 85, quoted in Osterman, *United States*, p. 37.

12. Ray S. Cline, *The CIA Under Reagan, Bush and Casey* (Washington: Acropolis, 1981), pp. 185–87. See also Grose, *Gentleman Spy*, pp. 419–27.

13. Bennett Kovrig of Johns Hopkins University conducted research late in the 1960s and assembled a comprehensive postmortem on the charges of outside support for the Hungarian rebels. See his *Myth of Liberation*, pp. 210–22. For additional documentation declassified later, see Grose, *Gentleman Spy*, p. 442.

14. Quoted in Evan Thomas, *The Very Best Men* (New York: Simon & Schuster, 1995), p. 146.

15. So recalled William Colby, as quoted ibid., pp. 147–48; see also pp. 318–20.

16. Lovett to the Taylor Board of Inquiry, May 11, 1961. See Grose, *Gentleman Spy*, p. 598, and following endnote.

17. The original Bruce-Lovett text resides, if anywhere, in White House files of the presidential foreign intelligence advisory board, which are inaccessible even by the CIA. The story of how the report can be cited, therefore, may be of interest. Lovett's testimony to the board of inquiry, quoted above, piqued the curiosity of then Attorney General Robert F. Kennedy, who proceeded to collect relevant documentation for his own files. After Kennedy's assassination in 1968, the Kennedy heirs gave a family friend, historian Arthur M. Schlesinger, Jr., unrestricted access to personal papers before they were turned over to the Kennedy Presidential Library and government control. Not yet knowing the exact context of highly classified records, Schlesinger typed extensive notes of what he found, including the Bruce-Lovett report to the White House. Because Freedom of Information Act appeals and the efforts of the CIA's own historians failed to unlock official access to this report, Schlesinger's notes, dotted with the abbreviations (easily decipherable) of a fast typist who knew he might never see the document again, stand as the only available text at large. Schlesinger kindly gave me a photocopy of his notes while I was writing the biography of Allen Dulles. They are cited in *Gentleman Spy*, pp. 445–48, and in slightly different excerpts in Schlesinger's own *Robert Kennedy and His Times* (Boston: Houghton Mifflin, 1978), pp. 454–57. The *Newsletter* of the Center for the Study of Intelligence (Washington), Spring 1995, pp. 3–4, contains a lighthearted account by Michael Warner of the CIA History Staff of the agency's futile efforts to locate the document.

18. Foreign Broadcast Information Service, SOV-89-049, Mar. 15, 1989, p. 84.

19. Victor Petrenko et al., *Europe-Asia Studies*, July 1995.

20. Yeltsin comment from Mar. 1993 and Havel's of Sept. 1995 are quoted on RFE/RL Web site, www.rferl.org.

Author's Note

This book arose in three stages. In the 1980s the Russian word *glasnost* entered the language of diplomacy and world politics, promising candor and openness where deception and secrecy had long prevailed. Those of us who had lived through the Cold War wondered if the bold new leader of the Soviet Union, Mikhail Gorbachev, could actually deliver on his promise. Over lunch one day in 1987, Michael Mandelbaum, my colleague at the Council on Foreign Relations, and I began brainstorming about ways to put *glasnost* to the test, not only about current problems but upon long-hidden episodes of history.

We started recalling vague generalities in memoirs and traditional histories about secret missions behind the Iron Curtain. We had grown up during the election campaigns of the 1950s, when "liberating the captive nations" of Eastern Europe seemed little more than an empty battle cry. With *glasnost* in the East, and Freedom of Information sentiments in the West, maybe the time had come to investigate whether there was any substance behind the dark and mysterious allusions lurking in the records. Another old friend, Michael Janeway, then an editor at Houghton Mifflin, was immediately interested in the idea, and turned me loose to give it a try. In 1988, even before I could ferret out any documentation, I set off for Munich to interview surviving veterans of early Cold War exploits congregated around the English Garden headquarters of Radio Free Europe and Radio Liberty.

Little did any of us imagine the upheaval immediately ahead: the Berlin Wall fell in 1989; communist regimes collapsed in the former Soviet satellites, and in 1991 the Soviet Union itself ceased to exist. Janeway called me one day and said, "Your book on Rollback is probably going to be different from what we expected!" Indeed so; no longer a test of *glasnost*, it held promise of opening a concealed episode in recent history that might help to explain the mutual suspicions and recriminations that started the world off on the Cold War.

The prospect of all the new information that could be anticipated, not only from *glasnost* but from the fall of communism, was overwhelming. But it would not be forthcoming quickly. I put Rollback aside and concentrated on my biography of Allen Dulles *(Gentleman Spy)*, collecting Rollback-related evidence all the while. By 1995, conditions were ripe to resume. Records and memoirs were trickling out from newly candid sources in the East, and from Washington came a flood of formerly secret documents of the early Cold War years, declassified and in some cases even posted on the internet for anyone who was interested — and who knew where to look. Other documents were quietly released to me after my appeals under the Freedom of Information Act. (These archives are described in the Notes on Sources.) They provided a context, at last, in which memoirs and anecdotes could be properly understood.

For this resumed effort, I owe primary and enduring gratitude to Professor Graham Allison of the Kennedy School of Government at Harvard. Graham, who had faith in the project even before we saw its full implications, appointed me to a research fellowship at the Belfer Center for Science and International Affairs. To him, Steve Miller, and the happy band of graduate students holed up in our long corridor of offices on the Charles, I express my thanks, for their patience and the stimulation of a community of scholars.

Tom Wallace in New York encouraged and provoked me from the start. Houghton Mifflin kept the project on its list for twelve years, through a bewildering series of editors culminating in Eric Chinski, who enthusiastically delivered the final sensitive prods to pound a cumbersome manuscript into shape.

Walter Pforzheimer and Lawrence Houston in Washington were the first to impress on me the central importance of George Kennan, even before I got my hands on the declassified documents to show it. I learned much from conversations with him over the years, and also with Frank Lindsay, Donald Fenton Jameson, and John Bross. I never met Michael Burke, but the relevant chapter in his memoir is more enlightening now that we can penetrate the obscurities of his CIA-imposed circumspection. Bill Coffin was visibly pained at the interest I expressed to him about this sorry episode in his early career.

As always, I am grateful for the help on matters great and small generously offered by my colleagues at the Council on Foreign Relations, notably Bill Hyland and Jim Hoge, plus the ever-kind Rosemary Hartman and Barbara Miller.

Claudia and our two daughters, Carolyn and Kim, long ago resigned themselves to my obsession with Rollback, but they cheerfully included me in their busy lives anyway. Carolyn's partner, June, never lost her enthusiasm for the rewriting of history. And their little daughter, Bronia, did her part in the final stage when she would visit, every morning dutifully picking up all the paper clips littering the floor around my desk from the night before.

Vineyard Haven and Cambridge
December 1999

Index

Abt, John, 64
Acheson, Dean, 82, 174, 175, 203, 209
Adams, Sherman, 211
Albania: Anglo-American political war-
  fare in, 154–59, 164; communist resis-
  tance in, 152, 156–59; OPC parachut-
  ing men into, 161
Alliluyeva, Svetlana, 236n32
Amerasia, 68, 81
American Committee for the Liberation
  of the Peoples of the USSR, 97, 129,
  131, 133–34, 233n18. See also Central
  Intelligence Agency (CIA); Office of
  Policy Coordination (OPC)
American Communist Party, 61, 63. See
  also Communism
American Federation of Labor, 110, 137,
  144, 213
American Slav Congress, 199
Amory, Robert, 214
Anders, Wladislaw, 176
Anti-Semitism, 167
Arbenz, Jacobo, 214
Arlington Hall: identifies Hiss as Soviet
  spy, 198; Philby's knowledge of, 159–
  60; wartime Soviet telegrams in, 88
Army Department, 183
Atomic Energy Commission, 141
Ausnit, Max, 169
Austria, 14, 28, 44

Bandera, Stepan, 46–47, 180, 182
Barbie, Klaus, 30–31

Bay of Pigs, 157n
BBC, 165
Beichman, Arnold, 137
Bell, Daniel, 140
Beneš, Edvard, 13, 14
Bentley, Elizabeth, 81, 83, 197, 198
Bergmanis, Augusts, 35
Beria, Lavrenty P., 186
Berle, Adolf A.: and Krivitsky's death, 65;
  meets with Chambers about gov-
  ernment spy ring, 64–65; notifies
  Roosevelt of USSR penetration of
  government, 65; represents Malaxa,
  169
Berlin Airlift, 215
Bevin, Ernest, 124, 154–55
Bidault, Georges, 124
Bishop, Robert: CIA's recruitment of, 39;
  and communism, 38; mental instabil-
  ity of, 30, 165, 168; and "rat line," 30,
  39; recruitment of candidates for polit-
  ical warfare, 168; in Romania, 37–40;
  and Wisner, 39, 168
Bissell, Richard M., 118, 217
Blum, Robert, 106, 108
Bohlen, Charles E., 7, 71, 73–75, 78
Braden, Spruille, 65
Braden, Thomas W., 141–42
Bridges, Styles, 122, 201
Britain: intelligence operations in
  Czechoslovakia, 37; and notification
  of USSR of Anglo-American espio-
  nage plans, 160–61, 170–72; political

Britain (*cont.*)
   warfare in Albania with U.S., 154–59;
   subsidizing WIN,
   177–78; tensions between U.S. and,
   182; training refugees for mission be-
   hind Iron Curtain, 34–35; and World
   War II, 13. *See also* Churchill,
   Winston
Bross, John, 178, 215, 216, 238n8
Brown, Irving, 110, 137
Broz, Josip. *See* Tito
Bruce, David, 218–19
Bruce-Lovett report, 218–19, 239n17
Bulgaria, 172, 203
Bullitt, William C., 57, 101, 113
Bullock, Alan, 19
Burgess, Guy, 236n15
Burke, Michael: and CIA "type," 146,
   148; leaving intelligence service, 213;
   meetings with Philby, 160–61; memoir
   by, 235n12; at NTS training base, 185–
   86; and OPC program in Albania,
   157–58; recruitment of refugees for po-
   litical warfare, 151–52
Burnham, James, 5–6, 208
Byrnes, James F., 49–50, 75, 87–89

Cambridge University, 56
Cannon, Cavendish, 153–54
Carnegie Endowment for International
   Peace, 195
Carol, King of Romania, 128
Carroll, Wallace, 149–51, 149n
Casey, William J., 19
Castro, Fidel, 214
Cates, Will, 133–35, 233n
Central Intelligence Agency (CIA): and
   Bay of Pigs, 157n; culture of, 235–
   36n14; establishment of, 95; focus
   moved from eastern Europe to Third
   World, 213–14; Hillenkoetter as direc-
   tor of, 101, 103, 108, 121, 144; historical
   recordkeeping of, 100–101, 233–34n22,
   235–36n14; history of, 233n8, 236n14;
   and Hungarian revolution of 1956, 217;

   infiltration into USSR, 184; inhibitions
   about Rollback operations, 101–2; and
   NSC 4-a, 96; objections to Bandera,
   181; OPC absorbed into, 145, 182,
   234n2; and "plausible deniability," 172;
   policy differences with OPC, 181; recruitment of Bishop, 39; and recruitment of USSR defectors, 95; resignation of officers from political warfare,
   212–13; rivalry with FBI, 230n22; in Romania, 167; sensitivity about financial
   matters, 233n5; Smith as director of,
   144–45
Central Intelligence Group (CIG), 88
Chamberlain, Neville, 12, 14
Chamberlin, Stephen J., 25
Chamberlin, William Henry, 174
Chambers, Whittaker: as accuser of Hiss,
   197; career in espionage, 63; conversa-
   tion with Berle, 195; interview with
   FBI, 65–66; and Krivitsky, 63–64; no-
   toriety of, 83
Chicago Tribune, 17n, 199
China, 198
Christian Science Monitor, 40
Churchill, Winston: election defeat after
   World War II, 69; Iron Curtain speech
   of, 22; and lack of intelligence on
   USSR, 22; and repatriation of USSR
   citizens after World War II, 20–21; and
   Truman, 22
CIA. *See* Central Intelligence Agency
   (CIA)
CIG. *See* Central Intelligence Group
Clay, Lucius D., 124, 138, 139
Clifford, Clark, 4, 91
Coffin, Margot, 147–48, 182–87
Coffin, William Sloan, 147–48, 151–52,
   213
Colby, William, 112
Cold War: American policy at beginning
   of, 32; congressional scrutiny of intelli-
   gence funding, 115; first battle of, 8,
   14–15; and Krivitsky's death, 62; and
   Marshall Plan, 93; and repatriation of

USSR citizens after World War II, 21; superpowers in, 15; and Truman Doctrine, 93. *See also* Iron Curtain; Political warfare

Columbia Broadcasting System, 213

Cominform, 117, 136

Comintern, 38, 58, 61, 117

Committee for a Free Albania, 158

Communism: American Communist Party, 61, 63; American public's attitude toward, 53–54, 201; in China, 198; conservatives' attitude toward, 53–68; containment of, 5–6; and Democratic Party, 194–99; eastern European resistance to, 32–49, 179–82; and fundamental Christianity, 54; liberals' attitude toward, 53–68; organized political warfare against, 7–8; as threat to capitalism, 14. *See also* Cold War; USSR

Congress: funding of political warfare, 204–5; Hoover's testimony before, 195–96; House of Representatives Select Committee on Un-American Activities, 55, 61, 196–97; knowledge of activities of CIA, 207–8; scrutiny of intelligence funding, 115; Senate Foreign Relations Committee, 207; support for training displaced persons to fight communism, 202–6

Congress for Cultural Freedom, 139–40, 142–43, 206, 213, 233–234n22

Cooper, Gary, 148

Correa, Mathias F., 105, 110

Counter-Intelligence Corps (CIC), 15, 26, 27–30, 46

Cronin, John, 82–83

Cuba, 157n, 214

Currie, Lauchlin, 64

Czechoslovakia: American Third Army in, 22; as Britain's sphere of intelligence operations, 37; Chamberlain's denial of crisis in, 12; and Iron Curtain, 13, 33–34; and parliamentary democracy, 33; porous border of, 44; Prague Spring of 1968, 219; and Radio Free Europe, 221; U.S. accused of spying in, 175–76; uprising in, 173–74

Czechoslovak Second (Intelligence) Bureau, 32–34

Daladier, Edouard, 57

Dallin, David, 130–31

Darling, Arthur, 100–101, 232n1

Davies, John Paton, 106, 187, 226n6

Davies, Joseph E., 73

Democratic Party, 194–99

Der Monat, 138

Dewey, John, 82

Dewey, Thomas E., 75, 107, 193, 194, 201

Dies, Martin, 55

Directorate of Operations (DO), 234n2

Directorate of Plans, 234n2

Displaced persons: congressional support for training in political warfare, 202–6; "disposal" of, 28–30; interrogation of, 27–28; recruitment for political warfare, 148, 151–52, 202–6; Romanians as, 166; smuggled to South America, 29–30; from USSR, 20–22, 29–30

Donovan, William J.: activism against communism, 102–3; career history of, 16; correspondence with Hillenkoetter, 103; discussion with USSR intelligence experts, 17; and Finnish offer for guerrilla warfare, 231n15; fired by Truman, 19, 144; as founding director of OSS, 16; and Hungary's relationship with Hitler, 22; plan for OSS in peacetime, 16–17n; policies of, 18; rivalry with Hoover, 17n; and Roosevelt, 19

Double agents, 35–38, 49, 179

Dragonovic, Krunoslav, 29, 39

Draper, William, 123

Duggan, Laurence, 64, 197–98

Dulles, Allen: biography of, 239n17, 242; and conflicts of intelligence agencies, 181; and covert operations, 105–7; as director of CIA, 208, 213–14; first meeting with Kennan, 106; and futility of

Dulles, Allen (cont.)
political warfare, 206, 213; and Hillenkoetter, 121; and Khrushchev's secret speech, 216–17; and Lindsay's report on failure of political warfare, 188–89; and McCarthyism, 210; and OSS, 105; and recording history of CIA, 236n14; recruitment as director of OPC, 98, 105–8, 109–10; "Relations between Secret Operations and Secret Intelligence" by, 106–7; representing Ausnit, 169; and uprising in Czechoslovakia, 174; and uprising in German Democratic Republic (East Germany), 238n8; and Wisner, 108–9, 187
Dulles, John Foster: and Dewey, 201; firing of Kennan from Foreign Service, 210; and McCarthyism, 210; and office of secretary of state, 204–5, 206, 208; and politics of anticommunism, 107, 188–89, 193–95, 198; Stalin's death, 211
Durrell, Lawrence, 234n9

Eastern Europe: and U.S. secret program of containment of communism, 6–8; USSR demarcation, 11–15. See also Iron Curtain; and specific countries
Eisenhower, Dwight D.: and Alpine redoubt myth, 19; attitude toward political warfare, 208, 212–14; election to presidency, 193, 205; and Nazis used in service of U.S., 25; and Nixon "slush fund," 170n; and OSS, 18; and Stalin's death, 211; and study of CIA clandestine operations, 218–19; and Yalta agreements, 22, 33
Elsey, George, 91
Encounter, 142
Estonia, 14, 34, 36, 162, 220
Ethridge, Mark, 87–88
Exchange Stabilization Fund (ESF), 115–16, 232n21

Farrell, James T., 138
Federal Bureau of Investigation (FBI):
break with White House, 195–96; and communism, 55; competitiveness with other intelligence agencies, 88, 230n22; illegal search and seizure activities of, 68; interview of Chambers, 65–66; on Krivitsky's death, 62; protection of Chambers, 65; rivalry with CIA, 230n22; and Truman administration, 81, 82; and USSR espionage in U.S., 66–67, 94
Felix, Christopher, 228n9. See also McCargar, James
Field, Noel, 2
Finland, 94, 231n15
Foreign Affairs, 4, 106
"Forest Brothers," 34, 36–37, 152, 163, 220–21
Forrestal, James V.: and Long Telegram, 4; notification of White House of communists in U.S. government, 81; and plight of eastern Europe, 14; recruitment of consultants to OPC, 105–6, 108; and recruitment of USSR defectors, 94; resignation as secretary of defense, 125; suicide of, 125n
France: Allied invasion of, 15, 17–18; clandestine assistance to anticommunist factions in, 97, 117; entrance into World War II, 13; and post–World War II reparations, 77; training camps for guerrillas in, 168
Franco, Francisco, 56
Freedom of Information Act, 239n17, 242
French Foreign Legion, 152

Gardner, Meredith, 88, 94
Gehlen, Reinhard, 24–25, 79–80, 105
Georgetown University, 54, 184
German Democratic Republic (East Germany), 12, 214–15. See also Germany; West Germany
Germany: and Allied invasion, 15; conditions after World War II, 19; intelligence about USSR during World

War II, 23–25; nonaggression pact with USSR, 59–61; Russian volunteer units during World War II, 20–21; training camps for guerrillas in, 168. *See also* German Democratic Republic (East Germany); Nazis; West Germany
Gillette, Guy, 207
Glasnost, 220–21, 241–42
Goebbels, Joseph, 11
Gorbachev, Mikhail, 241
Gottwald, Klement, 175
Gouzenko, Igor, 81, 83
Greece, 168
Grew, Joseph C., 54, 126
Grombach, John V., 42, 112
Gromyko, Andrei, 90
Gruenther, Alfred M., 108
Gubbins, Colin, 176, 180
Guerrilla warfare training, 94–95, 165, 168,
Gunther, John, 25, 41

Hall, Thomas, 39–41, 165
Hamilton, Ira, 40–41, 165
Harriman, W. Averell: and funding for OPC, 117; and Keenan, 1, 2, 110; and Marshall Plan funding of political warfare, 137; and Molotov's attendance at opening of United Nations, 71; and OSS, 17; resignation as ambassador to USSR, 1, 3; and Roosevelt's death, 69; and Stalin, 1, 69, 88; summary of Hopkins meeting with Stalin, 78; and Truman-Stalin relationship, 72–75
Harvey, George, 115
Havel, Vaclav, 221
Hayter, William, 156
Hazard, Elizabeth W., 228n5, 235nn7–8
Helms, Richard, 181
Henderson, Loy: attitude toward communism, 55; on Kennan, 1, 7; and Krivitsky, 58–60, 195
Hillenkoetter, Roscoe K., 101, 103, 108, 121, 144

Hiss, Alger: exposure of, 57–59, 64, 198; and Hopkins, 74; leaving government service, 93, 195; Roosevelt's knowledge of, 65; sympathy for Bolshevism, 2
Hitler, Adolf: American attitude toward, 53; defeat of, 2; and Poland, 13; and Sudetenland, 13. *See also* Nazis
Ho Chi Minh, 214
Hoffman, Paul, 117
Hood, William, 61, 229n5
Hook, Sidney, 54, 82, 136, 138
Hoover, J. Edgar: attitude about cooperating with USSR on intelligence, 17; break with White House, 195–96; on Chambers's espionage revelations, 66; on communism, 196; competitiveness with other intelligence agencies, 88; and decoded USSR cables, 197; disbelief in USSR espionage in U.S., 60–61; jealousy of Donovan, 17n; on Krivitsky's death, 62; and New Deal, 55; partnership with Shipley, 60; testimony before Congress, 195–96; and Truman administration, 81, 82
Hopkins, Harry: attitude toward communism, 88; illness of, 75, 76; repairing Truman-Stalin relationship, 73–74, 76–78; as source of information to USSR in World War II, 74; and Stalin, 74–75
Hornbeck, Stanley K., 58
House of Representatives Select Committee on Un-American Activities, 55, 61, 196–97
Houston, Lawrence R., 101–2, 114
Hughes, Emmet John, 205
Hull, Cordell, 75
Hungary: American intelligence in, 41–44; and Iron Curtain, 13; resistance to communism in, 32; revolution of 1956, 217, 219; Roosevelt's attitude about communist takeover of, 14; Smallholders party, 41–43; suppression of communist resistance movements in, 152; U.S. removal of politicians threatened by communism, 43

Immigration and Naturalization Service, 169

Intelligence: and "blowback," 165, 220; congressional scrutiny of, 115; Counter-Intelligence Corps (CIC), 15; double agents, 35–38, 49, 179; fate of agents in Rollback Operation, 153, 162, 170–75, 186–87; funding for, 114–18, 122, 128–29, 204; military intelligence, 15, 42, 67; moving attention from eastern Europe to Third World, 157n, 213–14; Office of Strategic Services (OSS), 15–16; overview of intelligence in 1940s, 15; "the Pond," 42; relationship between different government agencies of, 27, 67–68, 88, 181, 230n22; self-enriching missions in World War II, 15; SIGINT, 18; "Source 19," 74; title changes of American intelligence agencies, 234n2. *See also* Central Intelligence Agency (CIA)

Intermarium, 47–48

International Monetary Fund, 116

International Refugee Organization, 39

Iron Curtain: Churchill's speech about, 11; and Czechoslovakia, 13, 33–34; Goebbels's naming of, 11; and Hungary, 13; as metaphor of Cold War, 22; and Poland, 13; U.S. intelligence agencies understanding of cultures behind, 33; and Yugoslav Federation, 14. *See also* Cold War; Political warfare

Iron Guard, 166–67, 169

Italy, 38, 97, 117, 168

Jackson, C. D., 212, 215

Jackson, William H., 105

Jameson, Donald Fenton ("Jamie"), 183, 185, 236n32

Jebb, Gladwyn, 156

Jellicoe, George, 159

Jodl, Alfred, 20–21

Johnson, Louis, 125, 141

Josselson, Michael, 139–42, 206

Kennan, George F.: as ambassador to USSR, 208–9; and American Committee, 97; approval of Wisner's plan for political warfare, 124; attitude toward CIA, 103; attitude toward communism, 2, 5–6, 55, 79; contempt for military intelligence, 103; correspondence with Lovett, 110, 112; criticism of, 5–6; and dissolution of USSR, 222; fascination with secret intelligence, 7; fired as USSR ambassador, 209; and funding for OPC, 115; and guerrilla warfare against communism, 94–95; and Harriman, 1, 2, 110; Long Telegram of, 3–4, 39, 89–90; meeting with Allen Dulles, 106; and North Korea, 144; and NSC 4-a, 96; and OPC, 103–4, 112; Pennsylvania Bar Association speech, 209; political career of, 1–2, 88; and political warfare in Romania, 165; program for organized political warfare, 7–8, 87–99; and public organizations sponsoring political warfare, 126; and recruitment of USSR defectors, 94; response to criticism of USSR policy, 6; and secret program of communist containment, 93–99, 96–97; and violence in political warfare against communism, 98; and Whitney, 17; as "X" writing about USSR, 4–5, 106

Kennedy, John F., 113

Kennedy, Robert F., 218, 239n17

Kerensky, Alexander, 130, 132, 133

Kersten, Charles J., 202–4, 208, 212

Keynes, John Maynard, 198

Khrushchev, Nikita, 47, 182, 216–17

King, Mackenzie, 81

Koestler, Arthur, 138, 141

Krivitsky, Walter G.: arrival in U.S., 56; career in espionage, 56–57; and Chambers, 63–64; death of, 62, 65; as defector, 58; and Henderson, 58–60, 195; and House of Representatives Select Committee on Un-American Activities, 61; and Levine, 59, 60, 63

Laar, Mart, 220, 228n2
Lamphere, Robert, 197
Lane, Arthur Bliss, 177–78
Lansing, Robert, 54, 193
Lasky, Melvin Jonah, 138–40
Latvia, 14, 32, 34, 36, 55, 163
Lebid, Mykola, 46, 180
Leich, John Foster, 126, 128, 129
Lenin, Vladimir I., 54
Levine, Isaac Don: as accuser of
  Duggan, 198; and American Commit-
  tee for the Liberation of the Peoples of
  the USSR, 131–33; and communist
  threat in government, 201; creation of
  Plain Talk, 82; and Krivitsky, 59, 60,
  62, 63; *Saturday Evening Post* articles
  on Nazi-Soviet pact, 60–61
Lilienthal, David, 141
Lindsay, Frank: attitude toward OPC
  program in Albania, 156, 160; career
  history, 146–47; and CIA "type," 148–
  49; and dissolution of USSR, 221–22;
  and exploiting discontent in Russia,
  182; and failure of political warfare,
  188, 206; and financing WIN, 177; and
  French Foreign Legion, 166; leaving
  government service, 213; "Program for
  the Development of New Cold War
  Instruments" by, 237n39; recruitment
  of refugees for political warfare, 94,
  151–52
Lindsay, Margot Coffin, 147
Lippmann, Walter, 5, 14
Lithuania, 14, 34, 36
Lodge, Henry Cabot, 202, 212
Loeb, William, 201
Long Telegram, 3–4, 38, 89–90
Lovestone, Jay, 134
Lovett, Robert A., 108–10, 112, 218
Low, Robert, 158–59

MacArthur, Douglas II, 114n
Macdonald, Dwight, 136
Maclean, Donald, 56, 89, 92n, 122, 197
Malaxa, Nicolae, 169–70, 170n

Manacatide, Teodore, 40–41
Mansfield, Mike, 174
Mark, Eduard, 74
Markham, Reuben, 40
Marshall, George C., 71–73, 99, 108,
  146–47
Marshall Plan: as foundation of Cold
  War policy, 93; funding for OPC, 117,
  132, 204; limitations of, 194; original
  purpose of, 111; Truman's expectations
  of, 123
Masaryk, Tomaš, 13, 33
Mason, Gordon, 167, 235n7
McCargar, James, 42, 112, 158–59, 166,
  228n9
McCarthy, Joseph R., 113
McCarthy, Mary, 136
McCarthyism, 55, 61, 196–97, 210, 226n6
McCloy, John J., 82, 129
Melgunov, Sergei P., 131–32
Michael, King of Romania, 38, 128, 169
Mickelson, Sig, 127
Miller, Gerald, 100–101, 103, 104, 112, 115
Molotov, Vyacheslav, 69–71, 90–91
Moravec, Frantisek, 33–34, 227–28n1
Morocco, 48–49, 184
Morris, Louise Page, 113
Mossadegh, Mohammad, 214
Muggeridge, Malcolm, 161
Murphy, David, 184, 238n8
Murphy, Raymond, 137
Murphy, Robert, 93, 113, 124

Narodno-Trudovoy Soyus (NTS), 48–49,
  130, 133, 183–85, 220
National Catholic Welfare Conference,
  83
National Committee for a Free Europe,
  126–27
National Peasant Party, 169
National Security Council (NSC): and
  anticommunist rebellion in Albania,
  156–59; fear of provoking USSR with
  Rollback operations, 187; and funding
  of OPC, 116; and Kennan's program

National Security Council (NSC) (cont.) for organized political warfare, 7–8, 95–97; NSC Directive 10/2, 104, 112; and "plausible deniability," 172; and "psychological warfare," 95–96, 105

Nazis: intelligence on USSR, 23–25; nonaggression pact with USSR, 59–61; Red Army support of, 22; and SAFEHAVEN operation, 42; smuggled to South America, 30; trading expertise for clemency after World War II, 23–25, 28. See also Germany

Neff, Paul, 80, 95

New Deal: and communism, 53–68; and ethnic vote, 199; and expansion of federal government, 53; links with USSR espionage, 195; Republican opposition to, 82; Truman's attitude toward, 2. See also Roosevelt, Franklin D.

New Leader, 131, 138

New York Times, 49, 149n, 164, 165, 174–75, 217

New York University, 6, 54, 136

Nikolaevsky, Boris, 130

Nixon, Richard M., 83, 147, 170

North, John Ringling, 213

North Korea, 144, 161

Novikov, Nikolai, 90

Novoye Russkoy Slovo, 133

NSC. See National Security Council (NSC)

NSC 4-a, 96

NSC Directive 10/2, 104, 112, 166, 181, 188

NTS. See Narodnoy-Trudovoy Soyus (NTS)

Office of Policy Coordination (OPC): absorbed into CIA, 145, 182, 234n2; and American Committee for the Liberation of the Peoples of the USSR, 97, 129, 131, 133–34; attitude toward eastern European intellectuals, 127–28; creation of, 103–4; creation of National Committee for a Free Europe, 126–27;

and Department of Defense, 125; development of, 114; funding for, 114–18, 122, 128–29, 204; high-altitude balloons used by, 124–25; and Marshall Plan, 116–17; and parachuting men into Albania, 161–62; policy differences with CIA, 181; public knowledge of, 104, 164, 165; training camps in France, 168

Office of Strategic Services (OSS): abolishment of, 19, 25–26; access to SIGINT, 18; and Alpine redoubt myth, 18–19; collection of intelligence about USSR, 16–17; creation of, 15–16; hunting down war criminals, 23; and invasion of France, 18; leaks from, 68; plan for peacetime use of, 16–17n; X-2 counterespionage branch, 18

Offie, Carmel: Albania assignment for, 155, 158; and American Federation of Labor, 213; and Congress for Cultural Freedom, 139; death of, 114n; and Duchess of Windsor, 113; as homosexual, 113–14, 114n; knowledge of NTS, 183–84; leaving government service, 213; and OPC, 112–13, 134; and response to communist "peace offensive," 137; and Voice of America transmissions to Ukraine, 181

OPC. See Office of Policy Coordination

"Organization X," 122, 188

Orwell, George, 21, 138

OSS. See Office of Strategic Services (OSS)

Patton, George S., 22

Pennsylvania Bar Association, 209

Pentagon: and guerrilla training, 165; need for early-warning intelligence in Poland, 176; and "plausible deniability," 172

Philby, H. A. R. (Kim): on Anglo-American tensions, 182; background of, 159–60; on Bandera, 181; blamed for failures of Rollback operations, 163; and Burgess, 236n15; and "disinformation,"

182n; exposure of, 56; knowledge of Rollback operations in Albania, 160–61; knowledge of Ukraine resistance, 180; notifies USSR of Anglo-American espionage plans, 160–61, 170–72
Poland: and British intelligence, 176–79; communist police and resistance groups in, 173; cultural ties with Lithuania, 14; and Hitler, 13; and Iron Curtain, 13; and political presence of immigrants in U.S., 13; Red Army occupation of, 77; resistance to communism in, 32; and WIN, 176–79
Polish-Americans, 81–82, 199–200
Political warfare: and creation of OPC, 103–4; fate of agents involved in, 153, 162, 170–75, 186–87; funding of, 114–18; and guerrilla warfare, 94–95, 165, 168, 231n15; as noble cause, 111–12; operations in Albania, 154–59; public knowledge of, 8, 96–97, 101, 116, 164, 165; U.S. disclaims responsibility for, 8, 104, 172. *See also* Cold War; Dulles, Allen; Iron Curtain; Kennan, George; Office of Policy Coordination (OPC)
Poole, Dewitt C., 126
Popular Front Against Fascism, 58, 60–61, 82
Prague Spring of 1968, 219
Pravda, 121, 122, 162, 236n14
Prometheus, 48
Propaganda: "black propaganda," 103; tactics of Special Operations Executive (SOE) during World War II, 20, 22; USSR propaganda against U.S. and Britain, 87, 136–37, 161; western propaganda in Czechoslovakia, 125
Psychological Strategy Board, 212, 215
"Psychological warfare," 95–96, 105

Quinn, William, 26n

Radescu, Nicolae, 166, 170
Radio Free Europe: establishment of, 128; and Hungarian revolution, 217;

and political warfare, 134; public contributions to, 164; success of, 206, 213; Trifa commentaries on, 167; Yeltsin's tribute to, 221
Radio Liberty, 134, 213, 221
Rahr, Gleb, 48–49
"Rat line," 29–30, 39
Red Army: eastern European resistance to "liberation" by, 32–49; and Hungarian revolution of 1956, 217; occupation of Poland, 77; support of Nazi army, 22; Vlassov army's encouragement of defections from, 183. *See also* USSR
Reiss, Ignace, 57, 60, 62
Republican party, 82, 107, 201–2, 205
Resistance to communism: in Albania, 152, 156–59; Czechoslovak Second (Intelligence) Bureau, 32–34; "Forest Brothers," 34, 36–37, 152, 163, 220–21; in Hungary, 32, 41–44, 152; in Poland, 32–33, 173; in Romania, 37–41, 152; and Russian refugees, 47–49, 129–35, 148; in Ukraine, 152, 173; Ukrainian Insurgent Army (UPA), 44–46; in USSR, 32–49, 152, 156–59, 217, 219
Romania: anti-Semitism in, 167; Bishop's service in, 29, 37–40; diplomatic protest over U.S. parachuting agents into, 173; fascist sympathies, 166; forced landing of U.S. spy plane in, 174; Iron Guard, 166–67, 169; liquid wealth of, 168–69; National Peasant Party, 40; OSS operations in, 37–38, 43; resistance to communism in, 32; suppression of communist resistance movements in, 152; U.S. political warfare in, 165–68
Romanian Americans, 200
Roosevelt, Franklin D.: and cooperation with USSR on espionage and intelligence, 17; creation of OSS, 16; death of, 69–70; and Donovan, 19; Donovan's plan revealed to press, 17n; and Hopkins, 73; and New Deal, 53; opening diplomatic relations with USSR,

Roosevelt, Franklin D. (*cont.*)
55, 67; and Polish vote, 200; and repatriation of USSR citizens after World
War II, 20–21; and Stalin, 2, 17, 69;
sympathy for Bolshevism, 2, 14. *See
also* New Deal
Roosevelt, Kermit, 213–14
Russia Committee (UK), 155, 156, 162,
177
Russian émigrés, 47–49, 129–35, 148
Russian Liberation army, 130

SAFEHAVEN operation, 42
Salten, Felix, 63
Saltonstall, Leverett, 117–18
Saturday Evening Post, 60, 63, 142
SBONR. *See* Union of the Struggle for
the Liberation of the Peoples of Russia
(SBONR)
Schacht, Hjalmar, 23
Schlesinger, Arthur, Jr., 140, 239n17
Schuyler, Courtlandt Van Rensselaer,
37–40, 165
Sherwood, Robert, 78
Shipley, Ruth, 60
Short Course in the Secret War (Felix),
228n9
Sibert, Edwin, 24
SIGINT, 18, 24
Smallholders party, 40–42
Smith, Walter Bedell, 101, 126, 144–45,
170, 170n, 171n, 207, 233n8
SOE. *See* Special Operations Executive
(SOE)
"Source 19," 74
Special Operations Executive (SOE):
and Albania, 154–56; and Poland, 176–
79; propaganda tactics in World War
II, 20, 22
Spellman, Cardinal, 14
SSU. *See* Strategic Services Unit (SSU)
Stalin, Joseph: American attitude toward,
53; attitude toward France, 77; attitude
toward Truman, 70–73; awareness of
western intelligence operations in

USSR, 80–81; and Churchill, 74;
daughter of, 236n32; death of, 208, 211–
12, 216; and Harriman, 1, 88; and
Hopkins, 74–75, 77–78; and Kennan,
209; meeting with Hopkins, 77–78;
nonaggression pact with Hitler, 59–60;
and Popular Front Against Fascism,
58, 60; purges by, 56–57; and repatria-
tion of USSR citizens after World War
II, 20–21; and Roosevelt, 2, 17, 69–70,
74; and United Nations, 71. *See also*
USSR
Stimson, Henry L., 72–73
Strategic Services Unit (SSU), 26, 27, 49
Sudetenland, 13
Sudoplatov, Pavel, 47, 62, 74, 135, 180,
182, 182n
Sullivan, William, 83
Sullivan and Cromwell law firm, 126
Sulzberger, C. L., 49, 165

Taft, Robert A., 202, 205
Taubman, William, 72
Teheran Conference, 76
Thayer, Charles, 94, 147
Thompson, Dorothy, 65
Tildy, Zoltán, 43
Time, 63
Tiso, Joseph, 203
Tito, 12, 153–54, 153n
Training: Britain's training of refugees
for missions behind Iron Curtain, 33–
34; camps infiltrated by USSR agents,
162; Company 4000, 161; at Dachau,
161; guerrilla warfare training, 94–95,
165, 168, 231n15; of NTS, 185–86
Trifa, Valerian, 166
Trotsky, Leon, 54, 62
Troy, Thomas, 17n
Truman, Harry S.: abolishes OSS, 19, 25;
as anti-FBI, 196; approves Rollback op-
erations, 98; attitude toward USSR, 1,
2, 70, 89, 106; and Churchill, 11, 20–21;
and containment of communism, 6;
and formation of Central Intelligence

Group (CIG), 88; and immunity for Bedell Smith, 171n; and importance of keeping promises, 77–78; Kennan as political liability for, 209; as lame-duck president, 107; loyalty program of, 195–96; meeting with Molotov, 71–72; and New Deal, 2; and NSC 4-a, 96; and OPC, 104, 141; and political warfare against communism, 8, 96, 104–5, 123, 165–68; and Romania political warfare, 165–68; and Stalin, 72–75, 91; and Tito, 153; on USSR propaganda, 87; and western intelligence operations in USSR, 80–81

Truman Doctrine, 93, 111, 194

Ukraine: national identity of, 14; parachuting of agents into, 172–73; suppression of communist resistance movements in, 152, 173; Ukrainian Insurgent Army (UPA), 44–46, 179–82; welcome of Nazis as liberators, 45–46
Ukrainian Insurgent Army (UPA), 44–46, 179–82
Un-American Activities Committee. *See* House of Representatives Select Committee on Un-American Activities
Union of the Struggle for the Liberation of the Peoples of Russia (SBONR), 183
United Nations, 71, 77, 174
United States: cooperation with USSR in World War II, 1, 4; political presence of Polish immigrants in, 13; public support of Tito, 153; relations with USSR after World War II, 69–70, 76–77; response to USSR "peace offensive," 137–39; secret program of containment of eastern European communism, 6–8, 91–99; as superpower, 15; USSR espionage in, 59–61, 64, 89–90, 94. *See also* Central Intelligence Agency (CIA); National Security Council (NSC); Office of Policy Coordination (OPC); *and specific government officials*

United States Information Agency, 121
UPA. *See* Ukrainian Insurgent Army (UPA)
U.S. News & World Report, 122–23
USSR: and Alpine redoubt myth, 18–19; American public's attitude toward, 53–54, 76–77; atomic bomb testing by, 198; citizen emigration in twentieth century, 129–35; collapse of, 221, 241; containment policy by U.S., 5–6; co-operation with U.S. in World War II, 1, 4; curiosity about American spying methods, 17; displaced persons from, 20–22, 29–30; and double agents, 35–38, 49, 179; espionage in Latin America, 88–89; espionage in U.S., 57–61, 64, 89–90, 94; establishment of KI (Committee of Information), 135; expatriots smuggled to South America, 29–30; foreknowledge of Allied invasion of France, 74; and "Forest Brothers," 34; geographical demarcation of, 11–15; German intelligence about during World War II, 22–25; knowledge of U.S. intelligence operations, 121–22, 171–72; Lend-Lease aid from U.S., 1; nonaggression pact with Nazis, 59–61; occupation of Poland, 77; plutonium production in, 187; political warfare against West, 135–39; propaganda about West, 87, 136–37, 161; relations with U.S. after World War II, 69–70, 76–77; and repatriation of USSR citizens after World War II, 20–21, 28, 49; resistance to communism in, 32–49, 152, 156–59, 217, 219; response to Hungarian revolution of 1956, 217; response to Kersten amendment, 204–5; response to Stalin's death, 211–12, 216–18; and "Source 19," 74; and strategic military access from Albania, 156; and United Nations, 71; and U.S. spy plane's forced landing in Romania, 174. *See also* Red Army; Stalin, Joseph

Vandenberg, Arthur, 14, 81, 194, 71
Vlassov movement, 130, 150, 183
Voice of America, 181
Volhynia, 179, 182
Volunteer Freedom Corps, 202, 212
Vyshinksy, Andrey Y., 174

Wadsworth, George, 175–76
Wallace, Henry, 91, 92, 199
Walsh, Edmund A., 54, 82, 184
Washington, George, 115
Washington Post, 56, 209
Welles, Sumner, 55
West Germany, 173. *See also* German Democratic Republic (East Germany); Germany
White, Harry Dexter, 198
White Eagle over Serbia (Durrell), 234n9
Whitney, Thomas, 17
Wiley, Alexander, 6
Williams, Spencer, 131
Williams, Tennessee, 141
Wilson, Woodrow, 13, 45, 53, 154
WIN (Wolnosc I Niepodleglosc), 176–79, 188
Windsor, Duchess of, 113
Wisner, Frank G.: and Albania anticommunist rebellion, 156–59, 160; and Bishop, 39; clashes with CIA, 181; collaboration with fascism, 169; as director of OPC, 110–11, 112; and Allen Dulles, 108–9, 187; and exploiting discontent in Russia, 182; and financing of WIN, 177; fired from CIA, 218; and French Foreign Legion, 166; and funding of OPC, 115, 129; Kennan's approval of Wisner's political warfare plan, 124; and Khrushchev's secret speech, 216; knowledge of NTS, 183–84; and Lasky, 138–41; mental breakdown, 217–18; and Offie, 112–14; and public knowledge of political warfare, 204; and recruitment of displaced persons, 151–52; and Romania, 22, 37–38, 165; and Russian émigrés, 130; and Smith, 145; tour of eastern Europe by, 123–24; "Utilization of Refugees from USSR in US National Interests" by, 109

World War II: Allied invasion of France and Germany during, 15, 17–18, 74; and displaced persons, 20–22, 27–30, 151–52, 166, 202–6; and expansion of federal government, 53; France in, 13; and Great Britain, 13; Nazis trading Russian intelligence for clemency after, 23–25, 28; propaganda tactics used during, 20, 22; repatriation of USSR citizens after, 20–21; U.S. intelligence during, 74; U.S./USSR cooperation during, 1, 4. *See also* Displaced persons

"X article" (Foreign Affairs), 4
X-2, 18

Yale University, 100, 213
Yalta Conference, 22, 33, 76, 78
Yeltsin, Boris, 221
Yugoslav Federation, 14, 152–54

Zog I, King of Albania, 154–56, 158, 161